Marcel Pagnol

MANCHESTER
1824

Manchester University Press

French Film Directors

DIANA HOLMES and ROBERT INGRAM *series editors*
DUDLEY ANDREW *series consultant*

Chantal Akerman MARION SCHMID
Auterism from Assayas to Ozon: five directors KATE INCE
Jean-Jacques Beineix PHIL POWRIE
Luc Besson SUSAN HAYWARD
Bertrand Blier SUE HARRIS
Catherine Breillat DOUGLAS KEESEY
Robert Bresson KEITH READER
Leos Carax GARIN DOWD AND FERGUS DALEY
Claude Chabrol GUY AUSTIN
Henri-Georges Clouzot CHRISTOPHER LLOYD
Jean Cocteau JAMES WILLIAMS
Claire Denis MARTINE BEUGNET
Marguerite Duras RENATE GÜNTHER
Georges Franju KATE INCE
Jean-Luc Godard DOUGLAS MORREY
Mathieu Kassovitz WILL HIGBEE
Diane Kurys CARRIE TARR
Patrice Leconte LISA DOWNING
Louis Malle HUGO FREY
Georges Méliès ELIZABETH EZRA
François Ozon ANDREW ASIBONG
Maurice Pialat MARJA WAREHIME
Jean Renoir MARTIN O'SHAUGHNESSY
Alain Resnais EMMA WILSON
Jacques Rivette DOUGLAS MORREY AND ALISON SMITH
Alain Robbe-Grillet JOHN PHILLIPS
Eric Rohmer DEREK SCHILLING
Coline Serreau BRIGITTE ROLLET
André Téchiné BILL MARSHALL
François Truffaut DIANA HOLMES AND ROBERT INGRAM
Agnès Varda ALISON SMITH
Jean Vigo MICHAEL TEMPLE

FRENCH FILM DIRECTORS

Marcel Pagnol

BRETT BOWLES

Manchester University Press
MANCHESTER AND NEW YORK

distributed in the United States exclusively by Palgrave Macmillan

Copyright © Brett Bowles 2012

The right of Brett Bowles to be identified as the author of this work has been asserted by him in accordance with the Copyright, Designs and Patents Act 1988.

Published by Manchester University Press
Oxford Road, Manchester M13 9NR, UK
and Room 400, 175 Fifth Avenue, New York, NY 10010, USA
www.manchesteruniversitypress.co.uk

Distributed exclusively in the USA by
Palgrave, 175 Fifth Avenue, New York, NY 10010, USA

Distributed exclusively in Canada by
UBC Press, University of British Columbia, 2029 West Mall, Vancouver, BC, Canada V6T 1Z2

British Library Cataloguing-in-Publication Data
A catalogue record for this book is available from the British Library

Library of Congress Cataloging-in-Publication Data applied for

ISBN 978 0 7190 7381 6 *hardback*

First published 2012

The publisher has no responsibility for the persistence or accuracy of URLs for any external or third-party internet websites referred to in this book, and does not guarantee that any content on such websites is, or will remain, accurate or appropriate.

Typeset in Scala with Meta display
by Koinonia, Manchester
Printed in Great Britain
by TJ International Ltd, Padstow

Contents

LIST OF PLATES	*page* vi
SERIES EDITORS' FOREWORD	vii
ACKNOWLEDGEMENTS	ix
Introduction: Pagnol as auteur	1
1 **The emergence of a dramatic author**	11
2 **From theatre to cinema: Pagnol, Paramount, and *Marius* on-screen**	49
3 ***Cinématurgie* revisited**	85
4 **Another poetic realism**	147
5 **Pagnol and the French cinema industry**	198
Epilogue: Pagnol's legacy	237
FILMOGRAPHY	245
SELECT BIBLIOGRAPHY	261
INDEX	265

List of plates

1	Keep rolling!, *Mon Ciné*, 1935	page 136
2	An apprentice filmmaker, *Marius*, 1931	136
3	A love triangle, *Marius*, 1931	137
4	Seduction by jealousy, *Marius*, 1931	137
5	Shadows of temptation, *Marius*, 1931	138
6	Performing friendship, *Marius*, 1931	138
7	Unspoken truths, *Fanny*, 1932	139
8	A heavenly view, *César*, 1936	139
9	Decadence redeemed, *Angèle*, 1934	140
10	Constructed ruins, *Regain*, 1937	140
11	Familial bliss, *Angèle*, 1934	141
12	Adulterous chemistry, *La Femme du boulanger*, 1938	141
13	Domesticity regained, *La Femme du boulanger*, 1938	142
14	Conjugal frustration, *La Femme du boulanger*, 1938	142
15	Comedic pathos, *Jofroi*, 1933	143
16	Filmmaking *à la marseillaise*, *Angèle*, 1934	143
17	Atmospheric angst, *Fanny*, 1932	144
18	An economy of gazes, *Angèle*, 1934	145
19	Saturation marketing, *Regain*, 1934	145
20	Stardom by caricature, *Le Schpountz*, 1938	146
21	Human comedy on the Old Port, *César*, 1936	146

All plates are reproduced with the kind permission of Nicolas Pagnol and La Compagnie Méditerranéenne de Films. Copyright MPC (www.marcel-pagnol.com)

Series editors' foreword

To an anglophone audience, the combination of the words 'French' and 'cinema' evokes a particular kind of film: elegant and wordy, sexy but serious – an image as dependent upon national stereotypes as is that of the crudely commercial Hollywood blockbuster, which is not to say that either image is without foundation. Over the past two decades, this generalised sense of a significant relationship between French identity and film has been explored in scholarly books and articles, and has entered the curriculum at university level and, in Britain, at A-level. The study of film as art-form and (to a lesser extent) as industry, has become a popular and widespread element of French Studies, and French cinema has acquired an important place within Film Studies. Meanwhile, the growth in multi-screen and 'art-house' cinemas, together with the development of the video industry, has led to the greater availability of foreign-language films to an English-speaking audience. Responding to these developments, this series is designed for students and teachers seeking information and accessible but rigorous critical study of French cinema, and for the enthusiastic filmgoer who wants to know more.

The adoption of a director-based approach raises questions about auteurism. A series that categorises films not according to period or to genre (for example), but to the person who directed them, runs the risk of espousing a romantic view of film as the product of solitary inspiration. On this model, the critic's role might seem to be that of discovering continuities, revealing a necessarily coherent set of themes and motifs which correspond to the particular genius of the individual. This is not our aim: the auteur perspective on film, itself most clearly articulated in France in the early 1950s, will be interrogated in certain volumes of the series, and, throughout, the director will be treated as one highly significant element in a complex process of film production and reception which includes socio-economic and political determinants, the work of a large and highly skilled team of artists and technicians, the mechanisms of production and distribution, and the complex and multiply determined responses of spectators.

The work of some of the directors in the series is already well known outside France, that of others is less so – the aim is both to provide informative and original English-language studies of established figures, and to extend the range of French directors known to anglophone students of cinema. We intend the series to contribute to the promotion of the formal and informal study of French films, and to the pleasure of those who watch them.

DIANA HOLMES
ROBERT INGRAM

Acknowledgements

Like most academic monographs, this book had a long gestation period and was completed with support from many people and institutions. In 1996 a residential fellowship at the Camargo Foundation in Cassis, combined with a dissertation stipend from Pennsylvania State University, allowed me to take the essential first steps of conducting archival research in Paris and Marseilles, as well as seeing first-hand the fabled Vieux Port, the villages of La Treille, Le Castellet, and the rugged terrain in the surrounding countryside where Pagnol shot many of his films.

For his infectious enthusiasm and services as a tour guide, I owe a particular debt to the late Georges Berni, who for thirty years promoted Le Petit Monde de Marcel Pagnol exhibit in Aubagne. In Marseilles, I would especially like to thank the Archives Départementales des Bouches-du-Rhône in Marseilles and Aix-en-Provence for allowing me to consult rare copies of the journal *Fortunio* and documents related to Pagnol's copyright dispute with Jean Giono; the Bibliothèque de Marseilles à Vocation Régionale – L'Alcazar for sharing the fascinating unpublished correspondence between Pagnol and Jean Ballard. The Cinémathèque de Toulouse generously provided access to its 168-minute print of *César* – the only complete, original copy of the film known to exist – while the Archives Françaises du Film in Bois d'Arcy allowed me to screen an equally rare nitrate copy of *Direct au cœur*, Roger Lion's 1932 adaptation of an early play by Pagnol and Paul Nivoix.

Like many researchers of French nineteenth- and twentieth-century performing arts, I owe a great intellectual debt to Auguste Rondel (1858–1934) and his voluminous inventory of press clippings now housed in the Arts du Spectacle wing of the Bibliothèque Nationale. As one of Pagnol's earliest contacts in the theatre world of Marseilles, it seems fitting that Rondel provided me, though unknowingly and well in advance, much of the raw material needed to understand Pagnol's evolution as a playwright and his transition to filmmaking. Similar assistance was provided in Beverly Hills by the Special Collections department of the Margaret Herrick Library and the New York State Archives in Albany, both of which house extensive American censorship files on Pagnol's films. Above all, I would like to acknowledge the assistance of the Compagnie Méditerranéenne de Films in Boulogne-Billancourt, its former director Marianne Pagnol-Larroux, and her successor Nicolas Pagnol. Their generosity in granting me access to the company's voluminous press books, photo collections, and copy machine – despite my often critical take on their uncle/grandfather's work – enriched the project enormously. I will always have a fond memory of sipping Dom Perignon with Jacqueline Pagnol in her home on a chilly 11 November while discussing her late husband's career and her own starring roles in *Naïs*, *La Belle Meunière*, and *Manon des sources*.

As the book slowly evolved into its present form, funding and leave time were provided by the College of Liberal Arts and Sciences at Iowa State University, as well as its Center for Excellence in the Arts and Humanities. Intellectually and morally, many colleagues in the profession have inspired and supported me: Dudley Andrew, Richard Abel, David Culbert, Chris Faulkner, Lynn Higgins, Keith Reader, Steve Ungar, and Alan Williams, to name only a few. Alongside Matthew Frost and the rest of the production team at Manchester University Press, series editors Diana Holmes and Robert Ingram have my sincere gratitude for their feedback during the writing process and their patient belief that I could transform what was initially a narrowly focused socio-political reading of Pagnol's rural films into a more comprehensive work of cinema studies. I can only hope that the final product justifies the long wait.

Introduction: Pagnol as auteur

On 28 February 1995 an estimated 50,000 visitors descended on the town of Aubagne, located 15 kilometres east of Marseilles, to celebrate the centenary of Marcel Pagnol's birth. By midday traffic had blocked virtually all access roads and transformed several kilometres of the nearby national highway into a parking lot as motorists abandoned their vehicles on the shoulder and walked to town. Once there they discovered Aubagne as it had appeared a hundred years earlier through an old-fashioned Provençal fair complete with a farmer's market, demonstrations of traditional professions, acrobats, children's games, and a livestock display. After visiting 'Le Petit Monde de Marcel Pagnol', an expansive display of painted clay figurines depicting memorable scenes from his work, many fans left with their own handmade *santons* personifying their favourite Pagnol characters, including the filmmaker himself. Thousands of tourists also spilled over into the surrounding countryside to visit Pagnol's tomb in the nearby village of La Treille and other sites featured in his films and novels. The celebration confirmed Pagnol's status as a French cultural icon twenty-one years after his death and inaugurated a year-long series of events commemorating his life, including a travelling exhibition with stops in Paris, Marseilles, Lyon, and Monte Carlo as well as retrospective screenings of his films at the Modern Museum of Art in New York and the National Gallery in Washington, DC.

For Pagnol, cinema was the middle stage of an extraordinarily long and diverse career that began in boulevard theatre and ended in novels and memoirs. He excelled in all four genres, making him one of twentieth-century France's most popular and versatile dramatic authors. In addition to earning him international fame, fortune, and the distinction of being the first filmmaker admitted to the French Academy, Pagnol's work also generated substantial controversy. In 1930 at the height of his success as a playwright, Pagnol publicly 'converted' from stage to screen, claiming that the invention of talking motion pictures rendered both live theatre and silent film obsolete. He provocatively defined cinema as the visual embodiment of speech, casting the image and cinematic technique as supplements to the spoken word.

The outrage sparked by that position, which struck theatre professionals as a treasonous act of commercial opportunism and cinephiles as a wilful degradation of the so-called 'seventh art', followed Pagnol throughout his career. Though critics often denigrated his work as 'canned theatre', its popular appeal was immediate and durable. Pagnol's trilogy of films set in Marseilles – *Marius* (1931), *Fanny* (1932), and *César* (1936), the first two co-directed adaptations of his hit plays by the same name – scored unprecedented ticket sales and have remained among the best-loved classics of French cinema.

Pagnol's precocious commercial success afforded him a unique measure of financial and creative independence in an industry struggling to compete with Hollywood imports because of underfunding and organisational disarray. From the founding of his own production company in 1932 until his retirement from filmmaking in 1954, Pagnol served as his own writer, producer, director, and distributor, even building his own studio complex and acquiring two small cinemas in Marseilles. Surrounded by a loyal troupe of technicians, employees, and actors, he created an entirely self-sufficient, vertically integrated system for making and marketing films. In 1930s France, it was the only viable alternative to Paris and a model of efficiency that generated profit margins rivalling and often exceeding those of larger competitors based in the capital.

Convinced that only the public had the right to judge his work and vindicated by its consistent box-office performance, Pagnol gleefully antagonised critics in a variety of ways: by sometimes holding unannounced sneak previews of his films for the general public rather than private pre-release screenings for journalists; by drowning out negative reviews in a blitz of hyperbolic newspaper and magazine advertisements; finally, by attacking his detractors directly. In late 1933 Pagnol founded *Les Cahiers du film*, a short-lived publicity vehicle presented as a 'revue de doctrine cinématographique' (a journal of cinematic doctrine) whose purpose was to reaffirm his view of cinema as 'l'art d'imprimer, de fixer et de diffuser le théâtre' (the art of printing, definitively capturing, and disseminating theatre) (Pagnol 1933: 8) and to underscore commercial success of that formula. He went a step further in his 1949 essay *Critique des critiques* by characterising critics as envious, hypocritical assassins of true talent: 'des gens incapables d'agir ou de créer qui se donnent pour tâche, le plus sérieusement du monde, de juger les actions et les œuvres des autres' (persons incapable of doing or creating who in all seriousness assign themselves the task of judging others' actions and works) (Pagnol 1995: I, 1015). According to Pagnol, the arbitrary critical sabotage once endured by great authors such as Molière, Racine, and Stendhal was fortunately no longer possible thanks to the advent of modern marketing techniques that allowed direct communication between creative writers and their public. He concluded approvingly that 'c'est surtout dans le domaine du cinéma que l'autorité de la critique moderne pourrait être mesurée par un chiffre voisin de zéro' (with regard to cinema in particular, the authority of modern critics measures close to zero) (Pagnol 1995: I, 1033). This triumphant embrace of art-as-mass-commodity was of course anathema to most critics and many artists, only intensifying their disdain.

One of the first commentators to attempt a balanced reassessment of Pagnol was *Cahiers du cinéma* founder André Bazin, who in his 1959 classic *Qu'est-ce que le cinema?* devoted a chapter to the filmmaker as part of an extended reflection on the links between theatre and cinema. Bazin broke new ground by rejecting the longstanding tendency to dismiss Pagnol's work as the cinematic recycling of theatrical convention and by recognising the value of subordinating image to speech – especially the richly inflected, performative variety of French spoken in Marseilles – as the basis of social and psychological realism.

> L'accent ne constitue pas, chez Pagnol, un accessoire pittoresque, une note de couleur locale; il est consubstantiel au texte, et par-là, aux personnages. L'accent est la matière même de leur langage, leur réalisme ... Si Pagnol n'est pas le plus grand auteur de films parlants, il en est en tout cas quelque chose comme son génie. Le seul peut-être qui ait osé depuis 1930 une démesure verbale comparable à celle [la démesure visuelle] de Griffith ou de Stroheim au temps de l'image muette. Le seul auteur qui puisse lui être comparé aujourd'hui est

Chaplin et pour une raison précise: parce qu'il est aussi avec Pagnol le seul auteur-producteur libre.¹ (Bazin 1958–62: II, 121, 124)

Despite his admiration for Pagnol's creative independence and unrivalled talent as a screenwriter, Bazin deplored the end result of those qualities: a frequently self-indulgent style of filmmaking marked by slow pacing, static framing, extraordinarily long takes, overabundant dialogue, and uneven editing; in short, a blithe indifference to cinema's potential as a visual medium. He concluded in characteristically passionate terms by reaffirming his predecessors' negativity.

> Les centaines de millions que Pagnol a gagnés dans le cinéma, il ose les consacrer pour son plaisir à des monstres cinématographiques que la production organisée et rationnelle ne saurait même concevoir … Tout l'art de Chaplin est tendu vers sa propre critique et laisse un sentiment de la nécessité, de l'économie, et de la rigueur. Tout, au contraire, dans Pagnol contribue à un incroyable gâchis. Une plus grande absence de sens critique est difficilement concevable et relève d'une véritable pathologie de la création artistique.² (Bazin 1958–62: II, 124)

Justified in part by comparing Pagnol's work to that of accomplished peer directors from the 1930s such as Jean Vigo, Marcel Carné, and Jean Renoir, Bazin's scathing judgement was also influenced by the undeniably weak films Pagnol made late in his career, most notably *La Belle Meunière* (1948), a musical that recounted a fictional adventure of Franz Schubert's using experimental Rouxcolor technology and popular crooner Tino Rossi as the celebrated composer; and *Les Lettres de mon moulin* (1954), an incongruously burlesque rendering

---

1 Accent is for Pagnol not a quaint accessory, a note of local colour; it is consubstantial with the text and thus with the characters. Accent is the very substance of their language, their realism … If Pagnol is not the greatest author of talking films, he is in any event something like their genius. He is perhaps the only one who since 1930 has dared a verbal excess comparable to the visual excess of D.W. Griffith or Erich von Stroheim during cinema's silent era. The only author to whom he can be compared today is Charlie Chaplin, and for one specific reason: because alongside Pagnol he is the only independent writer-producer-director.

2 For his own pleasure, Pagnol dares invest the hundreds of millions he has earned from cinema in making cinematic monstrosities inconceivable to organised, rational production … Chaplin's entire art points to self-critique and creates a sense of necessity, economy, and rigour. On the contrary, everything in Pagnol's work contributes to an unbelievable mess. A more complete absence of critical judgment is hard to imagine and stems from a veritable pathology of artistic creation.

of three short stories by Alphonse Daudet. In addition, the three screen adaptations of *Topaze* (1932, 1936, 1951) – the first directed by Louis Gasnier for Paramount, the last two by Pagnol himself – never successfully captured the incisive social and moral critique or lived up to his original 1928 play.

Yet these shortcomings should not prevent acknowledging the maverick playwright-turned-director as a quintessential auteur whose work bears a unique personal stamp and constitutes one of the most intriguing and ambitious contributions to the development of French cinema. From his debut as a solo director in 1933, Pagnol's signature style depended not only on emphasising speech over visual technique, but on his embrace of realism through location shooting in the hills and villages of Provence, the use of actors with authentic local accents and often limited formal training, and the synchronous, on-site recording of sound. Deployed in a series of rural films adapted from short stories and novels by Jean Giono – starting with the improvised short feature *Jofroi* (1933) through to the big-budget hits *Angèle* (1934), *Regain* (1937), *La Femme du boulanger* (1938) – this realist mode of production always incorporated theatrically inspired scenes shot in studio. So did Pagnol's original screenplays, including *Merlusse* (1935), *Cigalon* (1935), *César*, and *La Fille du puisatier* (1940). His two best post-war films, *Naïs* (1945) and *Manon des sources* (1952) were photographed almost entirely on location and confirmed his seminal influence on Italian neo-realism (Leprohon 1976: 399–400). In France proponents of the new wave also identified strongly with Pagnol's independence as a producer-writer-director and collaborative, improvisational shooting practices, prompting admiring retrospectives in *Cahiers du cinéma* and *L'Avant-scène cinéma* (Guégan 1965; Labarthe 1965; Delahaye 1969; Gauteur 1970; Leprohon 1976).

In virtually every Pagnol film the combination of theatrical artifice and documentary realism is accompanied by another formal paradox – a constant oscillation between comedy and drama, genres he viewed as complementary rather than antagonistic. Echoing philosopher Henri Bergson's *Le rire: essai sur la signification du comique* (1900) and his own view of performative speech as the essence of cinema, Pagnol conceived laughter according to its social and psychological functions, defining it in his 1947 essay *Notes sur le rire* as 'un chant de triomphe; l'expression d'une supériorité momentanée et brusquement découverte du rieur sur le moqué' (a song of triumph; the expression of a sudden, momentary sense of superiority experienced by the laugher over the person being mocked) (Pagnol 1995: I, 980).

Like Bergson, Pagnol emphasised laughter's essential role in regulating society by identifying values, practices, and institutions in need of reform, but he added a new dimension to the theory by positing comedy as indispensable to creating the deep pathos necessary for effective drama. For Pagnol, true compassion and recognition of the ontological equality of all humans across artificially constructed social and cultural boundaries could emerge only following the sudden dissipation of laughter and the momentary feeling of superiority that sparked it. As he put it: 'Avoir pitié, c'est se sentir égal à une autre créature humaine qui souffre, et dont nous redoutons le sort pour nous-mêmes ... Egoïste par ses causes, elle est belle et noble dans ses conséquences. Elle est, comme le rire, le propre de l'homme, et le rire s'arrête où la pitié commence' (Pagnol 1995: I, 1006–7).[3]

By juxtaposing humankind's inherently selfish, competitive nature with its potential for compassion and solidarity, Pagnol draws on the humanistic tradition of Rabelais, Molière, and Chaplin, all of whom he cites as sources of inspiration. His belief in the social role of the artist as a comfort against injustice is expressed most directly in the following monologue from *Le Schpountz* (1938), which simultaneously satirised the disarray of the French cinema industry and refuted highbrow critics' scorn for popular comedy as a superficial, frivolous genre.

> Quand on fait rire sur la scène ou sur l'écran, on ne s'abaisse pas, bien au contraire ... Celui qui fait oublier un instant les petites misères – la fatigue, l'inquiétude, et la mort – celui qui fait rire des êtres qui ont tant de raisons de pleurer, celui-là leur donne la force de vivre, et on l'aime comme un bienfaiteur ... Le mérite est encore plus grand puisqu'il sacrifie son orgueil pour alléger notre misère. On devrait dire saint Molière; on pourrait dire saint Charlot ... Ne dites pas de mal du rire. Le rire, c'est une chose humaine, une vertu qui n'appartient qu'aux hommes et que Dieu, peut-être, leur a donnée pour les consoler d'être intelligents.[4] (Pagnol 1995: II, 727–8)

3 Feeling compassion means feeling equal to another human being who is suffering and whose fate we fear will befall us ... Selfish in its causes, compassion is lovely and noble in its consequences. Like laughter, it is uniquely human, and laughter stops where compassion begins.
4 When one makes others laugh on stage or on screen, one does not lower oneself, quite the contrary ... He who makes it possible to momentarily forget

If this passage offers further evidence of Pagnol's penchant for self-indulgence, it also suggests the extraordinarily rich social and cultural content of his films, which hinge on the reconciliation of tensions associated with France's difficult transition to modernity in the context of the Great Depression: the persistence of regional identity among increasingly strong national cohesion; the erasure of rural culture by urbanisation; generational conflict between parents who stress familial duty and children who seek self-fulfilment and independence; changes in traditional gender roles, particularly with regard to sexuality, and the consequences of that shift. In inter-war and immediate post-war years, these issues resonated strongly not only with French spectators, but with international audiences as well. Since then Pagnol's films have remained among the most marketable French exports to the rest of Europe, the Americas, and beyond thanks to his unique talent for crafting stories that are culturally specific yet remain broadly relatable to spectators worldwide.

In its attempt to balance the particular and the universal, as well as comedy and drama, Pagnol's representation of French society always risks caricature and cultural stereotyping. Even at the peak of his success in the 1930s, popular film magazines sometimes poked fun at his formulaic recycling of character types and themes, especially in the Mareilles Trilogy (see Figure 1). That same attitude resonates in the equivocal opening lines of Bazin's essay: 'Avec La Fontaine, Cocteau, et Jean-Paul Sartre, Pagnol complète l'Académie Française idéale de l'Américain moyen. Or, sa popularité internationale, Pagnol la doit d'abord paradoxalement au régionalisme de son œuvre' (Bazin 1958–62: II, 119).[5]

In France the unusual legacy of critical scorn and popular success attached to Pagnol's films has generated a voluminous yet largely superficial and repetitive corpus of publications aimed at the general

---

miseries such as fatigue, worry, and death – he who makes laugh those who have so many reasons to cry, he gives them the strength to live, and he is loved like a benefactor ... His worth is even greater since he sacrifices his pride to lighten our misery. We should say Saint Molière; we could say Saint Chaplin ... Don't speak ill of laughter. Laughter is a human thing, a virtue that belongs only to human beings and that God perhaps gave them to console them for being intelligent.

5 Alongside La Fontaine, Cocteau and Jean-Paul Sartre, Pagnol rounds out the average American's ideal French Academy. Yet, paradoxically, Pagnol owes his international popularity primarily to the regionalism of his work.

public: anecdotal memoirs by those who knew the man in some capacity (Audouard 1973; Castans 1975, 1978; Calmels 1978; Galabru 1999; Hernou 2005); novelistic biographies embellishing fact with imagined dialogue and other unverifiable inventions (Berni 1980, 1981; Castans 1987; Jelot-Blanc 1998; Ferrari and Pagnol 2000; Jelot-Blanc 2010); annotated collections of iconography (Bens 1994; Castans 1982, 1993); even illustrated guidebooks to the outdoor shooting locations of his films (Dariès 1995; More 1996; Dehayes and Pagnol 2002). This hagiographic tone persists even in the best French scholarship: Jean-Baptiste Luppi's meticulous account of Pagnol's life and early work until 1931 (Luppi 1995) and Claude Beylie's *Marcel Pagnol, ou le cinéma en liberté*, the first serious scholarly overview of his career as a filmmaker. First published in 1974 following Pagnol's death and revised twice since (1986 and 1995), it offers perceptive insights into recurring themes and a comprehensive filmography, but often sacrifices critical analysis to admiring description. As for English-language scholarship on Pagnol, it has been comparatively limited in scope and volume, ranging from useful though uneven overviews (Caldicott 1977; Michalczyk 1980) to insightful articles and book chapters focused primarily on the Marseilles trilogy (Vincendeau 1990, 2009; Andrew 1995; Heath 2004).

Taking up the challenge issued by Bazin fifty years ago, this book offers the first comprehensive, scrupulously documented, and unapologetically critical reading of Pagnol's cinema. Its aim is to highlight his singular contribution to classic French film as an auteur and businessman while at the same time evaluating the larger cultural and aesthetic stakes of his movies. Doing so means reconsidering Pagnol in several ways: first, by offering a reading of style and technique that links his theories on film, theatre, and the primacy of dialogue over image with French economic and social anxieties triggered by the arrival of talking cinema and the Great Depression; second, by framing his rural films as an alternative form of poetic realism that draws on a history of representations encompassing French painting, literature, and silent cinema; third, by mapping his complex personal and professional relations with influential contemporaries such as André Antoine, Jean Renoir, and René Clair; finally, by highlighting Pagnol's status in the 1930s as a successful industrialist and folk hero who combined quintessentially French artisanal production values with an innovative, highly efficient system of marketing and distribution modelled after Hollywood. Rather than adopting a strictly chronological approach, the book's five chapters are structured thematically, beginning with an overview that traces the emergence of Pagnol's signature style in theatre and ending with an epilogue that surveys the afterlife of his work in France since the mid-1970s.

References

Andrew, Dudley (1995), *Mists of Regret: Culture and Sensibility in Classic French Film*, Princeton, Princeton University Press.
Audouard, Yvan (1973), *Audouard raconte Pagnol*, Paris, Stock.
Bazin, André (1958–62), *Qu'est-ce que le cinéma?*, 4 vols, Paris, Editions du Cerf.
Bens, Jacques (1994), *Pagnol*, Paris, Seuil.
Berni, Georges (1980), *Marcel Pagnol: sa vie et son œuvre*, Aubagne, Editions Côte d'Azur.
Berni, Georges (1981), *Merveilleux Pagnol: l'histoire de ses œuvres à travers celle de sa carrière*, Monte-Carlo, Pastorelly.
Beylie, Claude (1995), *Marcel Pagnol, ou le cinéma en liberté*, 3rd edn, Paris, Fallois.
Biret, Philippe (1995), *A la rencontre de Marcel Pagnol*, Marseilles: Editions Laffitte.
Caldicott, C.E.J. (1977), *Marcel Pagnol*, Boston, Twayne Publishers.
Calmels, Norbert (1978), *Rencontres avec Marcel Pagnol*, Monte-Carlo, Pastorelly.
Castans, Raymond (1975), *Pagnol m'a raconté*, Marseilles, Editions de Provence.
Castans, Raymond (1978), *Il était une fois Marcel Pagnol*, Paris, Julliard.
Castans, Raymond (1982), *Les Films de Marcel Pagnol*, Paris, Julliard.
Castans, Raymond (1987), *Marcel Pagnol: biographie*, Paris, J.C. Lattès.
Castans, Raymond (1993), *Album Pagnol*, Paris, Fallois.
Dariès, Henri (1995), *Un bout de chemin avec Marcel Pagnol*, Aix-en-Provence, Edisud.
Dehayes, Thierry and Jacqueline Pagnol (2002), *Marcel Pagnol: lieux de vie, lieux de création*. Aix-en-Provence, Edisud.
Delahaye, Michel (1969), 'La Saga Pagnol', *Cahiers du cinéma* no. 213, June, 44–58.
Ferrari, Alain and Jacqueline Pagnol (2000), *La gloire de Pagnol*, Paris, Institut Lumière.
Galabru, Michel (1999), *Galabru raconte Pagnol*, Paris, Flammarion.
Gauteur, Claude (1970), 'Marcel Pagnol aujourd'hui', *L'Avant-scène cinéma* no. 105–6, July–September, 7–8.
Guégan, Gérard, Jean-André Fieschi and Jacques Rivette (1965), 'Une aventure de la parole: entretien avec Marcel Pagnol', *Cahiers du cinéma* no. 173, December, 24–37.
Hernou, Régine (2005), *Monsieur Pagnol et son clan*, Courtomer, ABM Editions.
Heath, Stephen (2004), *César*, London, British Film Institute.

Jelot-Blanc, Jean-Jacques (1998), *Pagnol inconnu*, Paris, Editions de La Treille.
Jelot-Blanc, Jean-Jacques (2010), *Pagnol et Raimu: l'histoire vraie*, Monaco, Editions Alphée.
Labarthe, André (1965), 'Pagnol entre centre et absence', *Cahiers du cinéma* no. 173, December, 66–71.
Leprohon, Pierre (1976), 'Marcel Pagnol', *Anthologie du cinéma* no. 88 (supplement to *L'Avant-scène cinéma*), May.
Luppi, Jean-Baptiste (1995), *De Pagnol Marcel à Marcel Pagnol: voyage aux sources de sa gloire*, Marseilles, Editions Paul Tacussel.
Michalczyk, John (1980), *The French Literary Filmmakers*, London, Associated University Presses, 39–61.
More, Julian (1996), *Les Chemins de Marcel Pagnol en Provence*, Paris, Ramsay.
Pagnol, Marcel (1933), 'Cinématurgie de Paris', in *Les Cahiers du film*, no. 1, December, 3–8.
Pagnol, Marcel (1995), *Œuvres complètes*, 3 vols, Paris, Fallois.
Vincendeau, Ginette (1990), 'In the Name of the Father: Marcel Pagnol's Trilogy *Marius* (1931), *Fanny* (1932), *César* (1936)', in Susan Hayward and Ginette Vincendeau (eds), *French Film: Texts and Contexts*, London, Routledge, 67–82.
Vincendeau, Ginette (2009), 'Marcel Pagnol, Vichy, and Classical French Cinema', *Studies in French Cinema* 9(1), March, 5–23.

1

The emergence of a dramatic author

Marcel Pagnol began his life in Aubagne, a small town in south-east France near Marseilles, on 28 February 1895, the same year that the Lumière brothers perfected the cinematograph and held the first public screenings in Paris. Although admiring commentators have often cited that chronological coincidence as a sign that Pagnol's fate was somehow cosmically intertwined with cinema, nothing in his family background or early years suggests any such predisposition. His ancestors were middling peasants and artisans anchored firmly in the region, since the mid-sixteenth century on his father's side and the early nineteenth on his mother's. The first of four children born to Joseph Pagnol, a public schoolteacher dedicated to promoting the secular values of the Republic, and to his wife Augustine, a seamstress and devout Catholic who had her son secretly baptised, Marcel enjoyed a happy and uneventful childhood. The Pagnols moved several times to facilitate Joseph's rise through the ranks, but in mid-1900 settled permanently in Marseilles just off La Canebière, approximately two kilometres north of the Vieux Port. Beginning in 1904 the family divided its time between the city and a rented summer house in the tranquil Marcellin valley between Marseilles and Aubagne. Later recounted with lyrical nostalgia in his novelistic memoir *Souvenirs d'enfance* (1957–59), the young Marcel's vacations in the countryside instilled in him a strong sense of regional identity and underscored the contrast between rural and urban culture, thereby providing the central themes for his future screenplays. Equally important, his exploration of the area also served as an unconscious, preliminary scouting of the outdoor locations where he would shoot many of his films.

To the consternation of his father, Pagnol was an underachiever as a student, described by his instructors as 'intelligent mais léger' ('intelligent but frivolous') and 'peu travailleur' ('not very hardworking') (Luppi 1995: 90). His class rank in science and maths remained consistently mediocre throughout middle and high school, but he gradually began to excel at languages after being forced to repeat a grade in 1907. His mother's untimely death in 1910 from pneumonia and father's remarriage two years later to a much younger woman appears not to have affected Pagnol adversely, for he won composition awards in Latin, English, and German on the way to receiving his baccalaureate in 1913. After graduation Marcel dutifully fulfilled his family's expectations by training to become a teacher like his father, paternal aunts, and uncle. Yet he dreamed of surpassing the banality of civil service through creative writing. During his final years at *lycée* he began publishing bucolic poems in a local literary magazine called *Massilia*, drawing inspiration from Virgil, nineteenth-century Provençal poet Frédéric Mistral, and his own summer adventures alongside best friend David 'Lili' Magnan (Luppi 1995: 94–100).

These first publications ignited an entrepreneurial spirit and an irrepressible ambition to achieve fame and fortune that would subsequently define his career as both playwright and filmmaker. Leading a team of recruited classmates, Marcel founded two literary magazines. The first, titled *Le Bohème*, folded after only two issues for lack of funding; the second, *Fortunio*, fared somewhat better, but the outbreak of the First World War in August 1914 interrupted its publication. Conscripted shortly thereafter, Pagnol served less than six months in all, receiving a medical discharge in May 1915 and escaping the murderous combat that killed 1.5 million Frenchmen, including his friend Lili and cousin André Pagnol.

In early 1916 he received a *licence ès lettres* degree from the University of Montpellier, married sweetheart Simonne Collin after a brief courtship, and embarked on a career teaching English that over the next three years took the couple from Pamiers to Aix-en-Provence and back to Marseilles (Luppi 1995: 139–52). The homecoming allowed him to revive *Fortunio* with the assistance of several former classmates. The magazine devoted roughly equal space to original literary works by local authors and criticism of books and plays, boasting a print run of about 800 by early 1921 (Luppi 1995: 163). More important, it provided Pagnol a forum for publishing sections of *Ulysse chez les Phéaciens* and *Catulle* – plays that drew directly on classical Greco-Roman literature – as well as two coming-of-age novellas inspired by the author's first loves, *La petite fille aux yeux sombres* (later reworked and published under the title *Pirouettes*) and *Les mémoires de Jacques Panier* (later revised and republished as *Le mariage de Peluque*). Well written though rather formulaic in their melodrama, these early works exemplify the twin creative strategies that would subsequently define Pagnol's dramatic writing: embellishing pre-existing stories and character types from various narrative traditions with references to his own experiences and Provençal culture.

Adapting to Paris

Significantly, there is no mention in Pagnol's voluminous autobiographical writings of his ever having any interest in or exposure to cinema prior to an unexpected transfer to Paris in mid-1922. Assigned to the Lycée Condorcet, one of France's most prestigious schools, Pagnol worked tirelessly to break into the literary world while continuing to teach full-time. His unpublished correspondence reveals a seething ambition to succeed by any possible means in the face of intense homesickness, recurring eye problems and migraines caused by overwork and poor diet, constant financial worries, and increasingly strained relations with Simonne. Sleeping little and writing up to ten hours a day, he was initially drawn to cinema not as a technology or a form of artistic expression, but as an expedient way to make money. In a characteristically vehement letter to *Fortunio* co-founder Jean Ballard from 27 November 1922, Pagnol argued that:

> les grandes manifestations de la pensée aujourd'hui n'ont pas 36 formes. Il n'y a que trois qui peuvent nous intéresser, quatre au plus: l'édition, en premier lieu, puis le théâtre (les théâtres parisiens font 7.000.000 de recette par semaine, selon *Comœdia*) puis la musique, puis le cinéma. Le reste n'intéresse personne et seuls les spécialistes lisent les journaux spéciaux. Je vous propose donc d'agrandir encore la place accordée aux livres, au théâtre, et à la musique. Le cinéma, lui, doit nous rapporter beaucoup d'argent à bref délai.[1] (Archives de la

---

[1] Today there are not 101 forms of great intellectual expression. There are only three that can interest us, four at the most: the printed word, first of all, then theatre (Parisian theatres take in 7 million francs weekly according to [the

Bibliothèque Municipale de Marseilles à Vocation Régionale, hereafter ABMVR)

He supported that position by demanding that the journal shift its focus from publishing original literary works to music, theatre, and film review columns: 'Celle du cinéma peut nous rapporter dix à douze mille francs par an. J'ai des propositions de la Paramount' (The cinema rubric can make us ten to twelve thousand francs a year. I have proposals from Paramount) (ABMVR, undated letter to Ballard, late 1922). These 'proposals' were likely not solicitations to purchase the rights to the mediocre plays and novels he was frenetically peddling, but offers to pay for favourable reviews of the company's new releases – a common practice at the time.

Pagnol appears not to have actually written any commissioned pieces for the American movie juggernaut or had much interest in cinema overall, for his regular review column in *Fortunio* focused almost exclusively on boulevard theatre (Pagnol 1922–24). The sole film critique he published was a scathing dismissal of Abel Gance's surrealist-influenced masterpiece *La Roue* that proclaimed the artistic inferiority of silent cinema to both theatre and the novel:

> La parfaite platitude de la production actuelle n'a jamais fait aucun doute pour personne, sauf pour les 'créateurs' de films, qui sont les premiers – et les seuls – à se reconnaître beaucoup de mérite. Cependant, il est indiscutable que le Septième Art a des possibilités égales à celles du théâtre, s'il m'est permis de comparer les deux; et, depuis toujours les intellectuels du monde attendent avec inquiétude le *cinégraphiste* de génie qui réalisera la première œuvre digne de ce nom.[2] (Pagnol 1923: 56)

Recasting the nearly unanimous acclaim that had greeted Gance's film as 'de la publicité moderne qui nous gonfle en forme de phare

---

daily arts paper] *Comœdia*), then music, then cinema. The rest doesn't interest anybody and only specialists read specialised journals. I am therefore proposing to further increase the space devoted to books, the theatre, and music. As for cinema, it can certainly pay off big for us in short order.

2 The utter flatness of today's productions has never been contested by anybody except for the 'creators' of films who are the first and only ones to acknowledge their worth. However, it is certain that the seventh art has a potential equal to that of theatre, if I may compare the two; and intellectuals worldwide are still anxiously awaiting the ingenious *cinégraphiste* who will produce the first work of art worthy of that name.

une très vulgaire vessie' (modern advertising that would have us see the most common candles as great beacons), Pagnol added:

> Parmi les 'trouvailles' que célèbre la critique, il faut signaler l'amour du mécanicien pour sa locomotive: il l'a *baptisée*. Est-il besoin de rappeler ici qu'Emile Zola a écrit *La Bête humaine*? M. Gance, par sa réalisation assez froide de cette conception émouvante, nous a montré quel abîme le sépare de l'homme de génie. La moindre page du célèbre roman vaut les 11.000 mètres de la pellicule ... Il n'y a donc là qu'un film assez banal, relevé par deux ou trois tentatives qui ne sont point géniales, mais simplement ingénieuses. En fin de compte, *La Roue* est assez loin d'être un bon film selon la formule.[3] (Pagnol 1923: 57)

Published under the pseudonym 'J-H Roche' to conceal his identity, these remarks constituted the reactionary manifesto of an ambitious, bitter young author who at the time felt unjustly excluded from an entertainment industry defined by rigid aesthetic codes and self-serving institutional practices rather than talent, hard work, or quality. The contempt he would feel throughout his career for professional critics is expressed here publicly for the first time, targeting by name the renowned Emile Vuillermoz for having praised Gance as a 'un génie qui a donné une orientation nouvelle au cinéma et provoqué une révolution dans l'esthétique moderne' (a genius whose work pointed cinema in a new direction and revolutionised modern aesthetics) (Pagnol 1923: 56). As a further protest against what he perceived as the commercial corruption of art, Pagnol often divided his play reviews into two sections respectively titled 'Théâtre' and 'Commerce', with the latter receiving summary, usually dismissive treatment.

Yet privately Pagnol was already coming to accept the necessity of financing and publicising his own work in a highly competitive environment. In his single-handed attempt to launch *Fortunio* in Paris, Pagnol did everything from negotiating advertising fees, subscription rates, and the cost of paper and printing to delivering the final copies

---

3 Chief among the 'innovations' celebrated by critics is the love of the mechanic for his locomotive, which he *named*. Is it necessary to recall that Emile Zola wrote *The Human Beast*? In his rather cold rendering of this moving idea, Mr Gance showed us the chasm that separates him from a man of genius. The least significant page of the famous novel is worth 11,000 metres of the film ... This leaves us with a rather banal film distinguished by two or three attempts which are the work not of genius, but of ingenuity. In the end, *The Wheel* is far from being a good film, even by formulaic standards.

to vendors, at times even reselling review copies of books received by the journal in order to keep it afloat (ABMVR, letter to Ballard, 1 February 1923). His natural talent for marketing is confirmed by the journal's shift from monthly to bi-monthly format in January 1923, a new cohort of Parisian advertisers, and a growing subscription list of around 250 by late spring (ABMVR, letter to Ballard, 29 April 1923). Along the way Pagnol also cultivated contacts with a number of high-profile personalities (novelist Henri Béraud, actor Edouard de Max, actor-directors Firmin Gémier and Charles Dullin), literary publishing houses (Gallimard, Hachette, Grasset, Albin Michel), arts newspapers or journals (*La Nouvelle Revue Française, Les Nouvelles littéraires, Le Mercure de France, Comœdia*), and boulevard theatres (Arts, Nouveautés, Variétés, Madeleine) that he would later use to good advantage (ABMVR, letter to Ballard, 19 March 1923). The experience convinced the future studio head, as he put it a decade later in *Les Cahiers du film*, that 'le commerce est le fumier qui nourrit la fleur de n'importe quel art' (business is the manure that nourishes the flower of all art) (Pagnol 1933: 3).

In that spirit of commercialism, the aspiring playwright rejected classically inspired drama as unmarketable to popular audiences hooked on topical plays treating current events, instead refocusing his work around socio-political satire. In late 1922 he and Paul Nivoix, a fellow transplant from Marseilles, co-authored 'Boxe' ('Boxing'), a three-act satirical play based loosely on the controversial fixed championship bout that had taken place in September between Georges Carpentier and Louis 'Battling Siki' Fall (ABMVR, letter to Gaston Mouren, 15 November 1922). While unsuccessfully trying to sell the manuscript as both a film treatment and a stage production, Pagnol set to work with Nivoix on *Tonton, ou Joseph veut rester pur*, a racy vaudevillian farce about a woman who attempts desperately to get pregnant immediately after the death of her rich husband so that she may access the fortune denied her by a pre-nuptial agreement (ABMVR, letter to Mouren, 15 November 1922). Signed Nivoix and 'Castro', another of Pagnol's early literary pseudonyms, the play was rehearsed briefly in December 1922 at a small neighbourhood theatre in the Belleville district of Paris, but not publicly performed until August 1923 when it was picked up by the Théâtre des Variétés in Marseilles to fill a one-week slot at the end of the season.

Encouraged by that first small taste of success, Pagnol soon began distancing himself from *Fortunio* in order to focus on his own projects and escape the hopeless feeling that he might never succeed as a solo author. 'Celui qui n'a rien écrit à 30 ans est un raté, un vrai raté', he confided to another friend in Marseilles. 'A 35 ans, il est irrémédiablement perdu' (He who hasn't published anything by the age of 30 is a failure, a true failure. At 35, he is irrevocably lost) (ABMVR, letter to Mouren, 10 March 1923). Though he continued to contribute occasional copy through late 1924, Pagnol effectively turned over control of the journal to Ballard in August 1923, when it first appeared with the subtitle *Cahiers du sud*. Under Ballard's leadership the journal returned to prioritising original prose and poetry over criticism and reviews, eventually adopting *Cahiers du sud* as its only appellation in January 1925 and enjoying a reputation for launching up-and-coming authors until it eventually ceased publication in 1966.

Modern classicism

While extricating himself from *Fortunio* Pagnol was still searching for a style of his own between classicism and modernism. Having already rejected traditional verse dialogue as commercially unviable, he also disliked contemporary dramatists such as André Gide and Jean Cocteau, 'des exemples à ne pas suivre qui défigurent prétentieusement la langue' (examples not to follow who pretentiously disfigure language). Posing again as 'J-H Roche', Pagnol expressed particular contempt for Cocteau's minimalist, avant-garde rendering of *Antigone*, which he claimed:

> a dépouillé la pièce de Sophocle de son incomparable lyrisme verbal et de la sonorité des vers antiques au profit d'un invisible porte-voix qui remplit très exactement la fonction des sous-titres au cinéma. Cette *Antigone* est brève, resserrée, toute en action; la plastique et le geste y ont une grande importance; elle est accompagnée d'une musique de scène; ce sont là toutes les caractéristiques d'un film. Cette *Antigone* est un film parlé.[4] (Pagnol 1923a: 182)

4 stripped Sophocles' play of its incomparable verbal lyricism and the ancient verses of their musicality in favour of an invisible narrator who serves exactly the same function as cinematic subtitles. This *Antigone* is truncated, tightly packed with action; plasticity and gesture are of primary importance; it is accompanied by stage music; these are all the characteristics of a film. This *Antigone* is a spoken film.

Rejecting experimental theatre and film as worthless, Pagnol set himself the task of forging an alternative form of modernism more stylistically conservative and easily accessible to the general public: 'ma doctrine est la suivante: fidélité absolue à la vieille langue; précision et simplicité. Langue classique et pure, autant que possible. Nos maîtres: Rabelais, Montaigne, La Fontaine, Molière, France. Classicisme, c'est-à-dire procédés classiques appliqués à l'âme et à la vie moderne'[5] (ABMVR, undated letter to Ballard, summer 1923).

While believing strongly in the necessity of direct language and social–moral critique, Pagnol struggled to reconcile two antagonistic narrative genres and performance styles, as his rather motley list of preferred authors suggests. The first was an exaggerated, farcical register stretching back to Rabelais and perpetuated in the early twentieth century by vaudeville, music hall, and café-concert. Pagnol and Nivoix knew that style well from the celebrated Alcazar theatre in Marseilles, having reproduced it themselves in *Tonton*. Yet under the tutelage of André Antoine both men had also developed a penchant for the sober, realistic vein of boulevard theatre. As founder of the experimental Théâtre Libre troupe in 1887, then director of the Théâtre des Menus Plaisirs (soon afterwards renamed Théâtre Antoine) and the Théâtre National de l'Odéon in the years preceding the First World War, Antoine had revolutionised modern drama by giving critical and popular legitimacy to naturalistic dialogue, performance, and *mise en scène* (Roussou 1954). Between 1917 and 1922, Antoine injected naturalism into cinema as well by becoming one of the first French directors to shoot feature films entirely on location (Esnault 1973; Chothia 1991: 171–88). After retiring from directing, Antoine devoted himself to film criticism and continued his long-standing practice of supporting rising authors by offering feedback on their manuscripts and recommending them to his extensive network of contacts in the industry (Roussou 1954: 343–7; Antoine 1962: 230–3).

Pagnol admired Antoine's skill both as a stage and screen director, later identifying him as 'mon maître bien aimé' (my cherished mentor) (Pagnol 1995: I, 1071) and 'celui à qui le théâtre du monde

---

5 My doctrine is as follows: absolute fidelity to the old language; precision and simplicity. Classical, pure language, as much as possible. Our models: Rabelais, [Michel de] Montaigne, [Jean] de la Fontaine, Molière, [Anatole] France. Classicism, which is to say classic techniques applied to modern life and the modern morals.

entier doit une reconnaissance éternelle' (he whom theatre across the world owes eternal gratitude) (Pagnol 1995: I, 169). Soon after meeting Antoine for the first time in November 1922, Pagnol sent him a series of letters soliciting advice on placing *Catulle* (Pagnol 1922). Though the play remained a dead letter, Pagnol and Antoine kept in touch thanks to the old master's involvement with a loose confederation of young journalists and playwrights who shared a love for the mordantly ironic, socially critical vein of modern theatre. The group, known unofficially as 'les moins de 30 ans' (the under thirties) or 'la coopérative des jeunes auteurs' (the young authors' cooperative) met regularly to discuss theatre and critique each others' work and included several future star playwrights, including Marcel Achard, Henri Jeanson, Léopold Marchard, Steve Passeur, and Jean Sarment (Pagnol 1995: I, 1065–9; Caldicott 1977: 47–9).

Influenced by Antoine, Pagnol and Nivoix soon abandoned the bawdy vaudeville of *Tonton* and optimistic satire of 'Boxe' in favour of naturalism, consciously modelling their next collaboration specifically after Octave Mirbeau and Henry Becque, the naturalist playwrights made famous years earlier by Antoine (Pagnol and Nivoix 1925). Whereas Becque's work, particularly *Les Corbeaux* (1882) and *La Parisienne* (1885), had condemned rampant bureaucratic corruption, greed, and bourgeois immorality, in the context of the mid-1920s Pagnol and Nivoix targeted the manipulation of collective mourning over the First World War. The result was a darkly ironic drama entitled *Les Marchands de gloire* in which an honest provincial bureaucrat stricken with grief over the disappearance of his son at Verdun is used by corrupt businessmen and their political cronies to take control of the government. When the missing son returns unexpectedly from a military hospital, he and his father, who has become minister of war pensions, bury the truth in order to protect their family's new-found power and wealth.

Following its premiere at the Théâtre de la Madeleine on 15 April 1925, the play enjoyed widespread critical acclaim for its sharp dialogue and darkly ironic socio-political critique, yet failed to win over the public and lasted only thirteen performances. Whether attributable to 'négligence dans le jeu des acteurs' (negligent acting) (Antoine 1925) or the play's 'cynisme trop poussé dans la peinture des maux' (excessive cynicism in its depiction of evil) (Dubech 1925), the failure left Pagnol bitterly disappointed. However, by the following summer the impact had been mitigated by a successful tour of local and regional theatres in the north-east, providing Pagnol the first substantial royalties of his career and much-needed confidence (ABMVR, undated letter to Ballard, summer 1925). A little over a year later, encouraged by the performance of a revised version of 'Boxe' entitled *Direct au cœur* at a theatre in Lille, Pagnol resigned from the Lycée Condorcet to concentrate fully on writing (ABMVR, letter to Ballard, 30 September 1926). At about the same time he split not only with Nivoix, but with wife Simonne as well in favour of a stage actress named Orane Demazis, who would remain his companion for the next thirteen years and star in most of his stage and screen productions.

The friction that Pagnol was experiencing between career advancement and love registered clearly in his next two plays, *Phaëton* (1926) and *Topaze* (1928), which modified the social realist style of *Les Marchands de gloire*. In *Phaëton*, a high schoolteacher named Jean Blaise attains international renown after discovering what he believes to be a previously unknown dialogue by Plato, only to learn twenty years later that the text is a fake. Having previously renounced everything else in his single-minded pursuit of his career, the ageing professor resigns his post at the Sorbonne and at the urging of a seemingly benevolent, ghost-like incarnation of his younger self, vows to make up for lost time by brusquely proposing to Cécile, an attractive former student who rejects him. A confrontation between Blaise's two selves ensues, with the younger man finally shooting and killing his double to avenge a life deprived of sensual pleasure, represented on stage by an imaginary Montmartre jazz club filled with music, dancing women, and flowing champagne.

Picked up by Rodolphe Darzens, an old friend of Antoine's who had recently become director of the Théâtre des Arts, the play debuted on 21 December 1926 under the new title *Jazz* – a change made to increase its popular appeal. Though Pagnol's insistence on balancing individual ambition and social relationships as the key to happiness was hardly original, echoing Goethe's *Faust* and Wilde's *The Picture of Dorian Gray*, *Jazz* was well received for its fusion of romanticism with social–psychological realism, its dialogue, and strong performances from bona-fide stars Harry Baur and Pierre Blanchar, who played old and young Blaise, respectively. The play was a minor box-office hit that exceeded all expectations, recording 110 shows over ten weeks and ending only because of a feud between Baur and Darzens (Baur 1926).

With his next creation, *Topaze*, Pagnol finally achieved that elusive stylistic balance, as well as the stardom and wealth that he had pursued so tenaciously since his adolescence. The title character is an idealistic schoolteacher named Albert Topaze whose selfless devotion to his social and intellectual mission is absolute. After the school's venal headmaster fires Topaze for refusing to change the failing grades of a student from an influential family, the naïve professor is tricked by a city councilman named Régis Castel-Bénac and his mistress Suzy Courtois into serving as a frontman for their illegal business activities and traffic of political influence.

When Topaze realises the truth he is at first paralysed with guilt and refuses to spend the substantial commission he receives on all transactions. A visit from the headmaster, who now treats his former colleague with respect instead of condescension, changes Topaze's attitude by making him realise the futility of adhering to high ethical standards. Committed to avenging the injustice he suffered as a result of his austere morality, Topaze quickly transforms into a Machiavellian crime boss, ousting Castel-Bénac from power and taking Suzy for himself. In the play's final scene he justifies his transformation to his old friend and fellow teacher Tamise:

> L'argent peut tout; il permet tout; il donne tout. Si je veux une maison moderne, une fausse dent invisible, la permission de faire gras le vendredi, mon éloge dans les journaux ou une femme dans mon lit, l'obtiendrai-je par des prières, le dévouement, ou la vertu? Il ne faut qu'entrouvrir ce coffre et dire un petit mot: 'Combien?' Regarde ces billets de banque, ils peuvent tenir dans ma poche, mais ils prendront la forme et la couleur de mon désir. Malgré les rêveurs, malgré les poètes et peut-être malgré mon cœur, j'ai appris la grande leçon: Tamise, les hommes ne sont pas bons. C'est la force qui gouverne le monde, et ces petits rectangles de papier bruissant, voilà la forme moderne de la force.[6] (Pagnol 1995: I, 453)

---

6 Money can do anything, make anything possible, provide anything. If I want a modern house, an invisible false tooth, permission to sleep late on Fridays, praise in the newspapers, or a woman in my bed, will I get any of them through prayer, loyalty, or virtue? It suffices to open one's wallet and speak the words 'how much?'. Look at these banknotes. They may be carried in my pocket, but they will take on the shape and colour of my desire. Despite all the dreamers, poets, and perhaps my own heart, I have learned the great lesson of life: Tamise, men are not good. It is power that governs the world, and these little rectangles of rustling paper are the modern form of power.

Topaze thus combines the biting social critique of *Les Marchands de gloire* with the plot structure of *Jazz*. However, whereas the latter plays end on a tragic, cynical note keeping with the naturalist tradition, *Topaze* adopts a lighter tone by turning the embrace of vice into a tool of social justice and reincorporating certain elements of vaudevillian performance and mise en scène into a realist framework. The casting of the play's male leads – André Lefaur as Topaze and Paul Pauley as Castel-Bénac – was crucial, for both men were well-known comic actors with substantial experience in light satire and music hall before moving into boulevard theatre and film (Chirat and Barrot 1983: 147–8, 177–9).

In the first two acts the characterisation of Topaze and Castel-Bénac is transparently playful but understated. Whereas the teacher exudes apparently immutable gullibility, probity, altruism, and poverty, the scheming city councilman personifies shameless iniquity, egotism, and affluence. The contrast is indicated visually not only by the men's appearance – Topaze wears a long, pointed beard, a ragged, stained tie, and a threadbare suit jacket while Castel-Bénac is immaculately clean shaven and coiffed in a custom three-piece suit – but by their respective work environments: on the one hand, a poorly appointed classroom decorated with tattered textbooks and morally edifying maxims hand printed in capital letters on construction paper, including 'Il vaut mieux souffrir le mal que de le faire' (Better to suffer evil than to perpetrate it), 'Bonne renommée vaut mieux que ceinture dorée' (A good reputation is worth more than a gilded appearance) and 'L'argent ne fait pas le bonheur' (Money can't buy happiness); on the other, a modern office boasting overstuffed leather chairs, a luxurious desk with drawers and a leather top, a massive freestanding safe, and a series of framed counter-maxims professionally executed in calligraphy including 'Soyez brefs' (Be brief), 'Le temps, c'est de l'argent' (Time is money) and 'Parlez chiffres' (Talk figures).

By emphatically setting up then subsequently dismissing the caricatural opposition between righteous destitution and evil materialism, Pagnol's denunciation of corrupt political and social institutions balances cynicism with an optimistic celebration of the wily individual who revolts against the system from within by turning its craven principles in his favour. As a modern-day bandit hero, Topaze personifies the quintessential trickster character prevalent in French folklore, *fabliaux*, and popular theatre since the medieval period. In a more direct sense the characters Topaze and Tamise were also

THE EMERGENCE OF A DRAMATIC AUTHOR 23

inspired by Pagnol's fellow schoolteachers and his father Joseph, who showed a quasi-religious commitment to the moral and intellectual formation of his students. As the playwright commented wistfully: 'Si mon père n'avait pas été paralysé par son idéal, par ses principes, par son respect des autres, il aurait pu réussir aussi bien que des hommes d'affaires, des courtiers, et des politiciens que j'avais rencontrés à Paris' (If my father had not been paralysed by his idealism, by his principles, by his respect for others, he could have succeeded just as well as any of the businessmen, courtiers, and politicians I met in Paris) (Pagnol 1995: I, 288).

Critics immediately appreciated the play's cultural lineage and innovative blending of styles. A columnist for *Le Journal* described the play as 'une vraie comédie humaine digne de notre grand Molière et de notre immense Rabelais; c'est vécu, léger, senti, profond, humain, cruellement divertissant; la satire sociale, d'une autorité et d'une âpreté singulières, demeure toujours infiniment spirituelle, légère, et gaie, sans jamais effleurer l'horrible pièce à thèse aux tirades vengeresses'[7] (de Pawlowski 1928). Pierre Brisson, the prominent drama critic for *Le Temps*, saw in *Topaze* 'un genre essentiellement composite qui rehausse le vaudeville, l'écartant de la pitrerie, lui donnant du piment et de la qualité. La pièce est drôle sans trop de pantalonnades, satirique sans cruauté, et sa violence superficielle n'est qu'une forme de la gaieté. En définitive, quelque chose comme un moyen terme entre Becque et Gandillot'[8] (Brisson 1928).

Having already recognised Pagnol's potential in laudatory reviews of *Les Marchands de gloire* and *Jazz*, Antoine took a special interest in the play. After initially suggesting Lefaur and Pauley for the male leads and placing *Topaze* at the Théâtre des Variétés (Pagnol 1995: I, 304–6), he publicly endorsed Pagnol's lighter take on social realism in the pages of *L'Information*, casting it as potentially revolutionary for a venue long associated with light comedy.

---

7 A true human comedy worthy of our great Molière and our immense Rabelais; it's lifelike, light, deeply felt, human, cruelly entertaining; the social satire, with its singularly bitter force, always remains witty, light, and gay, without ever coming close to the vengeful tirades of a didactic play.
8 An essentially hybrid genre that raises the level of vaudeville, distancing it from clowning, giving it bite and quality. The play is droll without being slapstick, satirical without being cruel, and its surface harshness is simply a form of gaiety. In the end, something like a middle ground between Becque and [nineteenth-century vaudeville playwright Léon] Gandillot.

> La pièce dégage une révolte indignée contre les mœurs présentes et risque de sonner étrangement sur les planches où fredonnèrent longtemps les marionnettes joyeuses de la vie parisienne. On pourrait craindre que sa tenue, sa généreuse colère parussent déplacées en pareil endroit. Selon l'accueil qu'elle recevrait en cas de réussite, le Théâtre des Variétés pourrait devenir une scène où il serait possible de ramener la grande comédie ... N'en déduisez pas cependant que *Topaze*, sous prétexte d'étudier un caractère et des mœurs observées en pleine vie, soit une pièce austère ou difficile. Vous vous divertirez d'un comique quelque peu amer et pourtant irrésistible. (Antoine 1928)[9]

The public proved Antoine right by greeting *Topaze* with a frenzied enthusiasm unseen in French theatre since the performance of Edmond Rostand's *Cyrano de Bergerac* in 1897. Following the play's premiere on 9 October 1928, its box-office receipts and number of consecutive performances shattered all existing records. In addition to amassing nearly a thousand shows in three seasons at the Variétés, it was also staged in virtually every major French provincial city by various travelling theatre companies (Anon. 1931). By the time the play's Parisian run finally ended in early March 1931, it had also been translated into fifteen foreign languages and staged an additional four thousand times worldwide, grossing an estimated twenty million francs in France and a hundred million abroad (Beaudu 1931). The play's cultural impact was sufficiently deep that the term 'Topaze' entered French popular usage as a synonym for any corrupt politician, prompting several circumspect municipal councilmen in Paris to issue press releases characterising Pagnol's work as pure fiction and denying involvement in any such wrongdoing (Nogué 1930). The sole distinction that escaped *Topaze* was incorporation into the repertoire of the Comédie Française, despite Antoine's repeated exhortations in his review column (Antoine 1928, 1929, 1929a).

For Pagnol *Topaze* marked the emergence of a clear personal style that successfully resolved the tensions present in his earlier work:

---

[9] The play offers an indignant revolt against current morals and risks sounding strange on a stage long occupied by the blithe stock characters of Parisian life. One might fear that the play's generous anger seem inappropriate to such a place. Based on the response that greets *Topaze*, the Variétés could again become a stage on which it is possible to perform great theatre ... However, do not conclude from these remarks that the study of character and morality as observed in real life makes *Topaze* an austere or contentious play. You will be entertained by a slightly bitter yet irresistible type of comedy.

vaudeville versus social realism; critical respect and artistic integrity versus commercial success; classicism versus modernism. By articulating moral and social critique around the motif of dissimulation and the incongruity between *être* (being or truth) and *paraître* (appearance), Pagnol's dramaturgy continues the classical tradition of Montaigne, La Fontaine, and Molière; yet his work is also thoroughly modern by positing identity and morality as fundamentally contingent and susceptible to change rather than innate and immutable, defined by gender or socio-economic class. Virtually all of Pagnol's protagonists, whether on stage or screen, undergo a profound transformation occasioned by conflicting ethical and material priorities. In *Les Marchands de gloire*, *Jazz*, and *Topaze*, the choice is formulated rather baldly by framing morality as an obstacle to wealth and power. In the wake of *Topaze* the choice would become more subtle, opposing duty towards one's family and/or community with the pursuit of selfish individual fulfilment, whether through adventure, as in *Marius*; sex, as in *Angèle*, *La Femme du boulanger*, and *Naïs*; or vengeance, as in *Manon des sources*.

Yet throughout Pagnol's work the irreparable disconnect between *être* and *paraître* remains the defining quality of modern society, in which traditional notions of ethics are no longer applicable. At the end of his tirade on the omnipotence of money, Topaze imagines offering his former pupils a revised morality lesson: 'Mes enfants, les proverbes collés aux murs de cette classe correspondaient peut-être jadis à une réalité disparue. Aujourd'hui, ils servent à lancer la foule sur une fausse piste pendant que les malins se partagent la proie. A notre époque, le mépris des proverbes, c'est le commencement de la fortune'[10] (Pagnol 1995: I, 456).

Pagnol and Nietzsche

The overwhelming critical and commercial success of *Topaze* relative to *Les Marchands de gloire* and *Jazz* also had a decisive impact on the way Pagnol conceived the function of tragedy and comedy. Revising

10 Children, the proverbs pasted to the walls of this classroom may have once reflected a reality that has now disappeared. Today, they serve only to set the masses on the wrong path while the clever divide the spoils among themselves. In our era, contempt for proverbs is the beginning of wealth.

the argument that cathartic tragedy serves to guide and correct spectators' conduct by eliciting horror towards treachery and pity for its suffering victims, Pagnol claims that catharsis should be understood 'au sens médical et physiologique du mot *purge*, car les hellénistes nous disent qu'Aristote ne l'a jamais employé au sens noble de *purification*' (in the medical, physiological sense of the word *purge*, for Hellenists tell us that Aristotle never used it with the noble meaning of *purification*) (Pagnol 1995: I, 38). For support he turns to Freud's *Beyond the Pleasure Principle*, which claims that the Id, or base instinct to self-gratification, can never be entirely eliminated, only repressed, and that such repression is the basis of human nature and civilisation. In so doing, Pagnol aligns himself explicitly with Rabelais, citing the famous exchange from *Le Tierce Livre* in which Doctor Rondibilis offers Panurge five remedies against carnal lust: wine, pharmacology, hard physical labour, fervent study, and sex. Panurge of course chooses the latter, leading Pagnol to conclude:

> C'est ainsi que la tragédie me purge en me faisant participer à un assassinat, un inceste, une vengeance, un viol; mais parce que mes instincts criminels sont affaiblis par leur longue captivité et par la discipline que je leur impose, il est aisé de les duper en les faisant complices d'un crime imaginaire joué sur la scène par des comédiens, dont je prends à mon compte les gestes et les sentiments. Détendus par cette courte sortie, mes monstres apaisés rentrent docilement dans leur cachot.[11] (Pagnol 1995: I, 40)

With regard to comedy, he rejects the classical notion of 'castigat ridendo mores' on the same grounds, arguing that:

> la comédie me purge de mon triste complexe d'infériorité et le remplace agréablement par un complexe de supériorité ... Je vois des personnages dupes de leurs propres défauts, qui à mon avis ne sont pas les miens – et cette supériorité passagère agit sur moi comme un tonique. Je ne crois pas que la vue de Monsieur Jourdain ou d'Harpagon ait jamais provoqué la conversion d'un seul Bourgeois ou d'un seul Avare. D'ailleurs, les spectateurs ne se reconnaissent jamais dans un héros qui fait rire, et ils ont bien raison, car les personnages

---

[11] Tragedy thus purges me by having me participate in a murder, an act of incest, vengeance, or theft; but because my criminal instincts are weakened by their long captivity and by the discipline to which I subject them, it is easy to placate them by implicating them in an imaginary crime played out on stage by actors, whose gestures and feelings I identify with. Calmed by this brief release, my pacified monsters return docilely to their dungeon.

du théâtre comique sont toujours des caricatures ... La vertu de la 'catharsis', c'est de répondre à ceux de nos désirs qui ne peuvent être satisfaits dans notre vie ordinaire.[12] (Pagnol 1995: I, 42)

The dramatist thus cannot reliably serve as a guardian of moral values or an agent of social reform and justice; his power is instead limited to offering spectators a temporary psychological and emotional mechanism for coping with a fundamentally unjust world unlikely to change and in which individuals are responsible only for themselves.

This view implicitly freed an exceptionally ambitious and talented author from the ethical and commercial constraints of social realism, allowing Pagnol to pursue commercial success by appealing to popular tastes while simultaneously adopting the persona of the intellectually superior, independent artist uncompromised by politics or base materialism and whose work supersedes conventional morality. As he candidly put it in a 1929 interview with a reporter who asked whether his success was deserved:

> Je l'ai farouchement voulu, aidé. Je suis têtu comme un taureau de la Camargue. Vous comprenez, je savais ce qu'il y avait en moi et ce que je pouvais faire. C'est l'essentiel: avant tout connaître son don et lui faire rendre son jus jusqu'à la peau comme un citron. Il faut avoir confiance en soi, une confiance tenace, presque indécente ... Le théâtre n'est pas une question d'écriture, mais de création de types 'nature'. J'ai horreur du théâtre littéraire et je ne peux pas sentir Henri Becque. Trop de fignolage! Trop de style! Quant au théâtre d'avant-garde, c'est du chiqué! Il n'y a pas de théâtre d'avant-garde, ni d'auteurs d'avant-garde. Il n'y a qu'un public qui se dit d'avant-garde pour se persuader qu'il est supérieur aux autres, une poignée de snobs, rien de plus.[13] (Ransan 1929)

12 Comedy purges me of my sad inferiority complex and pleasingly replaces it with a superiority complex ... I see characters deceived by their own flaws, which in my opinion are not my own – and this short-lived superiority has a tonic effect on me. I don't believe that the sight of Monsieur Jourdain [in Molière's *Le Bourgeois gentilhomme*] or of Harpagon [in Molière's *L'Avare*] ever prompted the reform of a single bourgeois or a single miser. Moreover, spectators never see themselves in a hero who makes them laugh, and they are indeed right, for in comic theatre the characters are always caricatures ... The virtue of 'catharsis' is to address those of our desires that cannot be satisfied in everyday life.

13 I wanted and promoted it fiercely. I am as stubborn as a bull from the Camargue. I knew what I had in me and what I was capable of. That's the most important thing: recognising one's gift and squeezing everything from it like the juice from a lemon. One has to have self-confidence, unshakeable, almost immodest confidence ... Theatre is not about the ability to write, but to create naturalistic

In both style and philosophical substance, there is a strongly Nietzschean dimension to Pagnol's view, which appropriates the ancient Greek dramatic tradition in a way that echoes the principle of 'superficial profundity', or the act of rejecting 'truth at any cost' in order to cultivate surface appearance. As the theorist of artistic will-to-power writes in *Die fröhliche Wissenschaft* (1887):

> Oh, those Greeks! They knew how to *live*: what is needed for that is to stop bravely at the surface, the fold, the skin; to worship appearance, to believe in forms, tones, words – in the whole Olympus of appearance! Those Greeks were superficial – *out of profundity*! And is not this precisely what we are coming back to, we daredevils of the spirit who have climbed the highest and most dangerous peak of current thought and looked around from up there, *looked down* from up there? Are we not, precisely in this respect – Greeks? Worshippers of forms, tones, words? And therefore – artists? (Nietzsche 1974: 38)

In his 1933–34 manifesto 'Cinématurgie de Paris' Pagnol echoes this sentiment by again dismissing strict adherence to social realism à la Becque and Antoine as detrimental to true art, which in his view requires only 'un effet de réel'; that is, a veneer of authenticity in acting, dialogue, and staging that exists only to showcase the talented writer-director's tweaking of reality for dramatic effect:

> Le chef d'œuvre de réalisme, c'est ce que vous verrez si vous vous asseyez à la terrasse d'un café pour regarder passer la rue, ou si vous percez un trou dans le mur pour surprendre la vie du voisin. C'est la négation même de l'art. Or, il y a un autre remède: au lieu de rendre vrai tout ce qui entoure l'acteur, supprimons la réalité de cet acteur. Les Grecs, avec les grands masques de plâtre, les hauts cothurnes et les draperies, mettaient l'acteur hors de la vie: les éclairages spéciaux de certains metteurs en scène tendent au même résultat, avec plus ou moins de bonheur. Ce résultat, le cinéma l'atteint pleinement et sans effort. IL NE PEUT PAS NE PAS L'ATTEINDRE.[14] (Pagnol 1934: 6)

---

type characters. I despise literary theatre and I can't stand Henry Becque. Too much polish! Too much style! As for avant-garde theatre, it's a sham. There is no real avant-garde theatre, nor any avant-garde authors. There are just spectators who call themselves avant-garde to convince themselves that they are better than everybody else, a bunch of snobs, nothing more.

14 The masterpiece of realism is what you will see if you sit on the terrace of a café to observe passing street life, or if you drill a hole in the wall to spy on your neighbour. This is the very negation of art. Yet there is a remedy: instead of rendering true everything around the actor, let's do away with the reality of

Pagnol would hold fast to that aesthetic and ideological position throughout his career as a filmmaker by cloaking various kinds of stock characters in irreproachably realistic, at times ethnographically precise situations, gestures, dialogue, and decors such as the farmhouse he had built for *Angèle* in the Marcellin valley and the ruined hilltop village created for *Regain*. From this angle, Pagnol's entire œuvre can be understood as a series of variations on and oppositions among social and cultural stereotypes: naïve, virtuous peasants versus cynical, corrupt city dwellers; greedy bourgeois versus generous artisans and farmers; women as alternatively manipulative vamps and helpless victims; men as cruel, powerful patriarchs or emasculated yet kindhearted protectors, to name only the most prominent configurations.

The inaugural Nietzschean moment for Pagnol, in both personal and aesthetic terms, occurs in the final scene of *Topaze* when the puritanical teacher-turned-corrupt politician convinces Tamise that immorality can paradoxically be justified on ethical grounds. Momentarily unable to refute his old friend's position that right and wrong are absolute categories impervious to relativism and that material wealth is unrelated to happiness, Topaze spies the tattered gloves Tamise is wearing and deplores his old friend's inability to replace them with an expensive fur-lined pair he has long wanted. In response to Tamise's protest that 'ils coûtent 60 francs; je ne puis pourtant pas les voler' (They cost 60 francs; I can't just steal them), Topaze concludes triumphantly: 'c'est à toi qu'on les vole puisque tu les mérites' (it's from you that they've been stolen since you deserve them) (Pagnol 1995: I, 458). Suddenly faced with the moral injustice of his own poverty, Tamise abandons his previous logic and agrees to work for Topaze in exchange for the implausible promise that they will henceforth conduct business honestly. By presenting a potentially revolutionary counter-ideology simultaneously with its critique, then intentionally leaving the issue unresolved at the final curtain, *Topaze* affords spectators the opportunity to reconcile the play's ethical message with their own personal sense of ethics and identity.

Introducing a small measure of justifiable transgression to restore social morality is essential to Pagnol's modernist recasting

---

the actor. The Greeks, with great plaster masks, high buskins and draperies, situated actors outside life: the special lighting used by certain directors tends towards the same effect, with more or less success. Cinema achieves this effect fully and without effort. IT CANNOT NOT ACHIEVE IT.

of classicism, echoing the polysemic ancient Greek concept of the *pharmakon* (meaning both 'poison' and 'remedy') explicated by Jacques Derrida in his famous essay 'La pharmacie de Platon' (Derrida 1972: 77–214). Just as the *pharmakos* ritual practised by the Greeks symbolically drove evil from the social body by physically casting from their cities a scapegoat maintained specifically for that purpose, Pagnol's most successful feature films systematically enact the purification of a community that has been progressively contaminated by secrets, lies and other forms of deception. In the Marseilles Trilogy, *Angèle*, and *La Fille du puisatier* the trigger is pre-marital sex and an illegitimate birth; in *La Femme du boulanger*, adultery; in *Manon des sources*, the blockage of a life-sustaining well and the death of Manon's father. The dysfunction and deep malaise present below the convivial, often comical surface of Pagnol's communities thus functions as a Derridean 'trace', always present yet scrupulously unacknowledged or actively concealed in dialogue because its revelation would endanger those it binds together. The result is a masterful dramatic tension that is always eventually resolved in the restoration of justice and social cohesion.

Consubstantial with this approach is Pagnol's view of laughter as a purgative, gleeful expression of superiority and power, which closely echoes Nietzsche's assertion in *Die fröhliche Wissenschaft* that 'Laughter means to gloat [sein schadenfroh], but with a clear conscience' (Nietzsche 1974: 207). Since Pagnol attributed the idea to Bergson, he perhaps did not realise that the French philosopher had himself been deeply influenced by Nietzsche (Weeks 2004: 1–2). Though the assertion that 'le rire, c'est une chose humaine, une vertu qui n'appartient qu'aux hommes et que Dieu, peut-être, leur a donnée pour les consoler d'être intelligents' (laughter is a human thing, a virtue that belongs only to human beings and that God perhaps gave them to console them for being intelligent) (Pagnol 1995: II, 727–8) does owe a clear debt to Bergson, it more closely echoes Nietzsche's famous aphorism from *Der Wille zur Macht*: 'Perhaps I know best why man alone laughs; he alone suffers so deeply that he *had* to invent laughter' (Nietzsche 1968: 56). Beyond explaining Pagnol's career-long contempt for professional critics and deference to box-office performance as the truest measure of a work's value, this affinity with Nietzsche constitutes a decisive step in his expression of modernist philosophy through literary devices borrowed from classicism.

If in one sense the intellectual genealogy from Nietzsche to Pagnol is oblique, filtered through the work of Aristotle, Plato, Bergson, Freud, and a host of literary authors, in another it is much more direct, for both men drew inspiration from the medieval Provençal troubadours. The title *Die fröhliche Wissenschaft* is Nietzsche's translation of the expression 'la gaya scienza' referring to the art of oral poetry. For Nietzsche, the phrase signified the 'unity of singer, knight, and free spirit', the perfect artist who used laughter 'to dance right over morality' (Nietzsche 1969: 294).

Regionalism lost and regained

Despite Pagnol's strong childhood affinity for the Greco-Latin cultural and literary heritage running from Virgil through the troubadours to Mistral's Félibrige movement, after moving to Paris he initially rejected regionalism as an element of dramatic composition. Hearing the refrain 'Ça fait trop province' ('it's too provincial') used by potential advertisers, vendors, publishers, and theatre directors to justify their rejection of *Fortunio* and his early solo works convinced the future author of the Marseilles trilogy to view eliminating all local colour as the essential precondition to national success. Pagnol's correspondence from the period is peppered with increasingly bitter tirades exhorting his co-editors to package the journal specifically for a Parisian audience by adapting to their tastes and prejudices. 'La grande question est la suivante' (The big question is the following), he wrote emphatically in December 1922:

> Faut-il faire une revue marseillaise ou une revue française? Il faut que dans la revue tout ce qui est régional (Riviera, Marseilles) soit imprimé sous un chapeau local. 'Vie à Marseilles' par exemple. Et si la revue est marseillaise, je vous affirme qu'il ne faut pas espérer la vente de 10 numéros à Paris, et pas une ligne de publicité. Vous ne pouvez imaginer combien les gens d'ici méprisent la Province, et tout particulièrement Marseilles. Nous ne méprisons pas autant les nègres. Une revue marseillaise ici ne peut être prise au sérieux, quand même elle serait écrite par Rostand.[15] (ABMVR, letter to Mouren, 27 November 1922)

15 Must the review be *marseillais* or French? Everything in the journal that is regional (Rivera, Marseilles) must be printed under a local heading. 'Life in Marseilles', for example. And if the journal is *marseillais*, I assure you that it won't sell ten copies in Paris, and not a single line of advertising. You can't

Marketing imperatives aside, during the difficult early years in Paris Pagnol felt a strong nostalgia for his home city and while writing *Topaze* worked gradually on a second manuscript about a young bartender from the Old Port torn between his desire to sail the world and his responsibilities to loved ones at home. Pagnol initially intended to have the play staged in Marseilles strictly for local consumption, but decided that it could succeed nationally after seeing a performance of Fernand Wicheler and Frantz Fonson's *Le Mariage de Mademoiselle Beulemans* (1910), a long-running hit melodrama that juxtaposes the young heroine's desire for independence with the marriage arranged by her overbearing, ambitious father, who owns a small brewery, to further his business interests. As Pagnol later acknowledged in a newspaper article celebrating the play's fiftieth anniversary, *Beulemans* served as an explicit model for *Marius* in both thematic content and characterisation (Pagnol 1960).

Echoing his Belgian predecessors, Pagnol anchors the universal themes of parent–child conflict and familial duty versus individual fulfilment in the specificities of local culture and language, but substitutes inter-war Marseilles for pre-war Brussels. Marius, the 22-year-old son of widower César Olivier, dreams of becoming a sailor and travelling the world, but feels obligated to help his father run the family Bar de la Marine. The irascible César is incapable of expressing his affection for Marius and still treats him like a child. Marius attempts to resign himself to a mundane, petty bourgeois life made bearable by his love for neighbourhood seafood vendor Fanny Cabanis. Even after the couple plans to marry, the lure of adventure at sea continues to torment Marius. When he has the opportunity to leave aboard a three-mast schooner headed for the Indian Ocean, Fanny selflessly urges him to go. He does so without telling César, who in the closing scene joyfully tells the devastated Fanny how much he is looking forward to the upcoming wedding.

Throughout *Marius* a parade of Provençal type characters join the action: Escartefigue the rotund, dull-witted, cuckold ferry boat captain; Panisse the lazy, rich sail vendor and lonely widower who also wants to marry Fanny; Fanny's mother Honorine, a voluble,

---

image how strong people's contempt is here for the provinces, and especially Marseilles. We don't feel as much contempt for negroes. A Marseilles journal can't be taken seriously here, even if it were written by [famed *Cyrano de Bergerac* author Edmond] Rostand.

demonstrative widow torn between her daughter's happiness and the financial security that Panisse offers. Collectively they personify the cultural stereotypes traditionally attributed to residents of Marseilles: a desire to savour life verging on laziness, emotional volatility and verbal excess, a love of exaggeration and lying, chauvinistic pride in their city, and a comical naïveté regarding life elsewhere.

Pagnol relished the opportunity to take personal revenge on those in the publishing industry who had previously dismissed him as a provincial hack and to revise the simplistic portrayal of Marseillais as inexhaustible spinners of tall tales and hot-tempered loafers. As he wrote to friend Carlo Rim in 1927 while completing *Marius*: 'Je me fous complètement de ce qu'on peut penser (et toi le premier!) du titre. Non, je ne tiens pas à glorifier le grotesque jobastre à barbichette dont les consternantes galéjades font s'esclaffer les spirituels Parisiens au dépens des Marseillais. Bien au contraire, je réhabiliterai Marius, j'en ferai un vrai héros digne de son auguste homonyme sans qui nous serions devenus Teutons!'[16] (Rim 1934: 52–3).

Taking his cue from Antoine, Pagnol assembled a cast of actors who grew up in or near Marseilles to ensure authenticity in their language and performance style. In addition to the nationally known Raimu (Jules Muraire) as César and Fernand Charpin as Panisse, Pagnol filled supporting roles with regulars from the Alcazar: Alida Rouffe as Honorine, Milly Mathis as her sister Claudine, Paul Dullac as Escartefigue, and Marcel Maupi as the ferry boat's stoker Innocent Mangiapan. As for Fanny and Marius, they were played respectively by Pagnol's companion Orane Demazis and Pierre Fresnay, a native Parisian and classically trained rising star who learned the Marseilles accent by living on site for two weeks prior to rehearsals (Fresnay and Possot 1975: 40). Together with Robert Vattier in the role of Monsieur Brun, the cast formed the core of an acting 'troupe' that would make the transition from theatre to film alongside Pagnol and remain with him through the end of the 1930s.

Complemented by the remarkable range of his actors, Pagnol's strategy to rehabilitate Marseilles on the national stage consists of

16 I don't give a damn about what people (especially you!) may think of the title. No, I'm not keen on glorifying the grotesque, goateed imbecile whose outlandish yarns make witty Parisians guffaw at the expense of the Marseillais. Quite the contrary, I'll rehabilitate Marius, I'll make him a true hero worthy of his noble namesake [the Roman general Gaius Marius, famous for winning the Cimbrian War] without whom we would have become Teutons!

validating the negative traits attributed to Marseillais just enough to make them redeeming. In this regard the one 'foreigner' in the insular community of the Old Port, a transplanted customs inspector from Lyon and regular patron of the bar named Monsieur Brun, plays an especially crucial role. His sympathetically wry attitude towards and commentary on the locals serves as a guide and point of identification for spectators, echoing the function of the chorus in classical Greek theatre.

The incorporation of regional dialect takes on a complementary function. Detailed linguistic analyses of morphology, syntax, phonetics, and especially vocabulary attest to Pagnol's exceptionally rich and accurate rendering of the popular French spoken in Marseilles at the time (Brun 1931; Rostaing 1942). In addition to providing realism and local colour, these particularities underscore moments of strong emotion and dramatic pathos, as when Panisse slips into Provençal to denounce César's cheating at cards, or Honorine learns that Marius and Fanny are sleeping together. In *Fanny* Pagnol emphatically rejects regional caricature and underscores the authenticity of his own representation by inserting a brief scene featuring an outrageously stereotypical Marseillais named Marius Tartarin. Copied directly on the outlandish protagonist from Alphonse Daudet's 1872 novel *Tartarin de Tarascon*, this Tartarin enters the bar spouting 'Ô bagasse, tron de l'air!'[17] in search of shellfish, bouillabaisse, and aioli. His ridiculously exaggerated accent baffles César, who immediately labels him 'un Parisien qui va se présenter aux élections' (a Parisian who is going to run for office) and gruffly informs Monsieur Brun that 'à Marseilles, on ne dit jamais "bagasse", on ne porte pas la barbe à deux pointes, on ne mange pas très souvent d'aïoli ... mais on construit vingt kilomètres de quai pour nourrir toute l'Europe avec la force de l'Afrique'[18] (Pagnol 1995: I, 625–6).

---

17 An idiomatic, slightly off-colour phrase expressing surprise or exasperation. 'Bagasse' is from the Provençal 'bagassa', meaning 'prostitute;' 'tron de l'air' is literally translated from Provençal as 'thunder of the air', but also commonly designates any high-spirited woman who is difficult to control.
18 A Parisian who is going to run for office. In Marseilles, we never say 'bagasse', we never grow double-pointed beards, and we don't eat aioli very often ... but we are building twenty kilometres of docks to feed all of Europe with the strength of Africa.

Social Realism in *Marius* and *Fanny*

Pagnol's effort to temper classic regional stereotypes also relied on a leavening of social realism in order to make his own melodramatic representation of Marseilles compelling. While stressing the picturesque aspects of the city and its residents, the stage versions of *Marius* and *Fanny* also subtly highlighted race and class conflict, thereby echoing a dual image of the city already firmly anchored in the popular imagination at the end of the 1920s. One the one hand, France's largest port signified squalor, indigence, vice, and uneasy ethnic mixing. Following a visit in early 1929, German cultural critic Walter Benjamin characterised the Old Port as a carcass rife with human bacteria.

> Marseilles: the yellow-studded maw of a seal with salt water running out between the teeth. When this gullet opens to catch the black and brown proletarian bodies thrown to it by shipping companies at regular timetable intervals, it exhales a stink of oil, urine, and printer's ink. This stench emanates from the tartar baking hard on the massive jaws composed of newspaper kiosks, lavatories, and oyster stalls. The harbour people are a bacillus culture, the porters and whores products of decomposition with only a passing resemblance to human beings. But the palate itself is pink, which is the colour of shame here, the colour of poverty. Hunchbacks wear it, as do beggar women. And the faded women of the rue Bouterie are given their only tint by the sole pieces of clothing they wear: pink shifts. (Benjamin 1999: 232)

Benjamin's view was common currency among French commentators as well. André Gide, who visited the Old Port in July 1932 to observe nephew Marc Allégret filming exterior scenes for *Fanny*, wrote despairingly of the crowd that gathered to watch:

> Plus de trois heures durant, mes regards cherchent en vain parmi le public quelque visage sur qui prendre plaisir à se poser. Les plus jeunes sont déjà stigmatisés par la misère. Chez les aînés, toutes les formes de l'égoïsme: veulerie, sournoiserie, ladrerie et même souvent cruauté. Qui dit aimer l'humanité s'éprend mystiquement de ce qu'elle pourrait être, de ce que sans doute elle serait sans cette monstrueuse atrophie.[19] (Gide 1977: 372–3)

19 For more than three hours my gaze searches the crowd in vain for a face on which it might find pleasure in settling. The youngest ones are already afflicted with misery, the older ones with every form of selfishness: cowardice, deceitfulness, avarice, and often even cruelty. Whoever claims to love humanity is

Yet as the proud gateway to France's massive colonial empire and exotic adventures real and imagined, Marseilles was also commonly associated with beauty, warmth, vitality, and passion for life. Pioneering investigative journalist Albert Londres described it as 'l'un des plus beaux ports du monde, le plus merveilleux kaléidoscope des côtes, un phare français qui balaye de sa lumière les cinq parties de la terre. Ici on embarque pour toutes les mers. On vous en montrera, des pays! On vous en fera connaître, des choses insoupçonnées!'[20] (Londres 1927: 7–8). André Suarès, co-editor of the prestigious *Nouvelle revue française*, summarised the paradoxical identity of his native city by referring to it as 'une fleur d'améthyste, un lit de lavande et de lilas' and 'un étincelant enfer peuplé d'une foule abjecte. Incessamment menacé d'une marée montante d'anarchie, l'antique et toujours jeune Marseilles, repaire de joie et d'énergie, repousse toujours les houles du chaos; une gaîté puissante refoule la marée dangereuse dans la mer, où elle se purifie'[21] (Suarès 1931: 9–10, 14–15).

On stage the first two scenes of *Marius* show both faces of the city by juxtaposing lyricism and comedy with pointedly realistic elements that would subsequently be excised from the screen adaptation. Marius gazes longingly at the ships in the harbour and expresses his wanderlust to Fanny and Escartefigue, but is suddenly interrupted by an Algerian who enters the bar and implores them to buy a rug after apologising for his body odour. Marius calls him a 'sale bicot' (dirty wog), the rug merchant exchanges words in Arabic with Fanny – whom we are told grew up in Oran (actress Orane Demazis' real birth city in Algeria) – and spits at Escartefigue as Marius chases him from the bar spouting epithets in Arabic (Pagnol 1931: 18–21). In the opening and closing scenes of the second act, a group of North Africans appears on the bar's terrace and sings melancholy songs

---

enamoured with what it could become, with what it would certainly be if not for this monstrous atrophy.

20 One of the world's most beautiful ports, the most marvellous kaleidoscope of coastline, a French beacon that bathes its light on the four corners of the earth. Here one embarks for every sea. You'll get to see so many countries, to experience so many unexpected things!

21 An amethyst flower, a bed of lavender and lilacs; a shimmering hell populated by an abject crowd. Eternally threatened by a rising tide of anarchy, the ancient yet forever young Marseilles, a repository of joy and energy, always throws back the swells of chaos; a powerful cheerfulness drives the dangerous tide back out to sea, where it is purified.

about serving France in the First World War. César initially tolerates them as paying clients, but when it comes time to close for the night and they want to stay, he chases them away with the insult 'sales moricauds' (dirty darkies), echoing Marius and identifying racism as integral to white petty bourgeois identity (Pagnol 1931: 95–7, 150–2).

Beyond these passing incidents, several other plot threads absent from the film underscore the problematic nature of race and class relations in inter-war Marseilles. Early in the first act, a young Malaysian woman described by Pagnol as 'petite, pieds nus, avec la peau cuivrée et une énorme chevelure crépue' (small, barefoot, with coppery skin and a huge, frizzy mane of hair) enters the bar and sells Marius breadfruit from Samoa. He smells it deeply and comments to Escartefigue that 'c'est drôle comme on voit les pays par leur odeur' (it's funny how one imagines countries by their smell), underscoring Marius' longing for exotic adventure, the erotic element of that exoticism, and his hesitancy to marry Fanny (Pagnol 1931: 45–6). Later on it is revealed that Honorine had a youthful inter-racial affair with a Sénégalais, who is referred to as a 'pauvre frisé' (poor curly-head) (Pagnol 1931: 60).

In addition, the original text of the play significantly amplifies the back-story on Fanny's Aunt Zoé, a prostitute who has long been absent from the family circle and serves as a cautionary tale for Fanny and Marius. As Honorine says of her fallen sister: 'la pauvre avait l'amour dans le sang et elle est tombée à la renverse de tous les sacs du Vieux Port' (the poor girl had love in her blood and she fell backward onto every sack in the port) (Pagnol 1931: 56–7, 231–2). The contrast is striking between the graphic image of Zoé servicing clients openly on the docks and the text that replaces it in the film version – César's obliquely poetic comment to Marius that 'l'honneur, c'est comme les allumettes, ça ne sert qu'une fois' (honour is like a match; it can only be used once). In another pointed reference to the depraved pleasures of Marseilles, the original text of *Marius* has Panisse suggest to César that his son's erratic behaviour with regard to Fanny might be the result of frequenting one of the city's drug dens to smoke opium 'comme un Chinois, avec un bambou' (like a Chinaman, with a bamboo pipe) (Pagnol 1931: 108).

The play also highlights class tensions among white Frenchmen by portraying Fanny and her mother as significantly more venal and calculating with regard to Panisse's marriage proposal. Rather than simply using Panisse's advances to make Marius jealous and elicit a counter-proposal from him – as in the film – on stage Fanny and her mother are genuinely tempted by the instant socio-economic promotion that Panisse offers their family. When Panisse approaches Honorine, her first priority is to establish his net worth (600,000 francs) and the dowry (100,000 francs) he promises by asking to examine his account books (Pagnol 1931: 62–6). The figures are so impressive that she consents despite openly recognising that 'les chemises de nuit n'ont pas de poches' (nightgowns have no pockets): the middle-aged Panisse will not be able to satisfy Fanny emotionally or sexually, and she will surely take lovers (Pagnol 1931: 65). Fanny herself happily imagines leaving her modest shellfish stand for 'un travail où on a des employés' (a job where one has employees) and a house with a maid (Pagnol 1931: 73, 89).

Even before her pregnancy and Marius' departure, Fanny seriously considers abandoning love in order to leave behind her precarious existence as a petty bourgeois *vendeuse* for the comfortable life of a moyen bourgeois *patronne*. Marius reproaches her bitterly – 'tu te vends' (you're selling yourself) (Pagnol 1931: 89) – but acknowledges that the opportunity is tempting since neither she nor he own a share of their parents' businesses and both will for the foreseeable future continue to earn only room and board in exchange for their labour (Pagnol 1931: 75). As unskilled service-sector employees, they are members of the era's so-called *classes moyennes* sandwiched between the *classe ouvrière* and the petite bourgeoisie, with little hope of ever surpassing the latter category.

While the stage version of *Fanny* de-emphasises the Cabanis women's initial venality by having Fanny marry Panisse to save her reputation and legitimise her baby, it still pointedly emphasises the incidental material and social benefits of doing so. Comfortably seated at a big oak table in her living room, Fanny questions an accountant about pending invoices and calculates the sail shop's liquid capital at over 200,000 francs; she subsequently tells her mother about accompanying Panisse to a gala performance of Fromental Halévy and Eugène Scribe's opera *La Juive* at which she met the mayor of Marseilles. Honorine, who is seen at the outset of *Marius* carefully counting a meagre profit of 91 francs from her fish stand, now listens to a luxury radio using headphones – expensive technology that allows her to enjoy music without waking the baby (Pagnol 1931: 55; Pagnol

1932: 169–71). In both screen adaptations, these pointed class references disappear.

So too does the most emphatic example of social realism in the stage version of *Marius*: the characterisation of Piquoiseau, the former sailor-turned-beggar, as a filthy, abject drunk whom Pagnol describes as 'ayant une bouteille de rhum vide, un béret de marin sale et fripé, un veston en loques, et un pantalon en lambeaux. Ses pieds nus sont noirs de crasse et de boue' (having an empty bottle of rum, a dirty, crumpled sailor's cap, a tattered jacket, and a torn pair of pants. His feet are black with grime and mud) (Pagnol 1931: 10). In the play Marius and César make Piquoiseau pay for his drinks in advance, and his only source of income is guiding visitors to the drug dens and brothels of the old neighbourhoods adjacent to the port. On-screen, however, Piquoiseau is no longer the personification of the city's squalid, miserable proletariat and his role is substantially reduced. His clothes are not in rags, he wears leather sandals rather than walking barefoot, and though dishevelled, he is generally clean and presentable during his brief moments on camera. No longer the personification of the *Lumpenproletariat*, in the film Piquoiseau takes on a more poetic role as an imp who gives voice to Marius' desire for seafaring adventure and constantly goads him to act on it.

Though all overt references to racial and socio-economic conflict disappeared from the film adaptation of *Marius* in 1931, they survived in print versions of the play until 1964. Coinciding with decolonisation, the first edition of Pagnol's complete works, and a resurgence of race and class debates in France, their removal definitively purged a beloved classic of any potentially controversial content. By that time, the author's original depiction of Marseilles had already been almost completely wiped from popular memory. A few brief glimpses of the city's dark underbelly do survive on screen in *Marius* – shots of real-life prostitutes at the entrance to an alley who call out to César as he goes to meet his lunch date; another group of prostitutes and sailors who briefly accost Fanny as she tries to follow Marius to the seedy club where he arranges to leave aboard a ship bound for the Indian Ocean – but no such material survived in *Fanny* or *César*, whose outdoor street sequences eliminate any hint of social critique, serving only to give the melodrama authenticity and emotional appeal. Fanny's dazed march to Notre Dame de la Garde after her doctor's visit underscores her emotional distress at being pregnant; her wedding procession with Panisse highlights her relief and his joy; César's breathless climb to the same church as Panisse lies dying suggests the irascible barkeep's emotional vulnerability and depth of feeling for his sick friend.

Gender, performance, and community

By softening the social realist dimension of *Marius* and *Fanny* on screen, Pagnol made his characters more sympathetic and forged a gentler satire of petty bourgeois culture that balanced vaudevillian comedy with remarkable dramatic pathos and psychoanalytical depth. In so doing, *Marius* and *Fanny* marked the final phase in the maturation of his dramaturgy by inaugurating what would become a career-long preoccupation with family dramas defined by two related narrative devices: the juxtaposition of self-sacrifice, duty and honour with selfish individual fulfilment; the use of performative language – often in bursts of excess to repress or sublimate difficult, potentially damaging truths and thereby ensure the unity of the family, the local community, and by extension, the social fabric of the nation. In so doing, the first two chapters of the Trilogy would permanently infuse Pagnol's work with a humanistic warmth and optimism absent from his early plays.

While César and Honorine's fits of exasperation directed at their children are superficially comedic, they are also powerful expressions of sublimated love that cannot be articulated overtly. Similarly, the exaggerated confrontations between the Olivier men and Panisse over Fanny produce hyperbolic verbal bravado (insults and threats of murder) as well as exaggerated physical posturing (feigned strangulation, kicks to the butt, and nose-to-nose stare-downs) but no actual violence, instead reinforcing social and gender solidarity by purging repressed male anxieties: the middle-aged Panisse's lack of virility compared to Marius; Marius' hesitancy to marry Fanny and renounce his wanderlust but unwillingness to let another man have her; César's desire to see Marius and Fanny marry in order to reintegrate a stabilising domestic female presence into the household, thereby compensating for the loss of his wife; finally, father and son's shared envy of and sense of inferiority towards the much richer Panisse.

The Bar de la Marine constitutes the social hub of a fragile phallocracy consisting of unmarried (and thus incomplete) or overtly emasculated men. In addition to Marius, César, and Panisse, there are Monsieur Brun, also a confirmed bachelor; Piquoiseau the beggar and drunk; and Escartefigue, who blithely accepts his unseen wife's infidelity but bristles when César breaks the taboo of mentioning it openly. Conversely, there is a vulnerable community of women revolving around Honorine and delineated spatially by her kitchen and fish stand opening onto the quay – a contrast between public and private space that underscores the tension regarding women's proper social roles. Honorine is the female equivalent of César in almost every respect: she has lost her spouse but shows no interest in remarrying; she is an irascible, emotive parent who sublimates her love for Fanny in tirades of exacerbation; she runs a small business that provides a modest living but not wealth; finally, she lives surrounded by women – her sister Claudine, Fanny, and her female employees. The defining taboo for the Cabanis family is the figure of Aunt Zoé, who got pregnant out of wedlock and was banished from the family into a life of prostitution.

Fanny's sexuality thus holds the potential both to definitively heal these damaged communities, by marrying Marius and bearing his children, as well as to definitively ruin them by choosing the wrong partner. The tension builds to an unresolved climax as Marius and Fanny sleep together in anticipation of their wedding, but he abruptly leaves for a two-year stint at sea. Only in *Fanny* does Pagnol realise the full psychological and social potential of the situation by having Fanny realise she is pregnant and marry Panisse in the interest of preserving family honour and legitimising the baby. In so doing, she renounces love for material comfort and enhanced social status while awaiting Marius' eventual return with a mix of hope, anger, and trepidation.

The social consequences of uncontrolled female sexuality, often personified in the figure of the unwed mother, would subsequently resurface throughout Pagnol's career as a filmmaker. The gender anxieties swirling around Pagnol's female protagonists has often led commentators to characterise his work as deeply patriarchal, even misogynistic. In a rare feminist critique of *Topaze* published shortly after the play's release, bestselling adventure novelist and *Paris-Soir* international affairs correspondent Elisabeth Sauvy-Tisseyre reproached Pagnol 'de n'être point un grand psychologue féminin' (for his limited insight into women's minds), noting that his female characters 'sont toutes des poupées semblables, marionnettes de comédie qui se jouent des hommes par intérêt et que l'auteur n'a pas su animer' (are all undifferentiated dolls, contrived marionettes who manipulate men to serve their own interests and to whom the author did not know how to give life) (Sauvy-Tisseyre 1928). More recently, Ginette Vincendeau has read the Trilogy as a 'declension on the name and nature of the father with, at their core, the character of César ... Simultaneously offering the image of perfect womanhood and the image of its transgression, these contradictory positions are of course defined by patriarchy. The "good" and especially "bad" aspects of the female heroine are shown as inherent to her "nature"' (Vincendeau 1990: 77, 79).

While this view can certainly be justified with reference to the content of the films and to Pagnol's fathering three children with three different women (British actress Kitty Murphy, Orane Demazis, and his secretary Yvonne Pouperon) while still legally married to Simonne Collin, it constitutes an incomplete reading of his gender politics. As Susan Hayward notes in her overview of gender in 1930s French cinema, Pagnol's films stand apart from other contemporaneous productions and are 'troubling for feminist critics of today because although on the one hand all the traditional male discourses are in place, on the other, strong representations of women are made' (Hayward 2005: 172–3), a point that Vincendeau has also recently acknowledged (Vincendeau 2009: 13–18). Following the populist strategy first deployed in the final scene of *Topaze* with regard to the ethics of business and politics, in the Trilogy Pagnol presents a reactionary social discourse on gender and power while simultaneously undermining it, thus leaving the issue unresolved and open to two radically opposed interpretations.

Although Fanny's sexuality represents a threat to the social fabric that must be neutralised by male authority, male sexual and/or social dysfunction is also present as a contributing causal factor to her 'transgression' of having pre-marital sex. Marius rejects his obligation to Fanny by going to sea after he has slept with her and they have planned their wedding, thereby forcing her to (in his words) 'sell herself' to the infertile (or perhaps impotent) middle-aged Panisse, who had always wanted children but been unable to have any with his late wife. Fanny's marriage to Panisse thus repairs both male and female sexual failings, restores the appearance of propriety, and ensures social cohesion. Rather than being unequivocally misogynistic, as critics have often contended, Pagnol's work is at root much more balanced in its gender politics and unremarkably traditionalist in its message: that men and women have a biological and social duty to each other that can be fulfilled only in the framework of marriage; conversely, that not doing so threatens not only the stability of gender roles, but the long-term continuity of the family unit and society as a whole. In this sense, the seemingly mundane little family melodrama played out in the Trilogy takes on a much more profound, mythic significance as a parable that dramatises the healing of a community previously fractured by gender taboos and dysfunction.

It should also be noted that Fanny's initial emotional martyrdom to César and Panisse's patriarchal will is substantially mitigated, and perhaps entirely offset by the enhanced social standing, confidence, and financial power she achieves running her much older husband's boat equipment business. Following Panisse's death, the end result is a rare form of female independence at once monetary and emotional, as she emphatically tells Marius. If in one sense it is possible to claim that César 'rewrites Fanny's future as a mother and the perpetuator of his own name' (Vincendeau 1990: 80) by suggesting that Marius and Fanny will marry and finally have legitimate children after Panisse's death, in another sense the patriarch is simply relishing the long-overdue, natural consequence of the couple's true love, which despite their separation was never in doubt. Ironically, given César's constant meddling in Marius and Fanny's affairs during the first two chapters of the Trilogy, in the end their reunion requires no effort on his part, the trials of their long separation having made their love even stronger than before, as the final scene of *César* makes clear. In this context, Pagnol's flouting traditional family morality in his own personal life after achieving fame is relevant not as evidence of misogyny, but simply as further proof of his exercising a Nietzschean prerogative that society grants accomplished artists.

Marius, *Fanny*, and the limits of theatre

Pagnol initially placed *Marius* with René Rocher at the Théâtre Antoine, but transferred the rights to the more lucrative Théâtre de Paris after its director Léon Volterra offered him a substantial advance (Antoine 1962: 248). The play premiered on 9 March 1929 and was an instant hit, catapulting its cast to instant national stardom and confirming Pagnol as France's most popular playwright. Critics almost unanimously appreciated the mix of comedy and pathos, the actors' ability to move between the two registers, and Pagnol's reworking of regional stereotypes. A columnist for the daily arts paper *Excelsior* commented that 'L'œuvre a un parfum, une couleur, un relief inoubliables. Ce n'est ni une caricature, ni une trahison. C'est *vrai*; c'est tour à tour comique et émouvant, et c'est joué à la perfection' (Méré 1929).[22] *L'Echo de Paris* went a step further, praising the play's 'humanité profonde' (profound humanity) and 'bonne humeur' (good cheer) while implicitly comparing its dramatic power to that of Racine's 1670 classic *Bérénice*:

> L'auteur nous montre ces braves Marseillais tel quels, avec une vérité, une mesure extraordinaires, vivants et gais, émouvants aussi, car un garçon de bar comme Marius et une simple écaillère comme Fanny, leurs amours sont aussi attachantes et leur séparation aussi poignante que de Titus et de la reine Bérénice. (Nohain 1929)[23]

As for André Antoine, his review highlighted the central role of performative language and Provençal dialect in forging a 'théâtre nouveau' (new type of theatre) that balanced caricature with realism:

> Les quatre actes de *Marius* réalisent à miracle le grouillement ensoleillé, la vie intense et si plaisamment frénétique de notre grand port. Le principal agrément de l'œuvre, c'est le dialogue coloré enveloppant le petit drame sentimental et le défilé des amusantes et pittoresques figures du terroir. (Antoine 1929)[24]

---

22 The work has an unforgettable fragrance, colour, and depth. It is neither a caricature nor a betrayal. It is *true*; its alternatively comic and touching and acted to perfection.

23 The author shows us these fine Marseilles folk as they are, with exceptional truth and even-handedness; lively, gay, and touching as well, for the love between a bar waiter like Marius and a simple fish vendor like Fanny is as captivating and their separation as poignant as that of Titus and Queen Bérénice.

24 In four acts *Marius* miraculously captures the sun-drenched bustle and the intense, pleasantly frenetic life of our great port. The work's main asset is

In all *Marius* ran for over two years and some 780 performances, leaving the stage in February 1931 only because of Volterra's pending contractual obligations with other playwrights (Anon. 1931a). Encouraged by both Volterra and spectators anxious to see the storyline resolved, by then Pagnol was already well into writing *Fanny* for the beginning of the autumn theatre season. The sequel did not debut until early December 1931, delayed by the loss of Raimu to a personal dispute with Volterra, Pierre Fresnay to a booking at another theatre, and Alida Rouffe to illness. Replacing the original cast in such a regionally specific, eagerly anticipated sequel – with Harry Baur, who had already worked with Pagnol in *Jazz*, as César; Antonin Berval as Marius; and Marguerite Chabert as Honorine – was a gamble, but the play drew even better reviews than its predecessor. In particular critics praised Pagnol's use of Fanny's pregnancy to accentuate pathos and social realism as a counterbalance to scenes of light, formulaic comedy and gentle caricature. The result, as one columnist put it, was reminiscent of Beaumarchais' *Le Mariage de Figaro* and *Le Barbier de Séville*, adding that 'Pagnol réussit ce que Diderot, Mercier, et même Beaumarchais ont manqué dans la tragédie bourgeoise du 18e siècle: il adopte et réhabilite l'horrible enfant bâtard' (Pagnol succeeds in doing what [Denis] Diderot, [Louis-Sébastien] Mercier, and [Pierre] Beaumarchais failed to in the eighteenth-century bourgeois tragedy: he adopts and rehabilitates the stigmatised bastard child) (Dubech 1931). As for Antoine, he wrote that '*Fanny* est d'une humanité profonde, certainement plus émouvante et plus directe, supérieure à tout ce que l'auteur nous avait montré jusqu'ici' (*Fanny* is deeply humanistic, clearly more moving and direct, superior to anything the author had previously shown us) (Antoine 1931). Even the notoriously difficult, socially conservative Pierre Brisson conceded that:

> Tous les attraits de *Marius* s'y retrouvent avec la même faconde, la même couleur, le même accent, les mêmes artifices et avec plusieurs épisodes qui trouvent dans le réalisme local une réussite encore plus complète. L'événement le plus banal, en s'y inscrivant, prend du relief et de la gaieté. M. Pagnol, folkloriste, est un vrai plaisir. Le Pagnol sentimental, protecteur des filles-mères et des droits sacrés de l'enfant, me paraît moins recommandable, ainsi que les sketches à ficelles du vieux répertoire. En somme, un sujet des plus graves, des

---

the colourful dialogue surrounding the simple love story and the parade of amusing, picturesque regional type characters.

plus moralisateurs qui mêle le style de Dumas fils aux revendications social-ibseniennes.[25] (Brisson 1931)

Although the absence of Raimu and Fresnay did undermine the play's continuity with *Marius* and its long-term drawing power, in the end it was Pagnol's rapidly developing interest in cinema that cut short *Fanny*'s theatrical run at just under 350 performances in September 1932. By that time, Paramount's screen version of *Marius* was about to be released nationally, Marc Allégret had just finished shooting *Fanny* for the film production company Pagnol had recently formed with Roger Richebé, and Louis Gasnier's rendering of *Topaze* for Paramount was nearly complete as well. Having already publicly announced his conversion from theatre to cinema, for the next twenty-five years Pagnol would devote himself exclusively to making movies.

References

Anon. (1931), '*Topaze* quitte les Variétés avant sa millième', *L'Œuvre*, 2 March.
Anon. (1931a), 'Tout a une fin: les deux dernières de *Marius* au Théâtre de Paris', *Comœdia*, 8 February.
Antoine, André (1925), 'Grave négligence', *Le Journal*, 29 April.
Antoine, André (1928), 'La Semaine théâtrale: *Topaze* aux Variétés', *L'Information financière, économique et politique*, 14 October.
Antoine, André (1929), 'La Semaine théâtrale: *Marius* au Théâtre de Paris', *L'Information financière, économique et politique*, 17 March.
Antoine, André (1929a), 'La Semaine théâtrale: réouverture des Variétés avec *Topaze*', *L'Information financière, économique et politique*, 29 September.
Antoine, André (1931), 'La Semaine théâtrale: *Fanny* au Théâtre de Paris', *L'Information financière, économique et politique*, 15 December.
Antoine, André-Paul (1962), *Antoine, père et fils: souvenirs du Paris littéraire et théâtral, 1900–1939*, Paris, Julliard.
Archives de la Bibliothèque de Marseilles à Vocation Régionale – L'Alcazar, Fonds Littéraire Méditerranéen, Correspondance Marcel Pagnol – Jean Ballard, JB MS 1018, 85 letters, 1922–69.

25 All the assets of *Marius* are again present, with the same loquaciousness, the same colour, the same accent, the same artificial devices, and several episodes that local realism allows to succeed even more fully. Framed in this way, the most mundane event takes on depth and cheerfulness. As a folklorist, Mr Pagnol is a true pleasure. The sentimental Pagnol, the protector of young, unwed mothers and the sacred rights of children, strikes me as less commendable, and the hackneyed, transparent comic sketches even less so. In sum, the topic is among the most serious, the most moralising, blending the style of [Alexandre] Dumas fils with social claims reminiscent of [Henrik] Ibsen.

THE EMERGENCE OF A DRAMATIC AUTHOR 47

Baur, Harry (1926), 'Débat autour de *Jazz*: une lettre de M. Harry Baur à M. Rodolphe Darzens', *Comœdia*, 29 December.

Beaudu, Edouard (1931), '*Topaze* aux quatre coins du monde', *L'Intransigeant*, 18 January.

Benjamin, Walter (1999), 'Marseilles', in Michael Jennings et al. (eds), *Walter Benjamin: Selected Writings, 1927–1934*, Cambridge, Harvard University Press, 232–6, originally published in *Neue schweizer Rundschau*, April 1929.

Brisson, Pierre (1928), 'Chronique théâtrale: *Topaze* aux Variétés', *Le Temps*, 15 October.

Brisson, Pierre (1931), 'Chronique théâtrale: *Fanny* au Théâtre de Paris', *Le Temps*, 7 December.

Brun, Auguste (1931), *Le français de Marseilles: étude du parler régional*, Marseilles, Institut Historique de Provence.

Caldicott, C.E.J. (1977), *Marcel Pagnol*, Boston, Twayne Publishers.

Chirat, Raymond and Olivier Barrot (1983), *Les Excentriques du cinéma français, 1929–1958*, Paris, Henri Veyrier.

Chothia, Jean (1991), *André Antoine*, Cambridge, Cambridge University Press.

De Pawlowski, Gaston (1928), '*Topaze*: les raisons d'une réussite', *Le Journal*, 13 October.

Derrida, Jacques (1972), *La Dissémination*, Paris, Seuil.

Dubech, Lucien (1925), 'Les raisons d'un échec', *L'Action Française*, 10 May.

Dubech, Lucien (1931), 'Au Théâtre de Paris: *Fanny*', *Candide*, 10 December.

Esnault, Philippe (1973), 'Antoine et le réalisme français', *La Revue du cinéma* no. 271, 3–64.

Fresnay, Pierre and François Possot (1975), *Pierre Fresnay*, Paris, Editions de la Table Ronde.

Gide, André (1997), *Journal: 1926–1950*, Paris, Gallimard.

Hayward, Susan and Will Higbee (2005), *French National Cinema*, 2nd edn, London, Routledge.

Londres, Albert (1927), *Marseilles, porte du sud*, Paris, Editions de France.

Luppi, Jean-Baptiste (1995), *De Pagnol Marcel à Marcel Pagnol: voyage aux sources de sa gloire*, Marseilles, Editions Paul Tacussel.

Méré, Charles (1929), '*Marius* au Théâtre de Paris', *Excelsoir*, 19 March.

Nietzsche, Friedrich (1968), *The Will to Power*, trans. and ed. Walter Kaufmann, New York, Vintage Books.

Nietzsche, Friedrich (1969), *On the Genealogy of Morals and Ecce Homo*, trans. and ed. Walter Kaufmann, New York, Vintage Books.

Nietzsche, Friedrich (1974), *The Gay Science*, trans. and ed. Walter Kaufmann, New York, Random House.

Nogué, Jean (1930), 'Connaissez-vous des Topaze au conseil municipal?', *Paris-Midi*, 29 October.

Nohain, Franc (1929), '*Marius* de Marcel Pagnol', *L'Echo de Paris*, 10 March.

Pagnol, Marcel (1922), Letter to André Antoine, Bibliothèque Nationale de France, Département des Arts du Spectacle, MS-78, 17 December.

Pagnol, Marcel (1922–24), 'Les Premières à Paris: les théâtres', *Fortunio* nos. 23–52, November 1922–April 1924.

Pagnol, Marcel [J-H Roche] (1923), 'Chronique cinématographique: *La Roue*', *Fortunio* no. 23, 15 January, 56–7.

Pagnol, Marcel [J-H Roche] (1923a), 'A l'Atelier: *Antigone* de Jean Cocteau', *Fortunio* no. 27, 15 March, 182–3.
Pagnol, Marcel and Paul Nivoix (1925), 'Confidences d'auteurs: *Les Marchands de gloire* au Théâtre de la Madeleine', *Le Soir*, 19 April.
Pagnol, Marcel (1931), *Marius: pièce en quatre actes et six tableaux*, Paris, Fasquelle.
Pagnol, Marcel (1932), *Fanny: pièce en trois actes et quatre tableaux*, Paris, Fasquelle.
Pagnol, Marcel (1933), 'Cinématurgie de Paris', *Les Cahiers du film* no. 1, December, 3–8.
Pagnol, Marcel (1934), 'Cinématurgie de Paris: le théâtre en conserve', *Les Cahiers du film* no. 2, January, 3–8.
Pagnol, Marcel (1960), 'Au Théâtre des Galeries: *Le Mariage de Mademoiselle Beulemans*', *Le Peuple belge*, 22 December.
Pagnol, Marcel (1995), *Œuvres complètes*, 3 vols, Paris, Fallois.
Ransan, André (1929), 'En déjeunant avec Marcel Pagnol', *Candide*, 24 October.
Rim, Carlo (1934), *Ma belle Marseilles*, Paris, Editions Denoël.
Rostaing, Charles (1942), 'Le français de Marseilles dans la Trilogie de Marcel Pagnol', *Le français moderne* no. 10, 29–44 and 117–31.
Roussou, Matei (1954), *André Antoine*, Paris, L'Arché.
Sauvy-Tisseyre, Elisabeth [Titaÿna] (1928), '*Topaze* de Marcel Pagnol', *Jazz* no. 1, December.
Suarès, André (1931), *Marsiho*, Paris, Grasset.
Vincendeau, Ginette (1990), 'In the Name of the Father: Marcel Pagnol's Trilogy: *Marius* (1931), *Fanny* (1932), *César* (1936)', in Susan Hayward and Ginette Vincendeau (eds), *French Film: Texts and Contexts*, London and New York, Routledge, 67–82.
Vincendeau, Ginette (2009), 'Marcel Pagnol, Vichy, and Classical French Cinema', *Studies in French Cinema* 9(1), March: 5–23.
Weeks, Mark (2004), 'Beyond a Joke: Nietzsche and the Birth of "Super-Laughter"', *Journal of Nietzsche Studies* no. 27, 1–17.

2

From theatre to cinema: Pagnol, Paramount and *Marius* on screen

Since the early 1930s critics and scholars have often inaccurately characterised Pagnol's films as 'théâtre photographié' (photographed theatre) or 'théâtre en conserve' (canned theatre), labels that the director himself sometimes defiantly appropriated to justify his defection from the stage and to generate publicity for his new career. While it is true that Pagnol conceived talking cinema as 'l'art d'imprimer, fixer, et diffuser le théâtre' (the art of recording, giving definitive form to, and disseminating theatre) (Pagnol 1933: 8), concurrently affirming the superiority of the writer over the *metteur en scène* and prioritising speech over image as the narrative essence of the seventh art, his view was far less reductive and 'anti-cinematic' than has often been asserted. From the outset Pagnol not only saw certain types of visual technique as crucial to crafting quality talking films; he recognised synchronous sound recording's power to enhance the realism of cinema, thereby liberating it from the artificial confines and conventions of both the stage and studio.

Working with Paramount and talented Hungarian director Alexander Korda, Pagnol first tested his ideas in mid-1931 by adapting *Marius* for the screen. The experience served as an informal apprenticeship for the maverick playwright, allowing him to learn the basics of movie-making and laying the foundation for his career as both a filmmaker and independent studio owner. Far more than a simple recording of the stage play brightened by a few exterior shots of Marseilles, *Marius* is a complex and innovative film that uses a variety of visual techniques and styles – most notably expressionism and realism – to enhance the effectiveness of Pagnol's dialogue and characterisation.

Theatre is dead, long live theatre!

Pagnol first entertained the notion of 'canning' theatrical performance in 1923–24 while writing reviews for *Fortunio*, but at the time the technical impossibility of recording sound and image simultaneously limited the idea to a conceit for disparaging plays whose writing he found inferior. Echoing his lament of Cocteau's *Antigone* as a 'film parlé' (spoken film) that replaced the 'incomparable lyrisme verbal' (incomparable verbal lyricism) of Sophocles' original with 'la plastique et le geste' (plasticity and gesture) (Pagnol 1923: 182), Pagnol offered an even more scathing review of Jean Variot's *Le chevalier sans nom*:

> En réalité, c'est un film, admirablement mis en scène et joué par Charles Dullin. Mais on aurait dû le tourner à la répétition générale et le projeter chaque soir. Cette combinaison cinématographique eût épargné aux fidèles de l'Atelier le texte de M. Variot. On ne saurait imaginer une prose plus laborieuse, plus lourde, plus creuse. Un aveugle trouverait la pièce exécrable; elle ferait la joie d'un sourd-muet.[1] (Pagnol 1924: 30)

Yet his attitude abruptly changed in early 1930 after seeing his first talkie, the Oscar-winning MGM musical *Broadway Melody* directed by Harry Beaumont, at the Palladium theatre in London (Pagnol 1995: II, 14–15). Pagnol returned home enthralled, and when invited by the general editor of *Le Journal* to contribute an article celebrating the six-hundredth performance of *Topaze* instead submitted a text under the misleadingly bland title 'Le film parlant offre à l'écrivain des ressources nouvelles' (Talking Film Offers the Writer New Resources). Its appearance on the front page of the 17 May 1930 edition – an unusual spot for a short arts piece in a major Parisian daily – inflamed the heated debate already under way in France about the impact of sound on cinema as an art and a business. In 1927–28 most sectors of the French entertainment industry initially had greeted the release of the first talkies in the United States and Britain with suspicion. For practitioners of theatre, music hall, vaudeville, and other performance genres, the new technology was an unwelcome

---

[1] In reality it's a film, admirably directed and acted by Charles Dullin. But its opening performance should have been recorded and then projected every evening. This cinematic trick would have spared the loyal patrons of the Atelier theatre Mr Variot's text. One couldn't imagine more laboured, heavy, empty prose. A blind person would find the play atrocious; it would delight a deaf mute.

competitor that usurped revenue and threatened their livelihoods; for silent filmmakers, it represented a commercial rival and lamentable contamination of cinema as a visual art. The huge box-office success of Warner Brothers' *The Jazz Singer*, which ran uninterrupted in Paris for nearly the whole of 1929, convincingly demonstrated the economic value of sound but left unresolved key technological and aesthetic questions, particularly the relative benefits of 'cinéma parlant' (films with dialogue and image recorded simultaneously) versus post-synchronised 'cinéma sonore', and how exactly these might be implemented to forge a specifically French, rather than American cultural style (O'Brien 2005: 64–77).

Pagnol's status as the country's most popular playwright put him in an ideal position to denounce talkies, but he took the opposite position, announcing its superiority to both live theatre and silent cinema. Pagnol claimed that talking film's capacity to capture the subtlest nuances of dialogue or appearance, those that would go unnoticed at a live stage production, instantly overcame the limitations of both theatre and silent film: on the one hand, the inevitable heterogeneity of the viewing experience, especially in large venues, and the necessarily unrealistic, declamatory performance of speech in order to be heard by all spectators; on the other, the lack of audible dialogue requiring the artificial, compensatory use of subtitles and exaggerated physical expression. By ensuring that 'tout spectateur verra l'image exactement comme l'objectif l'a vue, à la même distance et sous le même angle, et tout spectateur entendra les paroles de l'acteur comme les entendit la fidèle boîte ronde' (every spectator will see the image exactly as the camera lens saw it, at the same distance and at the same angle, and every spectator will hear the words of the actor just as the faithful round microphone heard them), talking cinema endowed dramatic art with an unprecedented degree of authenticity and emotional power, finally freeing the author and the actor to achieve their full potential while standardising the viewing experience for all spectators.

> Nous pourrons montrer au spectateur un visage à cinquante centimètres, comme s'il s'en approchait pour mieux voir se former et tomber une larme. Charlot nous a déjà montré, sur l'écran silencieux, l'incomparable puissance d'un cillement, ou d'un tremblement de lèvres. Nous pourrons écrire une scène chuchotée et la faire entendre à trois mille personnes sans changer le timbre ni la valeur du

chuchotement. Voilà un domaine nouveau: celui de la tragédie ou de la comédie purement psychologique qui pourra s'exprimer sans cris et sans gestes, avec une admirable simplicité et une mesure jusqu'ici inconnue, parce qu'inutile ... Voilà ce que nous apporte la merveilleuse découverte; nous sauterons la rampe, nous tournerons tout autour de la scène, nous ferons éclater tous les murs du théâtre, nous mettrons en morceaux le décor ou l'acteur. Pour la première fois, les auteurs dramatiques pourront réaliser des œuvres que ni Molière, ni Racine, ni Shakespeare n'ont eu les moyens de tenter.[2] (Pagnol 1930)

Throughout his career as a playwright Pagnol had disliked the inauthenticity of theatrical sets, especially the use of painted canvas scenery to represent outdoor locations. The day before *Marius* opened at the Théâtre de Paris in 1929, Pagnol cut a crucial night-time dockside scene because of his dissatisfaction with the backdrop and lighting, even though doing so forced him to rewrite the second and third acts at the last minute (Anon. 1929). He explained in a letter to the newspaper *Le Soir*: 'Eclairé par un clair de lune assez conventionnel, ce décor construit et peint pour un effet de nuit devenait ridicule' (Illuminated by a rather conventional moonlight lamp, the set built and painted to simulate night looked ridiculous) (Pagnol 1929). All the action thus took place in César's bar and on its terrace.

To make that set as authentic as possible, Pagnol and Raimu, who served as *metteur en scène*, employed staging techniques pioneered by André Antoine. Reviewers almost unanimously praised the wide range of naturalistic sound effects associated with the port (various ship's horns and whistles, motor noises, the clanking of mooring chains against the docks, accordion and guitar music played by sailors along the quay) and authentic props (cargo nets, barrels, wooden fish

2 We will be able to show the spectator a face at a distance of 50 centimetres, as though he were moving closer to better see a tear form and fall. On the silent screen Chaplin has already shown us the unequalled power of a blink or a trembling lip. We will be able to write a scene in whispers and have three thousand people hear it without changing either the timbre or the signification of the whisper. This is a new discipline: that of purely psychological tragedy or comedy which can be expressed without cries and gesticulation, with a wonderful simplicity and subtlety that until now was unknown and would have served no purpose ... Here is what this marvellous discovery offers us: we will leap over the footlights; we will film the stage from every angle; we will blow up all the theatre's walls; we will fragment the scenery or the actors. For the first time, dramatic authors we will be able to craft works of art that neither Molière, nor Racine, nor Shakespeare had the means to attempt.

stands), as well as the use of several three-dimensional tiers of space in front of the painted curtain representing the water and ships in port. Having the main actors and a changing parade of extras move through these spaces – the main room of the Bar de la Marine, its terrace, and the dock beyond – masked the artificiality of the backdrop just enough to preserve its atmospheric value (Nozière 1929; Méré 1929). As Lucien Dubech commented in *Candide*:

> Le décor, le cadre sont réglés à merveille. M. Raimu a su vraiment rendre la vie intense de ce port. On a l'impression d'être allé faire un tour au soleil sur le vieux port. A la terrasse, nous apercevons des filles, des marins, des passants. Un Arabe vend des tapis, une femme des oranges, une Malaise des fruits exotiques. Coups de sifflets, appels des sirènes, puis le calme pour le repos de midi. Les interprètes achèvent l'illusion, on sort en se demandant si l'on n'a pas vu de véritables Marseillais vivants.[3] (Dubech 1929)

Yet Antoine himself was more critical, writing that 'la mise en scène est suffisante, mais elle n'a point cependant évoqué chez nous avec toute l'intensité espérée les visions de là-bas. Le décor laisse apercevoir, par la porte ouverte, seulement quelques mâts des bateaux près du quai; nous eussions rêvé un horizon plus vaste, l'ouverture de la passe sur ce large auquel Marius ne cesse de rêver'[4] (Antoine 1929).

Antoine's disappointment was motivated less by the intrinsic quality of the play, which he summarised as 'un beau spectacle, à la fois populaire et de haut intérêt artistique' (a lovely spectacle, at once popular and of high artistic significance) than by a longstanding dissatisfaction with the artificiality of theatre in general. It was precisely this frustration that towards the end of his career had led him to progressively abandon directing for the stage in favour of naturalist cinema.

---

3 The sets and staging are executed marvellously. Mr Raimu knew how to capture the life in this port. One feels the sensation of having taken a walk in the sun through the Old Port. On the terrace we glimpse prostitutes, sailors, and passers-by. An Arab is selling rugs, a woman oranges, a Malaysian woman exotic fruits. Whistle blasts, siren calls, then the calm of the noon siesta. The actors complete the illusion; one leaves the theatre almost believing that one has seen actual living inhabitants of Marseilles.

4 The staging is acceptable, but it failed to deliver the intense atmosphere of the port that we had hoped for. Through the open door of the bar, the set affords us only a glimpse of a few ships' masts near the dock; we might have hoped for a broader horizon, opening up the passageway towards the open sea of which Marius continually dreams.

The eight films he made between 1915 and 1922 marked a stylistic revolution, shot entirely on site in settings ranging from the streets of Paris (*Le Coupable*, 1916) to the Breton coast (*Les Travailleurs de la mer*, 1917, from the Victor Hugo novel), the isolated farms of the Beauce (*La Terre*, 1919, from the Emile Zola novel), and the barge canals of Belgium (*L'Hirondelle et la mésange*, 1921). In each case Antoine shot using natural light, minimally modified sets, and many non-professional actors in supporting roles (Esnault 1958; Chothia 1991: 177–81).

While it is unlikely that Pagnol saw any of Antoine's movies, he was almost certainly aware of Antoine's views on cinema through their personal contact and the old master's numerous writings on film theory and practice. Indeed, an article Antoine published in 1919 under the title 'Propos sur le cinématographe' (Thoughts on Cinema) bears a striking resemblance to Pagnol's manifesto, starting with the exhortation that cinema be used to explode the artificial narrative conventions of stage production.

> Alors que l'ouvrage dramatique, qu'il soit théâtral ou littéraire, reste inexorablement soumis à la synthèse, à la limitation, à l'ordonnance des épisodes, au cinéma la multiplicité des images, la profusion des détails s'imposeront pour des suggestions qui ne sont restreintes par aucun obstacle matériel d'exécution ... On est simplement parti à faux, dès l'origine, en adoptant les directives et les méthodes théâtrales pour un art qui ne ressemble à rien de ce qui nous fut proposé jusqu'ici et qui réclame des moyens d'expression encore inemployés.[5] (Antoine 1919: 27–8)

Antoine also deplored silent cinema's depriving the actors of speech and disliked the use of exaggerated body language, eagerly anticipating the arrival of synchronous sound recording and other technologies which would finally allow film to become a complete dramatic art marked by realism and psychological nuance.

> Les conventions actuelles réglant le jeu du comédien fourvoyé au cinéma, ses puissances d'expression par le geste, paraissent d'une

---

5 While dramatic works, whether theatrical or literary, remain incontrovertibly subject to the structure, limits, and arrangement of narrative units, in cinema the variety of images and profusion of details offer a power of suggestion unrestricted by any logistical obstacle ... From the beginning cinema has taken the wrong path by applying theatrical rules and methods to a medium that in no way resembles its predecessors, and that demands using means of expression as yet not implemented.

fausseté et une raideur insupportables. Privé d'expression parlée, il devient inutilisable et inadapté pour l'action muette. Nous nous contentons dans ce pays du silence d'utiliser des artistes dont, si j'ose dire, les gestes font du bruit ... Lorsque l'écran, encore déshérité du relief, de la parole, et de la couleur, se sera enrichi de ces inévitables perfectionnements, nous pourrons seulement décider avec pleine sécurité si la production peut monter sans réserve au rang d'œuvre d'art. En attendant, il apparaît que l'œuvre d'un auteur cinématographique, qui doit être surtout un inventeur d'images, reste purement plastique et exactement le contraire de celle de l'auteur dramatique, aiguillé, lui, vers l'étude psychologique. (Antoine 1919: 27–9)[6]

Finally, Antoine shared Pagnol's enthusiasm at the camera's ability to standardise the viewing experience while offering the film author complete freedom and power to direct the viewer's gaze in any way he saw fit: 'L'un des apports inestimables du cinéma est de centupler les aspects d'un personnage, de décomposer ses mouvements, ses expressions, ses attitudes à l'infini, selon les distances et des formats sans cesse changeants, par la multiplication des tableaux et le déplacement incessant du spectateur'[7] (Antoine 1919: 30).

Whereas Antoine's call to explode the conventions of theatre and forge a new dramatic art remained largely unrealisable and thus uncontroversial during the silent era, Pagnol's articulation of the same vision just after the sonic boom drew widespread protests from representatives of both industries. Numerous theatre critics and fellow writers, especially admirers of his previous work, denounced mechanical reproduction and standardisation as inherently harmful

6 On-screen the conventions that normally regulate the actor's performance go astray, with his power of expression through gesture becoming intolerably false and stiff. Deprived of the spoken word, he loses his value and is unsuited for silent acting. In this silent realm, we must settle for using artists whose gestures, so to speak, make noise ... Though currently deprived of depth, speech, and colour, the screen will one day be enhanced by these technical improvements, and only then may we decide with total certainty whether film production can rise unhindered to the level of art. In the meantime, the work of a film author, who must above all be an inventor of images, remains exclusively plastic and precisely the opposite of that produced by the dramatic author, who devotes himself to the study of psychology.

7 One of cinema's invaluable qualities is its ability to show a hundred different aspects of a character, to infinitely dissect his movements, attitudes, and expressions by constantly changing perspectives and scales, through the proliferation of different settings and constant repositioning of the spectator.

to dramatic art, arguing that cinema was 'une mécanique inhumaine, des photos qui s'agitent sur une toile. Au théâtre, ce sont des personnages de chair et de sang. Ici la vérité, là, la fantaisie' (an inhuman mechanism, photos flickering on a canvas. In the theatre, the characters are made of flesh and blood. Here there is truth; there, fantasy) (Wolff 1930). For Pierre Brisson, even perfect recordings of the best plays could not offer the psychological and emotional communion between actors and audience during a live performance, thereby nullifying theatre's unique power to transform spectators with differing social characteristics into 'un seul être extraordinairement homogène' (a single, exceptionally homogeneous being) (Brisson 1930).

Conversely, cinema professionals did not object to Pagnol's defence of mechanical standardisation or his claim for the psychological and dramatic value of recorded speech. By mid-1930 France's top directors of the silent era – including Marcel L'Herbier, Abel Gance, Jacques Feyder, and René Clair – had already publicly acknowledged the artistic potential of incorporating spoken dialogue into visual narration (Abel 1988: II, 18–19, 38–42). What vexed them was the crude underestimation of cinematic technique that the maverick playwright used to justify his argument and his implicit assertion of the creative superiority of the writer and actor over the director, whose role Pagnol tellingly did not even bother to mention. He did however make the point explicitly in a follow-up piece published by *Comœdia*: 'Désormais le rôle du metteur en scène au cinéma sera pareil à celui du metteur en scène de théâtre. Beau rôle, certes, qui exige du goût, de l'imagination, et de grande qualités techniques, certes, mais nous voilà bien loin de l'autocrate qui arrange tout à son gré, même en dépit de l'auteur'[8] (Pagnol 1930a).

Clair, who had just achieved a masterful fusion of song, speech, and image in *Sous les toits de Paris* (1930), answered Pagnol by name in a scathing article titled 'Les auteurs de films n'ont pas besoin de vous' (Film Authors Don't Need You):

> Sous prétexte que le cinéma contient un bon nombre d'incapables, M. Pagnol affecte d'ignorer qu'il est des auteurs de films qui sont plus proprement auteurs de leurs œuvres que beaucoup d'auteurs drama-

[8] Henceforth the role of the film director will be exactly equivalent to that of the stage director. Clearly, an important role that requires taste, imagination, and substantial technical expertise, but we have left behind the autocrat who arranges everything as he pleases, even in spite of the author.

tiques ne le sont des leurs. Or il se trouve que tous les films auxquels notre souvenir peut s'attacher ont été faits sans le concours des auteurs de romans et de comédie ... Le cinéma parlant n'existera que si l'on trouve la formule qui lui est propre, s'il peut se dégager de l'influence du théâtre et de la littérature, si l'on fait de lui autre chose qu'*un art d'imitation*. A cette forme d'expression nouvelle il faut des hommes nouveaux. Ces hommes, nous ne les trouverons pas parmi ceux qui ont déjà consacré leur activité au théâtre et à la littérature. Ceux-ci sont déjà déformés, perdus pour le cinéma duquel ils peuvent sans doute tirer quelque bénéfice matériel, mais à qui ils ne peuvent apporter aucun bénéfice spirituel.[9] (Clair 1930)

Rather than an intentional slur, as Clair obviously took it, Pagnol's view of the director as a minor partner in the filmmaking process was the result of ignorance and the naïve projection of his own prior experience in boulevard theatre onto cinema. Not only did Pagnol have limited exposure to film and know nothing of shooting or recording techniques; the *mise en scène* of his plays had always been a matter of secondary creative importance, absent from the initial writing process and improvised during rehearsals in collaboration with actors and theatre owners. Harry Baur had taken primary responsibility for staging *Jazz*, Variétés head Max Maurey for *Topaze*, and Raimu for *Marius*, with each theatre's respective *directeur de la scène* and *régisseur* providing technical and logistical advice. Pagnol can thus perhaps be excused for misconceiving the cinematic *metteur en scène* as a technician whose role was limited to helping execute the writer's vision.

If in one sense Clair misconstrued Pagnol's intentions, he was right to assert that his rival's endorsement of talking pictures was motivated by commercial opportunism. Picking up on Pagnol's passing remark that Maurice Chevalier's latest film had been seen by nearly as many spectators in eight weeks as *Topaze* in two years, Clair

9 On the pretext that the cinema has a good number of incompetents, Mr Pagnol pretends not to know that there are film authors who are more genuinely authors of their work than many dramatic authors are of theirs. As it happens, all the films that we find memorable were made without the input of novelists or playwrights ... Talking cinema will survive only if it finds its own form, if it breaks free from the influence of theatre and literature, if it becomes something other than *an art of imitation*. This new form of expression requires new men. These men will not be found among those who have devoted their efforts to theatre and literature. They are already warped, lost to cinema, from which they can no doubt extract some material profit, but to which they cannot contribute any intellectual benefit.

attacked: 'cet auteur, étonné d'apprendre que les recettes produites en deux mois par un film étaient plus fortes que celles d'une de ses pièces, se sentit soudain attiré par l'écran' (this author, astonished to learn that a film earned more in two months than one of his plays in a year, suddenly felt drawn to the screen) (Clair 1930: 3). The accusation implied not just venality, but hypocrisy as well. Contrary to Pagnol's habit of flaunting his plays' earnings in the press – he claimed to have pocketed 16,000,000 francs in royalties from *Topaze* alone by May 1930 – and writing indignant rectification letters when box-office receipts were underreported (Pagnol 1930b, 1930c), his articles in *Le Journal* and *Comœdia* justified talking cinema in terms of aesthetic progress and democratising access to quality entertainment, conspicuously eliding the huge financial pay-off of adapting his plays for the screen.

By the mid-1930 the massive popularity and economic power of sound cinema were fuelling the wholesale defection of capital and personnel (writers, directors, distributors, and venue owners as well as performers) from theatre and other live performance arts into talkies (Andrew 1995: 115–27). The case of Pagnol's friend, Théâtre de Paris owner Léon Volterra, was typical. In early 1930 Volterra diversified his business interests by converting his other theatre, the Marigny, into a sound cinema. Virtually all the top-grossing French films of 1929–30 brought to the screen pre-existing vaudeville, music hall, or theatrical acts, most with only minimal modification. Even the exceptions that achieved something more than simple transposition, such as Clair's *Sous les toits de Paris*, still prominently featured some form of diegetic performance, especially song and dance (O'Brien 2005: 54–63; Crisp 2002: 305–8).

In order to meet steadily growing demand for the new commodity, film producers needed a steady supply of ready-made material, and boulevard theatre provided the most convenient and profitable source. The more recent and popular the play, the greater its box-office appeal as a movie – hence the enormous value of *Topaze* and *Marius*. When Pagnol's article appeared in print, many of his peers in the theatre world had already sold the adaptation rights to their plays or had been hired to write dialogue for the screen. The most prominent example was Yves Mirande, under contract on both counts with MGM in Hollywood (Andrew 1995: 95–6). Seen in context, Pagnol's view of talkies was far less revolutionary than either he or his hagiographers would subsequently claim. It was simply the aesthetic justification of an undeniable economic reality that French cinema's most distinguished directors had already accepted as a necessity of survival, but worried would damage the integrity and development of cinema as an autonomous art.

Though not explicitly acknowledged by either Clair or Pagnol, the debate also involved significant reforms to French intellectual property law, which prior to 1930 did not contain clear provisions guaranteeing writers' royalties or creative rights related to adaptations of their work. Typically authors were paid only a flat sum up front and participated in the adaptation process only in so far as the producer deemed appropriate. Twelve days before Pagnol's article appeared, the Société des Auteurs et des Compositeurs Dramatiques (SACD), a national guild for writers in the performing arts, signed an agreement with the French national film union, La Chambre Syndicale de la Cinématographie, outlining a standard contract for adapted work (Méré 1930). In addition to receiving an initial payment for adaptation rights, writers would receive a percentage of ticket sales after the film's release, and enjoy a 'droit de regard' (right of access and input) during production. Conversely, producers retained the power to veto proposed changes if these were unreasonable in nature, occurred late in the project, or threatened its financial viability.

An identical agreement was signed on 20 May 1930 between the cinema union and the Société des Gens de Lettres, the national guild for prose authors (Rageot 1930). The new contracts drew strong praise from writers favourably disposed to talking cinema, but disgust and equally loud protests from those opposed to the new medium. At a dinner held by another national literary guild, La Société des Poètes, popular playwright and drama critic René Fauchois denounced the new guidelines as an act of treason that would fatally degrade literature and theatre, leading a cohort of his colleagues in cries of 'à bas le cinéma!' (down with cinema!) (Boissy 1930).

The larger issue at stake for both French theatre and film professionals was the fear that talkies would serve as a potent vehicle of American cultural and economic imperialism, exacerbating a process of degradation which according to many commentators was already well under way. For novelist and playwright Paul Morand, one of the era's most vocal exponents of anti-American thought, Hollywood talkies were no less than a moral and intellectual contagion infecting the French spirit. As he put it in an indignant article published by the *New York Times*:

> Theatre proprietors for the most part are looking only for financial success and care little about the quality of the product. The people care still less. The cinema initiated them, they run around in Fords or Buicks, they smoke Camels or Luckies, and they shave with Squibb's or Colgate's. But the dramatic authors are by way of the sound films reduced to poverty, like the French musicians professionally menaced by the negroes with saxophones in Montmartre. (Morand 1930)

Aside from venting his notorious racism, Morand was reacting to the fact that the dominance French cinema had enjoyed until the First World War – by some estimates 70 per cent or more of the world market – had been gradually usurped by the United States during the 1920s. Pagnol's stance in favour of cinema as a mass-market industrial commodity, as well as his failure to address issues of national style and intellectual quality, thus exposed him to suspicion of complicity with the American talkies flooding into France and made adapting his work for the screen a delicate proposition.

Pagnol's apprenticeship at Paramount

Pagnol's controversial declarations had the effect of a marketing prospectus, attracting contract offers from several studios. Among them was Paramount, which in late April 1930 had opened a massive new production centre in Joinville-le-Pont, located 25 kilometres east of Paris. At a total investment of over 11 million dollars, the studios boasted six sound stages, ample space for exterior sets, editing facilities, and a development laboratory, surpassing in size and technology all native competitors – Pathé-Natan, Gaumont-Franco-Aubert, and Braunberger–Richebé – as well as the German company Tobis, the only other foreign interest with a production site on French soil (Anon. 1931). Created to circumvent new French regulations limiting the number of imported films and preventing foreign companies from transferring a large percentage of the revenue they earned in France back to their home countries, the Cinéstudio Continental, as it was officially known, exemplified Paramount's ambition to expand its already substantial market share into a position of unquestioned dominance.

Whereas talkies for the European market had previously been made in Hollywood with imported talent – an expensive but successful strategy responsible for dual-language hits such as Josef von Sternberg's *Der blaue Engel/The Blue Angel* (1930), as well as the Maurice Chevalier vehicles *La grande mare/The Big Pond* (1930) and *Le petit café/Playboy of Paris* (1930) – Joinville allowed Paramount to cut costs by two-thirds and to expand its geographic reach beyond France and Germany (Anon. 1930). By concurrently shooting a single screenplay in up to four different languages using the same sets, technicians, and often director, Paramount intended to colonise key smaller markets with limited native production capabilities such as Spain, Sweden, Italy, Poland, and Czechoslovakia. In operation six days a week and up to twenty hours a day, the studios referred to by locals as the 'Tower of Babel' churned out three hundred movies in three years, with French productions accounting for approximately 70 per cent of the total (Waldman 1998: vii–xi).

Marius had initially caught the eye of a Paramount story scout in Paris only days after its premiere in March 1929, but the idea of making a screen adaptation for the American market was rejected because of the play's 'slowness in action, unsatisfactory romance, and unhappy ending' (Farley 1929). However, by mid-1930 its success on stage and Paramount's effort to colonise the French market transformed *Marius* into an indispensable acquisition. Sometime during June or July Joinville head Robert Kane offered 500,000 francs (approximately $20,000) for the rights to *Marius*, but Pagnol, citing the standard contract provisions negotiated by the SACD, instead demanded a percentage of the box-office receipts and creative control over the production, stipulating in particular that the full cast of the original stage version be hired (Pagnol 1995: II, 31–2). In addition to violating the studio's normal practice of paying authors a flat sum for their work and using salaried house actors under long-term contract, these conditions challenged the strict top-down hierarchy in which executives wielded authority over directors or screenwriters.

Though the deal immediately fell through, Kane extended Pagnol an open invitation to spend time at the studios, no doubt in the hope of convincing him to reconsider. The aspiring filmmaker spent much of the late summer and early fall at Joinville studying every aspect of production, from editing, lab processing, set design, camerawork, and sound recording to financing, marketing, and distribution. As he later remembered: 'Prenant des notes comme un écolier, j'ai appris les rudiments de l'Art et de l'Industrie Cinématographiques. S'il m'a été possible plus tard de réaliser des films, tout en dirigeant un laboratoire, des studios et des agences de distribution, c'est à l'amitié de Robert T. Kane que je le dois'[10] (Pagnol 1995: II, 29–30).

Although Pagnol admired the efficiency and profitability of Paramount's tight vertical integration, he deplored the studio's dismissive treatment of writers – 'des auteurs à qui on n'achète qu'un titre' (authors from whom one purchases only a title) – and the mutilation of their work by the script department, 'un bureau dans lequel plusieurs personnes qui n'ont jamais réussi à écrire un roman ni une pièce de théâtre, dépècent et recuisent les œuvres des autres' (an office in which several people who have never managed to write a novel or a play dismember and re-cook the work of others) (Pagnol 1995: II, 26). During his informal apprenticeship Pagnol defended and radicalised his declarations about talking cinema in a flurry of interviews and articles, proclaiming that 'd'ici cinq ans, le théâtre n'existera plus; il n'y aura plus une seule salle de théâtre ouverte à Paris' (five years from now theatre will no longer exist; there will not be a single venue open in Paris) (Pagnol 1930d) while lamenting talkies as

> un trésor entre les mains des maladroits qui le gaspillent. Il y a des metteurs en scène qu'on n'accepterait pas comme troisième régisseur au théâtre, des vedettes qui ne seraient pas engagées comme figurants. Il faut comprendre, balayer, rebâtir. (Chantal 1930)[11]

At the same time Paramount's strategy of copying American hits for the French market was proving ineffective, generating disappointing box-office figures and a rising stream of complaints from spectators, distributors, and theatre owners (Anon. 1930a, 1930b). According to Ukrainian expatriate journalist Ilya Ehrenbourg, who published a scathing tongue-in-cheek account describing Joinville as 'une usine de rêves, où les décors sont plus honnêtes que les gens' (a dream factory, where the sets are more authentic than the people),

---

10 Taking notes like a schoolboy, I learned the basics of film art and business. If later on I was able to make films while running a laboratory, studios, and distribution agencies, I owe it to the friendship of Robert T. Kane.

11 a treasure controlled by incompetents who are wasting it. There are directors who would not be hired as third stage managers in the theatre, star actors who wouldn't be hired as extras. We must understand this, clean house, and rebuild.

the problem was not the films' technical quality or production values, but the insipid, moralising tone of American-written screenplays, lack of psychological complexity in the characters, and predictably facile happy endings (Ehrenbourg 1932: 118–19). Cameraman Osmond Borradaile reported that the sentiment was especially strong among the French technicians working at Joinville, who expressed 'nothing but condemnation' during breaks in the staff cafeteria (Borradaile and Hadley 2002: 42–3).

Ever the astute marketer, Pagnol capitalised on this dissatisfaction by positioning himself as a vocal advocate of high quality and a defender of quintessentially French filmmaking. In a September 1930 interview he expressed his desire to write a script for Maurice Chevalier and German expatriate director Ernest Lubitsch, the pair responsible for Paramount's hit musical *The Love Parade* (1929):

> La grande satisfaction que j'éprouve en me consacrant au cinéma parlant, c'est que Paramount me donne le pouvoir de faire un film français, joué en français par des Français et dont seront tirées des versions étrangères, alors que jusqu'ici les grandes productions interprétées par nos compatriotes comme Chevalier étaient des productions américaines 'traduites' seulement en français. Ce sera du cinéma de chez nous.[12] (Pagnol 1930e)

Shortly thereafter he announced having prepared a film treatment of *Marius* and raised the possibility of directing it himself (Pagnol 1930d).

Likely conceived as a tactic to pressure Paramount into offering the favourable contract he was seeking, Pagnol's announcement coincided with Paramount's public acknowledgement that appealing to the French public necessitated acquiring home-grown stage or screenplays and preserving their integrity on-screen by retaining original dialogue and actors – a practice already under way at small French production companies such as Braunberger–Richebé in its adaptation of Sacha Guitry's play *Le Blanc et le noir*, and Albatros Films in its treatment of Marcel Achard's *Jean de la lune* (Anon.

12 The great satisfaction that I feel in devoting myself to talking cinema comes from Paramount's giving me the power to make a French film, acted in French by Frenchmen and which will be adapted into foreign versions, whereas until now the big productions featuring our countrymen such as Chevalier were American productions 'translated' only into French. This time it will be our own native cinema.

1930b, 1930c). In early October 1930 Paramount executives relented to Pagnol's demands, paying him $2,157.83 (55,000 francs) for the rights to *Marius*, creative control over the adaptation, and a percentage of the film's ticket sales to be determined according to total production expenses (Anon. 1930d). Shortly thereafter, Kane charged Pagnol with forming an advisory committee of notable French writers to recommend and evaluate new production material (Anon. 1930e, Pagnol 1995: II, 33–4). Though short-lived, it resulted in the acquisition of several popular plays including Yves Mirande's comedy *Un Homme en habit*, which in mid-1931 became the first bona fide hit to come out of Joinville. By that time Paramount had ambitiously expanded the new model to the rest of Europe, with over thirty such 'native' projects under contract in five different languages (Anon. 1931b).

Marius from stage to screen

This shift in market conditions and production strategy created the perfect atmosphere for adapting *Marius*. All that remained was the crucial task of finding a director with the personality and professional credentials to satisfy the potentially antagonistic expectations of both Paramount and Pagnol. While the studio required strict adherence to a budget and timeline, the author's contract guaranteed him not only supervisory rights over the production, but top billing on the film's marketing materials (Pagnol 1995: II, 35–6). The man Kane recruited for the job was Alexander Korda, a seasoned director with a résumé of more than forty feature films and a rare breadth of international experience acquired in his native Budapest, Vienna, Berlin, and Hollywood (Kulick 1975: 13–58) (see Figure 2). At First National Pictures Korda had proved his ability to work within the confines of the American studio hierarchy while maintaining a commitment to quality and adding touches of originality, as exemplified by the historical satire *The Private Life of Helen of Troy* (1927).

Better still, Korda had five sound films to his credit, a background in screenwriting, and a talent for adaptation, with six of his ten Hollywood pictures based on plays or short stories. He was known for preserving the integrity of his source material through faithful characterisation and recycled dialogue, judiciously using camerawork and editing to draw out key dramatic elements and render them visually.

Korda was also personally well suited to collaborate with Pagnol. They were both ambitious, disliked the absurd nature of studio bureaucracy, and craved independence, Korda having ended his short stint at Fox in mid-1930 after refusing an executive producer's last-minute demand to re-edit an already completed picture (Kulick 1975: 54–5). 'In Hollywood', he quipped to an interviewer, 'the stupidest producer on the lot can give orders to a director like me, and everybody's nephew is a producer. I should have come here as a producer myself, or better yet, as a nephew' (Waldman 1998: 85–6).

Despite their maverick tendencies, both Pagnol and Korda were savvy enough to recognise that working for Paramount was a crucial step in building the start-up capital and reputation needed to found their own production companies, which would occur almost simultaneously in 1933. With that shared goal in mind, Korda and Pagnol clicked from their introduction sometime in early 1931. After seeing *Marius* on stage, Korda agreed that the play's structure and dialogue should be kept essentially intact and that the original cast should reappear in the film. 'Je ne crois pas qu'on ait pu voir jamais des artistes aussi profondément intégrés dans leurs personnages' (I don't think we have ever seen artists who inhabit their characters more fully), he told an interviewer. 'Ils les vivent comme ils respirent' (For them it's as natural as breathing) (Bessy 1931). Crucially, he even managed to win over the irascible Raimu, who initially derided the presence of 'un Tartare venu d'Olivoï pour nous tirer la photographie!' (a Tartar who's come from Hollywood to take our photo) and signed his contract less than two weeks before shooting was scheduled to begin (Pagnol 1995: II, 37).

The issue of how to adapt the play visually arose early in the production process. Pagnol took the lead by showing his colleagues a rough shooting script he had completed several months earlier. Kane thought it 'réussi' (successful), with Korda suggesting 'quelques coupures' (a few cuts) that Pagnol accepted 'sans la moindre hésitation' (without the least hesitation) (Pagnol 1995: II, 36–7). The original document has unfortunately disappeared, but Pagnol described his vision for the film's opening in a December 1930 interview. This sweeping aerial sequence offers the first concrete illustration of his manifesto in *Le Journal*, testifying to the knowledge he had acquired during his internship at Paramount and to the richness of his nascent cinematic imagination.

Le *Marius* du cinéma, ce sera autre chose que le *Marius* du théâtre – les murs de toile abattus, le décor changeant, l'horizon. Au début de *Marius*, du ciel. En bas, à huit cents mètres, tout Marseilles! Une carte géographique de la ville, de la mer. Puis on se rapproche, on survole, on distingue les rues, les quais, le port! Ses fumées, ses halètements, ses sifflements, ses sirènes, ses appels, sa voix entière, immense, multiple, grondante. Le pont transbordeur, les grands bateaux qui viennent de l'autre côté de la terre, qui apportent dans leur mâture un reflet des tropiques et dans le cœur de leurs marins la nostalgie des îles lointaines, des cieux qui ont plus d'étoiles que les nôtres. Partout, du soleil, du soleil de Provence, du soleil comme il n'en fait qu'à Marseilles! On approche encore, c'est le Vieux Port, et tout à coup, on entre dans le Bar de la Marine, devant le comptoir de zinc de César. Tout le port, qui résume tout le monde, et dans le bar, entre les murs où sont peints les bateaux, Marius, prisonnier.[13] (Chantal 1930)

Rather than 'canning' theatre by recording a stage performance from a single vantage point with an immobile camera, as his detractors would often assert, Pagnol wanted to enhance the realism of his work and free himself from the stage through the use of location shooting, natural light, mobile camerawork, and ambient sound. His approach to talking film should thus be understood not as inherently opposed to the visual properties of cinema, but as an obsessive drive to achieve and definitively preserve the highest possible quality of dramatic performance.

Pagnol's proposed opening, though still bearing the stamp of literary lyricism rather than technical precision, makes relatively sophisticated use of images to express key motifs handled on stage through direct expository dialogue. Rather than emerging slowly over the

13 *Marius* on film will be something different than *Marius* in the theatre, with the canvas walls torn down, changing scenery, and the horizon. At the beginning of *Marius*, the sky. Eight hundred metres below, all of Marseilles! A geographic map of the city, of the sea. We draw closer, fly overhead, distinguish streets, the docks, the port! Its smoke, its panting, its whistles, its sirens, its calls, its whole immense, varied, rumbling voice. The mechanical bridge, the great ships that come from the other side of the globe, that carry in their sail rigging a reflection of the tropics and in the hearts of their sailors nostalgia for distant islands, for skies that have more stars than ours. Everywhere, sun, the sun of Provence, sun as it shines only in Marseilles! We draw closer still – it's the Old Port – and suddenly, we enter the Bar de la Marine, before us César's counter. The whole port, which is a microcosm of the whole world, and in the bar, surrounded by walls with boats painted on them, Marius, imprisoned.

course of the first two acts, Marius' burning desire to escape from the suffocating confines of his native city and his father's authority to the open sky and sea is immediately apparent, captured metaphorically by the heat of the Mediterranean sun and the panoramic tilt-down view of the port that progressively narrows before coming to rest on the bar counter under César's gaze. In terms of its dramatic function, this is a subtle subjective shot that characterises Marius as a caged bird, his flight into the bar establishing the trajectory that he will later follow in reverse to escape.

The second important opposition alluded to visually is that of modernity against tradition – symbolised respectively by the *pont transbordeur*, a towering mechanical iron bridge spanning the Old Port, and the rigging of old-fashioned sailboats crafted from wood and canvas. As an expansion of the generational conflict between Marius and César, as well as that of individual freedom and fulfilment versus familial duty and self-denial, the contrast between symbols of past and present introduces the question of progress and nostalgia, thereby effectively enriching the specific culture of Marseilles and circumstances of the Olivier family with a universal dimension.

The key elements of Pagnol's vision survive largely unmodified in the establishing sequence of the finished film. The first shot is a low-angle close-up of billowing sails that pans to the left, down, back to the right and up, stopping at the top of the schooner's highest mast; followed by a panoramic high-angle looking out towards the sea that pans east from the *pont transbordeur* on the Old Port to reveal the entire city, coastline, and a steamboat headed for the open water beyond; then a perfectly matched counter-shot looking inland from the sea that pans west from Notre Dame-de-la-Garde cathedral back into the heart of the port, revealing the schooner anchored at the dock, the adjacent street with Panisse napping outside his sail shop, and finally the Bar de la Marine, identified by a quick, panning close-up of its lettered awning.

Next we see medium-range one-shots of César sleeping in a booth and Marius washing glasses behind the bar looking through the open doorway at the schooner. As he walks outside, Fanny comes into frame but Marius looks past her, his attention focused entirely on the ship. A brief close-up of Marius in profile cuts to a subjective shot that shows his gaze moving over the sails in exactly the same pattern as before – up, left, down, then right. Yet this time the camera swings full circle, returning to the same view of Marius in profile, which thanks to a quick cut away to Fanny we now recognise as a subjective shot from her perspective: she has been watching him, understood his longing gaze towards the sea, and wants him to look at her instead, as expressed in her shrill greeting that snaps him out of his reverie: 'Ô Marius! A quoi tu penses?' (Oh, Marius! What are you thinking about?). 'A toi, peut-être' (Maybe about you), he answers playfully, prompting her to retort in kind: 'Menteur! Tu penses à moi quand tu me vois' (Liar! You think about me when you see me) (see Figure 3).

Though clearly inspired by Pagnol's motifs and imagery, the screen version reworks and enriches them through the masterful combination of visual and aural technique. While the panoramic shot/countershot signifies Marius' desire for freedom and imprisonment in the bar, father-son conflict is suggested by contrasting Marius' restless preoccupation with César's tranquil sleep, a state of literal unconsciousness that betrays his sedentary, complacent mentality. Korda emphasises this opposition though a conflation of related but distinct sounds: on the one hand, the deep, resounding whistle of a steamship leaving the port, which instantly mesmerises Marius and pulls his gaze away from Fanny out to the sea, followed by the shrill whine of the coffee percolator in the bar, which immediately wakes César but Marius does not hear even after the ship's whistle has faded away. Significantly, the effect on was not part of Pagnol's original stage version, which incorporated only the ship whistle as a signifier of Marius' wanderlust (Pagnol 1931: 25–6).

Perhaps the most impressive aspect of the opening sequence is the triangular exchange of glances between Marius, Fanny, and the harbour that Korda uses to introduce the shifting geometry of desire that will serve as the narrative thread of the entire trilogy. Marius longs for the sea, just as Fanny longs for him and attempts to make him jealous, first by recounting her recent date with another suitor named Victor (a story appropriately cut short by the steamship's whistle), and later by flirting with Panisse in the bar. The pleasure she takes in observing Marius' angry confrontation with the older man is obvious, captured deftly by Korda in a shot that shows a smiling Fanny looking intently at Marius while he accuses Panisse of lechery (see Figure 4). In the ensuing competition between them, César initially conspires to help Marius win Fanny, but after Marius chooses the sea and leaves Fanny pregnant, he is obliged to side with his old friend to ensure the well-being of his grandson. Only after Panisse's death in the third instalment of the Trilogy, *César*, will Marius, Fanny, and César be reunited harmoniously, their individual desires finally reconciled with their familial obligations.

The first few minutes of *Marius* succinctly illustrate the nature of Pagnol's collaboration with Korda, who deftly managed to add narrative complexity and psychological depth to the play without changing its core elements. As he explained shortly before the film's release: 'Une pièce de théâtre comme un roman ont en soi leur élément cinématique. Nous avons pu compléter certaines scènes, préciser leur sens, leur portée, leur atmosphère. Quoi qu'on puisse prétendre, le cinéma pourra parfois être le complément du théâtre et non sa simple copie'[14] (Bessy 1931). Pagnol was equally pleased with the result, telling interviewers that he found the film 'bien supérieur à la pièce' (substantially better than the play) and that 'la mise en scène d'Alexandre Korda a su traduire excellemment ma pensée' (Korda's directing expressed my vision superbly) (Anon. 1931b, Bernier 1931).

Though Pagnol later recalled that the production served as a second, more formal apprenticeship – 'Alexandre ne tourna jamais un plan sans m'expliquer ce qu'il voulait faire, et pourquoi il le faisait' (Alexander never shot anything without explaining to me what he wanted to do and why he was doing it) (Pagnol 1995: II, 37) – Korda never received proper credit, his contribution overshadowed by a lack of archives specifying the exact division of labour, Pagnol's self-serving notion of authorship, and contractual prerogatives as 'premier superviseur' (first supervisor), which ensured that all publicity for the film would bear the phrase '*Marius* de Marcel Pagnol', with 'mise en scène d'Alexandre Korda' (directed by Alexander Korda) appearing below in a smaller font (Masson 1931).

Many influential critics dismissed Korda as no more than a recording technician who, in the words of Emile Vuillermoz, 'a tout simplement installé son appareil dans le trou du souffleur' (simply set up his camera in the prompter's box) (Vuillermoz 1931). Lucien Rebatet noted approvingly that Korda's name did not appear at all on the cover of the programme distributed to spectators, commenting

---

14 A play and a novel both inherently contain a cinematic element. We were able to complement certain scenes, specify their meaning, their impact, their atmosphere. Contrary to what some claim, cinema can on occasion complement theatre and not simply copy it.

that 'il n'avait qu'à s'effacer, il a su le faire avec assez d'élégance' (he had only to make himself inconspicuous, and he did so with appropriate elegance) (Rebatet 1931). However, in his memoirs Pierre Fresnay identifies Korda as the driving creative force behind the film, both in terms of camerawork and guiding the actors:

> Dans cette vaste bouilloire qu'était la Paramount se tenait un personnage fin et grand qui fumait un énorme cigare et qui ne disait presque jamais rien, mais n'en pensait pas moins et voyait très juste ... Il a été l'homme nécessaire, indispensable, et discret. Il n'a jamais écarté les traditions qui avaient pu naître au cours des représentations théâtrales, et il faisait son travail avec un calme souverain. Il parlait toujours bas, et toutes ses suggestions étaient délicates et pertinentes.[15] (Fresnay 1975)

Marius and German expressionism

While Pagnol always made a point of touting *Marius* as purely French in style and as inaugurating a new genre of talking cinema free from the influence of silent film, the crucial narrative importance of high-contrast lighting reveals a clear debt to German expressionism and the so-called *Straßefilm*. Korda knew the genre and the technique well, having directed a prime example, *Das unbekannte Morgen* (1922), in Berlin starring Werner Krauss (Kulick 1975: 37–8). The man responsible for lighting and set design on *Marius* was Alfred Junge, a talented art director who had worked extensively in Berlin during the 1920s and would later win an Oscar for his work on the Hollywood noir classic *Black Narcissus* (1948).

In *Marius* Junge consistently mixes zones of intense light and shadow within the frame to register moments of intense emotional and psychological turmoil for Marius and Fanny, as well as to indicate visually the evolution of their plight. Rather than permeating the entire film, much of which takes place in bright sunlight with little or no shadow, the effect is associated with four crucial locations,

15 In the vast stew that was Paramount, there stood a tall, slender figure who smoked an enormous cigar and almost never spoke, but thought and saw clearly ... He was the just the man we needed, essential and unobtrusive. He never eliminated aspects of our performance that had been acquired during the run of the stage play and he went about his job with a masterful serenity. He always spoke softly, and all his suggestions were tactful and relevant.

none of which were part of the original stage production: a seedy underground club near the port where Marius meets sailors to arrange his departure; the dock from which he finally departs after two aborted attempts; finally, Marius and Fanny's bedrooms, where they experience love and despair most powerfully.

In the club scene, Marius physically and metaphorically descends from the brilliantly sunny street above, where Fanny awaits his return, through a doorway and into the shadows. Once seated at a table to discuss his passport papers, he and four sailors are brightly illuminated by an overhead lamp, but their long, black shadows look down from the wall at Marius like malevolent wraiths tempting him to pursue his selfish dream and expressing the inner torment he feels at preparing to leave César and Fanny. Realising why Marius has abruptly left her at the bar, she experiences a sudden wave of despair and returns home, passing from the uniformly bright public space of the street into the variegated private space of her bedroom. Here the lighting is geometric in its precision, the room and Fanny's bed divided exactly in half between sunlight and shadow. She lies face down with her head in the darkness, sobbing on her pillow until her mother enters and, from the bright half of the room, offers to solve the problem by speaking to César. Fanny, sitting up in a medium-range one-shot, suddenly turns hopeful, as signified by the alternating streaks of light and shadow cascading across her body.

The lighting also helps sustain the dramatic and psychological tension as Marius attempts to renounce sailing and commit to Fanny. In a pair of short night sequences, he visits the docks to contemplate the object of his guilty desire: a three-mast sailboat whose massive hull is, in classic expressionist fashion, unrealistically well illuminated, while the deck, sails and rigging remain bathed in shadow that deepens gradually as it ascends towards the black sky behind. In the first scene Marius is accompanied by Piquoiseau, the former sailor-turned-beggar who goads him to leave with the promise of exotic adventure and leads him aboard from the light of the wharf onto the darkened deck. Later on, as Marius confesses to Fanny his undiminished longing for the sea and how it first came over him after observing a sailboat from the Leeward Islands, the long shot/countershot sequence of their conversation is intercut with three brief shots of a crew preparing to depart on an identical three-master, which again bears highly differentiated zones of light and shadow.

Beyond illustrating Marius' emotional struggle, here the lighting links the private indoor space that he and Fanny occupy – the foyer of César's bar – with the dock just outside the closed door. Recalling the earlier scene in Fanny's room, the bar contains an area of intense brightness, which Marius occupies as he finally tells Fanny his true feelings, and an area of shadow, to which Fanny suddenly retreats when she realises that Marius still desperately needs to sail. Nearly surprised by César, the couple retreat together into Marius' bedroom, where they stand against the wall in a brilliant rectangle of white light, embrace passionately, then move unseen towards Marius' bed in the dark foreground. At the same time, the camera zooms away back towards the white wall and pans slowly upward and to the right, revealing a painting of a huge steamboat, an 'exotic' African wooden mask, a nautical map of the Mediterranean, and a framed drawing of two merchant sailboats, but not a single image of or gift from Fanny. Though physically present in Marius' life and room, she is clearly not the object of his most compelling desire and will ultimately lose him to the sea.

While the point is clear for spectators, it is not for the heroine, who convinces herself that Marius will stay following their tryst. The tipping point occurs in a third and final night scene which begins with a brilliantly front-lit close-up of Marius and Fanny sitting at a dockside table deciding how to decorate their room after their wedding. His head and shoulders bowed and his expression wistful, Marius makes an effort to concentrate, but the sudden whistle of a ship – the same sound used in the film's opening sequence – captures his imagination and snaps him erect, as though awakened from a dream, in parallel to César's awakening by the coffee percolator. Piquoiseau abruptly emerges from the darkness to tempt Marius anew and the camera cuts to a medium-range profile shot of the trio now covered in alternating stripes of light and shadow projected by the back-lit slats of a dock partition (see Figure 5). Marius steals away to discuss a last-minute opening on a freighter, but Fanny follows them to eavesdrop and Marius bitterly refuses the position because of his obligation to her.

Moments later when they return to her house, the camera travels with them through the wall from the dark exterior staircase into the equally black kitchen. Fanny touches a match to the overhead oil lamp and is immediately bathed in bright light. Her strained expression, seen in close-up as she blows out the match and lifts her head, instantly expresses the weight of the terrible choice she faces: prove her love to Marius by setting him free to sail and in so doing suffer the terrible pain of his absence, or say nothing and keep him captive, thus saddling herself with the unbearable guilt. Fanny will choose self-sacrifice the next morning, but for the moment she remains tormented. In a medium-range two shot of her bedroom intercut with shot/counter-shot close-ups in profile, Marius waits on her bed while she turns her back and walks to the window, contemplating the lighthouse in the harbour – an appropriately phallic dual signifier of her love for Marius and his attraction to the sea – as its spinning beacon alternatively brightens and plunges the set into shadow.

The climactic final confrontation between Marius and Fanny in his bedroom also makes good use of lighting by showing the tortured bartender curled up tightly against headboard of his bed, head in hands, then moving quickly into the brightly lit background towards Fanny when she opens the door. Gesticulating emphatically with a wild look in his eyes, Marius tells her:

> Il y a un bateau à quai, à gauche, tu l'as vu, hein? J'ai une place à bord, je suis inscrit sur le rôle. Tout à l'heure on est venu m'appeler. Je n'avais que mon sac à prendre, il est prêt. Et maintenant encore, si je voulais partir, je n'aurais que le quai à traverser. Et pourtant, comme tu vois, je reste ici avec toi.[16]

Though effective in its original theatrical form, Korda gives the moment a specifically cinematic dimension and psychological depth by using another quintessential technique of German expressionism: the rapid-fire montage of subjective, often visually distorted shots and sound to register mental anguish.

During Marius' agonised tirade, his image is replaced by a series of seven two-second shots showing the ship's crew preparing to sail. An initial view of the entire ship and surrounding quay gives way to mid-range images of sailors working feverishly on the bow and above the deck in various sections of the rigging, then sliding down out of frame as the sails unfurl. While these shots are realistic and thus easily intelligible, the next one carries out a sudden, disorienting shift in angle and distance: now seen in close-up, the sails occupy the entire

16 There's a ship at the dock, on the left; you saw it, right? I have a spot on board; I'm on the crew manifest. They came to call me a moment ago. I just had to pick up my bag; it's ready. And still now, if I wanted to leave, all I would have to do is cross the dock. And yet, as you see, I'm staying here with you.

frame and are canted at a 45-degree angle. Crucially, this is a skewed variation on the subjective shot employed at the outset of the film to capture Marius' gaze, the juxtaposition indicating that his unfulfilled wanderlust has evolved from longing to near-madness. Like the audience, Fanny understands, and sets him free 'd'épouser la mer' (to marry the sea), as she puts it, instead of her.

It should also be noted that in *Marius* the lighting plays an integral role in the spatial and affective construction of gender, which does not always follow biological stereotypes. On the one hand, actions set in the seedy music hall and on the docks, public places bustling with activity and dominated by shades of darkness, are defined as masculine by association with Marius' yearning to sail. On the other, moments of vulnerability and abnegation are coded as feminine, occurring in intensely lit private spaces inhabited by only two persons, with bedrooms being of particular importance. The key exception is the Bar de la Marine, a male-dominated public site normally steeped in sunlight and characterised by verbal and physical bravado, as in the near-fight between Marius and Panisse over Fanny or the card game in which César and Escartefigue attempt to cheat Monsieur Brun and Panisse.

However, on two crucial occasions the bar becomes a private space that reveals positive, 'feminine' aspects of César and Marius. The first is the conversation during which César, seated alone with Marius at the breakfast table awash in bright morning light, warns his son not to leave Fanny after sleeping with her, closing with the famous line that 'l'honneur, c'est comme les allumettes, ça ne sert qu'une fois' (honour is like a match; it can only be used once). In so doing, César exhibits his only moment of 'motherly' conduct in the film, substituting transparent affection for his usual sublimation of love through exasperation. The gender reversal implicit in his transformation from distant, irascible patriarch into nurturing confidant is further reinforced by a brief shot of him cooking breakfast for Marius in the kitchen, a task and space strongly associated with women.

A second episode of 'feminisation' occurs in the night-time scene where Marius admits to Fanny his irrepressible desire for the sea, the brilliant light that surrounds him during his confession symbolising the moral value of truth and redeeming the selfish, socially destructive desire he has pursued in the club and on the docks. As noted in Chapter 1, this subversion of classic gender stereotypes should be seen as typical of Pagnol's consistently populist approach to moral, social and political issues, which involved presenting strong ideological positions while simultaneously critiquing them. Just as *Topaze* can be seen as an equivocal reflection on the survival of ethics in an inherently corrupt, unjust capitalist system, the Marseilles trilogy offers an ambivalent take on the emotional and social consequences of pre-marital sex and arranged marriage between younger women and older men.

The lighting in *Marius* draws out these themes in subtle yet powerful fashion, merging with camera movement, sound, and editing to give the film version a visual richness that it lacked on stage. Korda's patient recycling of key metaphors – ships' masts and sails to represent youthful male lust for adventure and rejection of patriarchal authority; whistles to disclose controlling, unconscious priorities; light to mark truthfulness, emotional intimacy, and torturous, self-sacrifice; shadow to suggest repressed or sublimated desire, temptation, and socially destructive self-indulgence – echoes the work of expressionist masters such as Friedrich Murnau, Carl Theodor Dreyer, and Fritz Lang. The 'Germanic' influence on French poetic realism is well documented (Elsaesser and Vincendeau 1983; Phillips 2004), especially with regard to lighting and set design, but it is usually associated with directors such as René Clair, Jean Renoir and Marcel Carné. While Korda's involvement does make *Marius* an anomaly both within the Trilogy and Pagnol's overall career as a director, the film deserves to be remembered precisely for that reason as a particularly successful example of Franco-German stylistic convergence.

Marius and French realism

If the 'German' contribution consisted essentially of adding psychological depth through artificial lighting, it was the realism provided by location shooting that gave the movie a quintessentially 'French' feel and made it the first concrete manifestation of Pagnol's desire to free dramatic art from the confines of the stage and studio. When pre-production for the screen version of *Marius* began in April 1931, Pagnol requested approval for several weeks of filming in the Old Port. Kane initially resisted, adhering to Paramount's standard practice of making pictures entirely at Joinville in the interest of time and budget. However, he relented after Pagnol and Korda protested the inauthenticity of the sets Junge designed for the wharf and Bar de la Marine (Pagnol 1931a). Korda subsequently recruited his brother Vincent, a painter living on the Riviera, to serve as co-art director on the picture, and sent him to scout locations in Marseilles. Guided by Pagnol's old friend Jean Ballard, Vincent made detailed sketches of the port and adjoining neighbourhoods that served as the basis for planning the outdoor shooting and constructing matching sets at the studios (Ballard 1931).

Spanning six weeks from late June through early August, filming was split evenly between Joinville and Marseilles (Anon. 1931c, 1931d; Chantal 1931). *Marius* was Paramount's first European production to make use of extensive location shooting, a move that substantially increased the studio's usual three-week timeline and $85,000 budget for a three-language picture (Anon 1931a). *Variety* reported that *Marius* cost $80,000 exclusive of the Swedish and German versions shot simultaneously under the titles *Längtan till havet* (Longing for the Sea, directed by John Brunius) and *Zum goldenen Anker* (The Golden Anchor, also directed by Korda) (Anon. 1931e). Even that figure may have been low, as French journalists reported daily expenses in Marseilles of 80,000 francs, or about $3,000 (Anon. 1931f), and Pagnol himself later told an interviewer 'il faut bien l'avouer, on jouait aux sous' (I have to admit, we were playing with money) (Vermorel 1933). Paramount tolerated the expenditures only because it needed the film to prove its commitment to satisfying the French market with home-grown, culturally appropriate material. A five-page ad that ran in France's largest corporate film journal during May and June 1931 reassured distributors and theatre owners that 'Paramount connaît vos inquiétudes et prépare une programmation qui répondra exactement à ce que désire votre clientèle. *Marius* à l'écran montrera toute la beauté, toute la lumière des paysages, toute l'atmosphère que la scène ne pouvait que nous suggérer. Ce sera un beau voyage au pays du soleil'[17] (Anon 1931g).

The logistics of shooting in the Old Port at the height of summer were complicated as well as expensive. According to local newspapers, crowds of curious onlookers were so large and boisterous that a large

---

17 Paramount understands your worries and is preparing a program of films that will satisfy your clients completely. *Marius* on-screen will show all the beauty, all the sunny landscapes, all the atmosphere to which the stage version could only refer indirectly.

police presence was necessary to keep the set clear and relatively quiet during filming. The night-time dock sequences choreographed by Junge were a particular challenge because they required simultaneously illuminating massive sailboats and large sections of the dock. A Paramount cameraman who remained at Joinville remembered having to construct makeshift lights for another film being made concurrently because Korda 'had pinched all the lamps from the studio' (Borradaile and Hadley 2002: 44). An eyewitness on the set reported the lights being so numerous and bright that they initially blinded a group of prostitutes and derelicts lingering along the docks, causing them to cry out and fall over (Anon. 1931c).

The cost and effort paid substantial aesthetic dividends, endowing *Marius* with a depth of authenticity unmatched in France since the advent of talking cinema. The inimitable summer sunlight of the Mediterranean that drenches the daytime outdoor scenes creates a cheerful, expansive atmosphere that by contrast intensifies the psychological turmoil and feeling of entrapment that Marius and Fanny experience during the expressionist night-time scenes indoors.

As one critic noted: 'C'est l'image qui donne au film sa poésie simple et ses vertus de sincérité. L'atmosphère est créée avec un rare bonheur par des vues d'intérieur précisément étudiées, par ces coins du Vieux Port, de ses rues, de ses maisons balafrées, de ses types si divers et si nettement marqués'[18] (Bizet 1931).

In its balance of studio and location shots, *Marius* represents a middle ground between the German and Swedish versions. Whereas the former incorporates almost no footage from Marseilles and eliminates other elements (such as the famous card game) that Paramount producer Jacob Karol deemed 'too local' in nature, *Längtan till havet* extends the length of the establishing sequence to show daily life in the streets surrounding the port and subsequently replaces several comic, theatrical scenes with additional aerial views of the city and harbour. In so doing, director John Brunius translates the film's 'exotic' appeal visually, rather than relying on the highly inflected, characteristically southern speech of the French-language version (Rossholm 2006: 159–60).

18 It is the images that give the film its simple poetry and admirable sincerity. The atmosphere is exceptionally well created by shots of carefully designed interiors and by the Old Port, its various nooks, streets, dilapidated houses, and varied, distinctive inhabitants.

The less extensive use of documentary-style footage in *Marius* underscores the highly selective nature of Pagnol's realism, which incorporates location shots not in the interest of exoticism or social-realist critique, but to lend melodrama an air of authenticity while giving it psychological and emotional depth. In that sense, the flashes of daily life captured on the port are no less artificial, no less dictated by narrative and aesthetic imperatives than Junge's expressionist lighting. Pagnol's detractors seized on this objection, charging that the screen version of *Marius* 'n'a contribué que quelques vues banales de Marseilles et quelques décors supplémentaires' (contributed only a few banal shots of Marseilles and a few extra sets) (Champeaux 1931) and that the very premise of the film was 'difficile à admettre' (difficult to accept), for three-mast trading ships such as the one that torments Marius had been obsolete since the mid-nineteenth century and all commercial traffic had been rerouted to a deeper port built farther up the coast (Fayard 1931). By 1931, the only three-mast sailboats still using the Old Port were tourist attractions that sometimes ferried visitors to nearby If island, whose château served as the prison in Alexandre Dumas' *L'homme au masque de fer*.

Many of Pagnol's supporters also conceded the point, but regarded his leavening of melodrama with realism as an aesthetic innovation that gave *Marius* a unique blend of nostalgic lyricism and palpable authenticity, distinguishing it from most other adapted plays. Screenwriter and freelance journalist Henri-André Legrand praised *Marius* as a unique combination of palpable authenticity and nostalgic lyricism, citing as evidence the tracking shot in which César walks along the quay to meet his girlfriend.

> Conduits avec maîtrise avec le réalisateur, nous avons vu le Vieux Port, ses mâts et ses cheminées; nous avons parcouru les ruelles grouillantes où chacun interpelle et où, jusque dans les moindres recoins, le soleil dur appuie ses taches dansantes. L'image accomplit ce miracle d'être à la fois prodigieusement concrète et prodigieusement évocatrice. Ainsi, sans nuire aucunement à la beauté de la pièce, le film en a rendu la compréhension plus unanime ... Bien souvent, la transposition au cinéma des comédies du boulevard donnent un résultat lamentable qui n'a rien de commun avec ce film. On doit espérer que l'exemple de *Marius* montrera la bonne voie aux producteurs.[19]

19 Masterfully guided by the director, we've seen the Old Port onto which César's shop opens, the port's masts and smokestacks; we've heard the laughter of

(Legrand 1931)

Three short sequences illustrate the multiple benefits of shooting on site in natural light: the panoramic high-angle views of the port, city, and coastline – all shot from a hot-air balloon – that open the film; a 20-second two-shot showing Panisse speaking with Fanny at her fish stall; and a tracking shot of César walking from the bar to the nearby café where he has a secret lunch date. As Panisse flirts with Fanny, the lettered awning and beaded doorway screen of the bar behind them sway in the breeze, then a series of four extras – an old man in a sailor's coat, a woman with a shopping net, and two French legionnaires in uniform – pass in front of the camera and briefly obscure the actors from view. By purposefully violating a traditional rule of studio filming, the shot injects a fleeting but crucial moment of documentary realism into the action, thereby balancing and opening up the more theatrical scenes inside the bar that precede and follow it.

The same is true to an even greater degree of the 45-second mobile shot that follows César to his date. Absent from the stage version, it offers an exceptionally dense image of the quayside street spread across three spatial layers. A diverse array of people (sailors, nuns, children playing, couples holding hands) and objects (bicycles, carts, storefronts, vendors' stalls, dogs) move through both the background and foreground, occasionally blocking César from sight and drawing his attention. After shaking hands with a passing man, he briefly stops to reject the come-on of a prostitute who calls out to him from an alley where she and her several other women are scouting potential clients. In addition to adding atmospheric value, the interaction serves an important dramatic function by underscoring César's desire for female companionship and presumably sex (in the person of his unseen date, whom Marius reports is a buxom Dutch woman) without falling into moral impropriety (represented by the prostitutes) or dishonouring the memory of his late wife. César's plight causes him

---

sailors who quiver at the sound of ship's whistles; we've travelled through the teeming alleys where everybody calls out to each other, and where the harsh sun casts its dancing spots into the smallest corners. The images perform the miracle of being both thoroughly concrete and immensely evocative. Thus, without in any way undermining the beauty of the play, the film made it more complete and accessible ... Quite often the screen adaptation of popular stage comedies yields a lamentable result that has nothing in common with this film. One must hope that *Marius* will show producers the right approach to take.

substantial embarrassment that remains unexpressed throughout the film. Rather than touting his sexual exploits in stereotypical macho fashion, he justifies his departure to Marius and Monsieur Brun in a string of awkward excuses. Here again, as in his affectionate face-to-face conversations with Marius, César is 'feminised' as a nurturing parent whose primary concern is his family reputation and the welfare of his son, whom he still perceives as a child who could be hurt by his father frequenting a woman other than his mother.

For an author who had always resented the narrative limitations of theatrical staging, the ability to change settings as often as necessary and the use of parallel editing had the added benefit of eliminating artificial stage entrances and exits, as well as the surplus of expository dialogue that sustained the plot by summarised off-stage action but also undermined subtlety. Contrary to the claims of influential critics incensed by Pagnol's approach to cinema, *Marius* is far from 'du théâtre mécanique sans aucun effort d'adaptation' (mechanical theatre that makes no attempt at adaptation) (Vuillermoz 1931) and demonstrates neither a 'pauvreté d'imagination' (poverty of imagination) nor a 'négligence de tout ce qui est la puissance et la raison du cinéma' (a neglect of all that is the power and essence of cinema) (Soupault 1931).

Occasionally, though, even critics keen to denounce Pagnol on principle grudgingly acknowledged the film's improvement on the play. Contradicting his own previous claim that 'on n'a pas pu ajouter à *Marius* une seule trouvaille visuelle, et ce n'est presque jamais du cinéma' (not a single visual innovation was added to *Marius*, which is almost never cinematic), Jean Fayard concluded that 'grâce à l'effet de gros plans, aux changements d'angle de vue, Raimu m'a paru meilleur encore [qu'au théâtre], plus drôle et plus truculent dans les scènes burlesques, plus discret et touchant dans la scène où il avoue à son fils sa tendresse paternelle'[20] (Fayard 1931). Georges Champeaux followed suit, asserting that 'on n'a pas traduit la pièce dans la langue du cinéma; on l'a simplement recopiée' (the play has not been translated into the language of film; it has simply been recopied), only to admit that the tracking shots and close-ups of Raimu 'démontrent la

20 Thanks to the effect of close-ups and changes in viewing angles, Raimu struck me as even better [than on stage], more droll and irascible in the farcical scenes, more subdued and touching in the scene where he confesses his paternal tenderness to his son.

supériorité du cinéma. Se déplaçant avec le personnage, la caméra fait de lui le centre mouvant du tableau et nous donne la sensation de marcher dans ses pas' (demonstrate the superiority of cinema. By moving with the character, the camera makes him the mobile centre of the frame and gives us the feeling of walking in his shoes) (Champeaux 1931). Ironically, the latter comment describes exactly the effect Antoine and Pagnol envisaged in their respective manifestoes.

After the film's completion Paramount executives were dissatisfied with the excessive cost and length of *Marius*, recommending that it be cut from 132 minutes to the standard 75–80 minutes to allow more daily screenings and maximise profits. However, Kane and Pagnol managed to preserve the integrity of the film by citing spectators' overwhelmingly positive response to an impromptu test screening held in Paris (Anon. 1931h). In the end only about ten minutes of comic sketches unrelated to the plot were removed, including one long sequence in which a crane lifts Piquoiseau from a ship on which he has tried to stow away in the coal bin (Cambien 1931).

Unconcerned with quibbles over length and the aesthetics of theatrical adaptation, the public made *Marius* an immediate box-office hit upon its release in October 1931. The picture was by far the most popular of the season, attracting an estimated 650,000 spectators during its initial run in Paris and at least that many outside the capital (Crisp 2002: 311). According to *Variety*, it grossed a record $6,200 (155,000 francs) on its first Sunday (Anon. 1931i). Pagnol reported that it averaged a million francs ($40,000) a week through to the end of the year, and that demand was so strong in the provinces that Paramount used the film as a 'locomotive' to move its entire inventory. For independent cinema owners, securing a week of exclusive rights to *Marius* required renting nineteen additional Paramount films at the same price, effectively locking them into the studio's national distribution circuit for four full months (Pagnol 1995: II, 39). At the peak of its popularity, there were a whopping 200 copies of *Marius* in circulation (more than four times the industry norm) and 150 daily screenings (Pagnol 1995: I, 612). This unprecedented success not only vindicated Pagnol's belief in using talking cinema to reinvent theatre; it provided him the liquid capital and confidence he needed to move towards directing and producing films on his own – a step that the ever-ambitious author would take the following year with *Fanny*.

References

Abel, Richard (1988), *French Film Theory and Criticism: a History/Anthology*, 2 vols, Princeton, Princeton University Press.

Andrew, Dudley (1995), *Mists of Regret: Culture and Sensibility in Classic French Film*, Princeton, Princeton University Press.

Anon. (1929), 'Une scène supprimée de *Marius*', *Comœdia*, 10 March.

Anon. (1930), 'Paramount Turns 'Em Out in Paris for One-Third of Home Cost', *Variety*, 22 October.

Anon. (1930a), 'French Disdain for Foreign Versions Becoming Stronger', *Variety*, 10 December.

Anon. (1930b), 'Original Stories for Foreign Markets Look Like General American Production Policy', *Variety*, 10 December.

Anon. (1930c), 'French Yarns by Paramount', *Variety*, 24 December.

Anon. (1930d), Paramount Studios Comptroller's Report, Margaret Herrick Library, Special Collections, Paramount Pictures Scripts, Production File no. 1131, 9 October.

Anon. (1930e), 'Paris Prize Contest for Native French Stories', *Variety*, 31 December.

Anon. (1931), 'Paramount's Joinville Policy', 14 January.

Anon. (1931a), 'In Five Languages, All Made Abroad', *Variety*, 22 April 1931.

Anon. (1931b), 'Ayant laissé *Marius* à Joinville, Marcel Pagnol va s'occuper de *Fanny* à Juan-les-Pins', *Paris-Midi*, 13 August.

Anon. (1931c), 'On tourne *Marius* à Joinville', *Aux écoutes*, 23 June.

Anon. (1931d), 'On tourne *Marius* de Marcel Pagnol', *Le Petit Marseillais*, 7 July.

Anon. (1931e), '*Marius*', *Variety*, 27 October.

Anon. (1931f), '*Marius* chez lui: la célèbre pièce de Pagnol a été filmée cette nuit aux Pierres-Plates', *Le Petit Provençal*, 7 July.

Anon. (1931g), 'Paramount connaît vous inquiétudes', *La Cinématographie française*, 9 May.

Anon. (1931h), 'Trying Supers Out on French Before Editing', *Variety*, 20 October.

Anon. (1931i), 'Paris' Good Week-End', *Variety*, 20 October.

Antoine, André (1919), 'Propos sur le cinématographe', *Le Film* no. 166, December, reprinted in *1895: Bulletin de l'Association française de recherche sur l'histoire du cinéma*, 'Antoine cinéaste', no. 8–9, May 1990, 27–32.

Antoine, André (1929), 'La Semaine théâtrale: *Marius* au Théâtre de Paris', *L'Information financière, économique et politique*, 17 March.

Ballard, Jean (1931), Letter to Marcel Pagnol, Archives de la Bibliothèque de Marseilles à Vocation Régionale – L'Alcazar, Fonds Littéraire Méditerranéen, 30 June.

Bernier, Jacques (1931), 'Un succès, *Marius*', *Ciné-Miroir*, 14 October.

Bessy, Maurice (1931), 'Marcel Pagnol et Alexandre Korda nous parlent de *Marius*', *Ciné-Miroir*, 2 October.

Bizet, René (1931), 'Un grand film français: *Marius* de Marcel Pagnol', *Pour Vous*, 15 October.

Boissy, Gabriel (1930), 'Les poètes avec ou contre le cinéma', *Comœdia*, 19 June.

Borradaile, Osmond and Anita Hadley (2002), *Life through a Lens: Memoirs of a Cinematographer*, Montreal, McGill-Queen's University Press.

Brisson, Pierre (1930), 'Théâtre et cinéma: à propos d'un article de Marcel Pagnol', *Le Temps*, 26 May.

Cambien, Odile (1931), 'Mihalesco nous parle de *Marius*, ou l'invitation au voyage', *Cinémonde* no. 150, 3 September.

Champeaux, Georges (1931), '*Marius*', *Gringoire*, 16 October.

Chantal, Suzanne (1930), 'Opinions sur le film parlant: "un trésor qu'on gaspille", nous dit Marcel Pagnol', *Cinémonde*, 4 December.

Chantal, Suzanne (1931), '*Marius* n'est plus à St. Maurice', *Cinémonde*, 6 August.

Chothia, Jean (1991), *André Antoine*, Cambridge, Cambridge University Press.

Clair, René (1930), 'Les auteurs de films n'ont pas besoin de vous', *Pour Vous* no. 85, 3 July.

Crisp, Colin (2002), *Genre, Myth, and Convention in the French Cinema, 1929–1939*, Bloomington, Indiana University Press.

Dubech, Lucien (1929), 'Formidable triomphe au Théâtre de Paris de *Marius*', *Candide*, 14 March.

Elsaesser, Thomas and Ginette Vincendeau (1983), *Les Cinéastes allemands en France: les années 30*, Paris, Goethe Institute.

Ehrenbourg, Ilya (1932), *Usine de rêves*, Paris, Gallimard.

Esnault, Philippe (1958), 'Faut-il réhabiliter Antoine?', *Cinéma* no. 25, March, 58–85.

Farley, Frank (1929), Report on *Marius* sent to Paramount's New York production office, Margaret Herrick Library, Special Collections, Paramount Pictures scripts, Production File no. 1131, 11 March.

Fayard, Jean (1931), '*Marius*', *Candide*, 19 October.

Kulick, Karol (1975), *Alexander Korda: The Man Who Could Work Miracles*, London, W.H. Allen.

Legrand, Henri-André (1931), 'Notes d'un spectateur: en voyant *Marius* et en se souvenant de *Jean de la Lune*', *Comœdia*, 13 October.

Masson, Jean (1931), 'Marcel Pagnol, "superviseur", offre à boire à Joinville', *Pour Vous* no. 136, 25 June.

Méré, Charles (1929), 'Avant *Marius*', *Excelsior*, 7 March.

Méré, Charles (1930), 'Déclarations de Monsieur Charles Méré, président de la Société des Auteurs, relatives à l'accord intervenu entre la Société des Auteurs et la Chambre Syndicale de la Cinématographie', *Comœdia*, 8 May.

Morand, Paul (1930), 'A Protest from France', *New York Times*, 12 January.

Nozière, Franck (1929), 'Un grand succès: *Marius*', *L'Avenir*, 10 March.

O'Brien, Charles (2005), *Cinema's Conversion to Sound: Technology and Film Style in France and the US*, Bloomington, Indiana University Press.

Pagnol, Marcel [J-H Roche] (1923), 'A L'Atelier: *Antigone* de Jean Cocteau', *Fortunio* no. 27, 15 March.

Pagnol, Marcel [J-H Roche] (1924), 'Au Théâtre de l'Atelier: *Le chevalier sans nom* de Jean Variot', *Fortunio* no. 46, 1 January.

Pagnol, Marcel (1929), 'Une lettre de Marcel Pagnol à propos de *Marius*', *Le Soir*, 22 March.

Pagnol, Marcel (1930), 'Le film parlant offre à l'écrivain des ressources nouvelles', *Le Journal*, 17 May.

Pagnol, Marcel (1930a), 'Les ennemis du cinéma parlé', *Comœdia*, 6 June.

Pagnol, Marcel (1930b), 'La véridique histoire de *Topaze*', *Bravo: tous les spectacles*, March.

Pagnol, Marcel (1930c), 'Marcel Pagnol nous écrit pour mettre au point certaines informations concernant ses pièces', *Paris-Midi*, 29 October.

Pagnol, Marcel (1930d), 'Marcel Pagnol et Maurice Chevalier: il est question d'une collaboration', *L'Intransigeant*, 24 September.

Pagnol, Marcel (1930e), 'Marcel Pagnol, écrirait-il des scénarios?', *Comœdia*, 16 September.

Pagnol, Marcel (1931), *Marius: pièce en quatre actes et six tableaux*, Paris, Fasquelle.

Pagnol, Marcel (1933), 'Cinématurgie de Paris', *Les Cahiers du film*, no. 1, December, 3–8.

Pagnol, Marcel (1931a), Letter to Jean Ballard, Archives de la Bibliothèque de Marseilles à Vocation Régionale – L'Alcazar, Fonds Littéraire Méditerranéen, 27 May.

Pagnol, Marcel (1995), *Œuvres complètes*, 3 vols, Paris, Fallois.

Phillips, Alastair (2004), *City of Darkness, City of Light: Emigré Filmmakers in Paris, 1929–1939*, Amsterdam, Amsterdam University Press.

Rageot, Gaston (1930), 'Les droits des collaborateurs du film ont été établis hier par un traité signé hier par à la Société des Gens de Lettres', *Le Journal*, 21 May.

Rebatet, Lucien [François Vinneuil] (1931), '*Marius*', *L'Action française*, 16 October.

Rossholm, Anna Sofia (2006), 'Film, Theatre and the Translation of the Local: *Marius* in Sweden', in Rossholm, *Reproducing Languages, Translating Bodies: Approaches to Speech, Translation and Cultural Identity in Early European Sound Film*, Stockholm, Stockholm University Press, 144–60.

Soupault, Philippe (1931), '*Marius*, un film de Marcel Pagnol', *L'Europe nouvelle*, 31 October.

Vermorel, Claude (1933), 'En laissant parler Marcel Pagnol à l'heure du dessert', *Pour Vous*, 2 February.

Vuillermoz, Emile (1931), '*Marius*', *Le Temps*, 10 October.

Waldman, Harry (1998), *Paramount in Paris: 300 Films Produced at the Joinville Studios, 1930–1933*, London, Scarecrow Press.

Wolff, Pierre (1930), 'Le film parlant rétablit la gloire du poète', *Paris-Soir*, 31 May.

3

Cinématurgie revisted

Despite their mutually lucrative partnership in making *Marius*, Pagnol ran afoul of Paramount over the adaptation of *Topaze* in early 1932 as the worsening of the Great Depression threatened the solvency of the Joinville complex and made reducing expenses more imperative than ever for the American juggernaut. In a directive sent to Paris in April 1932, Paramount founder Jesse Lasky acknowledged that the 'tremendous success' of *Marius* stemmed from 'the atmospheric shots of the docks and the picturesque scenery of the waterfront', but dictated that *Topaze* follow a different production model: 'Our company is greatly in need of program pictures that can stand up through the outstanding interest and vitality of the stories themselves without any great expense in cast, direction, or production value' (Lasky 1932).

Having already sent Alexander Korda to work at Paramount's London branch, studio executives prevented Robert Kane from producing *Topaze*, vetoed Pagnol's renewed demands for supervisory privileges, and exercised the company's right of first refusal to adapt *Fanny* (Pagnol 1995: II, 42–3; Richebé 1977: 91–2). Pagnol withdrew from the project in disgust to craft a screen version of *Fanny* that would be free from all foreign influence. 'Ce sera un film qui n'aura rien d'américain', he told an interviewer, 'un film marseillais qui ne sera fait que par des Marseillais et où je veux mettre le plus d'images de notre splendide ville et le plus de lumière possible dans le plein air. A mon goût, dans *Marius* il n'y avait pas assez de ces images. Mais cette fois je suis libre, je vais travailler à ma guise'[1] (Pagnol 1932).

---

1 It will be a film with nothing American, a Marseilles film that will be made only by Marseillais and in which I want to put as many images of our splendid city as

The other Marseillais involved was Roger Richebé, who ran a profitable chain of cinemas in southern France and co-owned a small production company/studio with Pierre Braunberger in the Paris suburb of Boulogne-Billancourt. Founded in mid-1930, theirs was one of only a few small French production companies not crushed at the outset of the sound era by Paramount, Pathé-Natan, and Tobis (Richebé 1977: 53–4). Known for its commitment to experimentation and high quality, as evidenced by Jean Renoir's *La Chienne* (1931), Braunberger–Richebé took a holistic approach to adapting popular plays by respecting their structure and dialogue while adding visual interest and complexity (Andrew 1995: 93–4). In so doing, the company distinguished itself from its giant competitors, which tended either to transpose stage productions essentially unchanged or modify them beyond recognition (Harlé 1930).

Richebé enjoyed the distinction of being the first film producer to sign Raimu to a long-term contract and initially rejected entreaties from Paramount to release him temporarily for *Marius*. Pagnol persuaded Richebé to relent, but only in exchange for exclusive screening rights to the film in his chain of cinemas, several of which competed directly with Paramount's in large-market cities (Richebé 1977: 85–6). At Richebé's suggestion, he and Pagnol formed a new company – La Société des Films Marcel Pagnol – to make and distribute *Fanny*, dividing expenses and profits equally. For Pagnol the arrangement was ideal since it provided all the material and logistical support he needed (an experienced producer, a studio equipped with the latest Western Electric sound equipment, an established distribution network), reduced his financial risk, and allowed him to maintain creative control of the project (Richebé 1977: 92–3; Agay 1932).

The director Richebé recruited to work with Pagnol, Marc Allégret, had both a strong command of visual vocabulary, as demonstrated in the remarkable documentary *Voyage au Congo* (1927) commissioned by his uncle André Gide, and a straightforward approach to theatrical adaptation acquired from making six sound pictures in 1930–31, including Sacha Guitry's hit *Le Blanc et le noir*, a Richebé production starring Raimu. As Allégret told an interviewer: 'Mon rôle est de servir le texte, de diriger le jeu des acteurs, de donner au film son movement en utilisant une technique simple. Le metteur en scène doit collaborer

---

possible, shot in natural light and the open air. In *Marius* there were not enough of these images. But this time I am free and shall work as I like.

avec l'auteur, à qui il peut avoir à demander de modifier son dialogue selon les nécessités du moment'[2] (Vidal 1932).

Which language? Image and speech in the Trilogy

Following Korda's example, Allégret used subtle cinematic technique and location shooting to enhance the realism and psychological depth of Pagnol's original narrative. The most effective instance occurs when the camera follows the heroine for three full minutes through the busy streets from the doctor's office, where she has just confirmed her pregnancy with Marius' baby, to Notre Dame de la Garde high atop the hill overlooking the port. After a tight opening shot registers her pallid face and stunned expression, parallel tracking from across the street emphasises her emotional frailty and solitude as she is visually swallowed up by the busy urban landscape of cars, shops, trolleys, and other pedestrians. Though nearly run into on two occasions by men who turn and shoot her irritated glances, she continues to teeter forward, stopping momentarily to lean on a light pole for support and twice absently laying her forearm and hand across her stomach. As Fanny climbs the steps to the church, a slow, high-angle pan reveals the port below, bisected by the channel to the sea that has stolen Marius from her. Inside a tilt-down close-up captures her kneeling at the altar, tearfully begging for forgiveness, strength, and Marius' safe return to legitimise their baby.

This is arguably the most purely cinematic sequence of any Pagnol film, devoid of dialogue but using non-diegetic music, ambient sound and camerawork to complement Orane Demazis' wonderfully understated performance. 'Dans toute cette partie', commented one reviewer, 'nul ne songe à se demander si *Fanny* est du cinéma ou du théâtre. Il y a une force irrésistible dans les images et l'interprétation qui abolit tout esprit critique' (In this segment, nobody dreams of asking whether *Fanny* is cinema or theatre. There is an irresistible power in the images and the acting that precludes any criticism) (Lehmann 1932). Even reviewers generally hostile to Pagnol were impressed, with Georges Champeaux noting approvingly that 'cette

2 My job is to serve the text, to direct the actors, to give the film movement by using simple techniques. The director must work with the author, whom he may have to ask to modify the dialogue as the need arises.

vision de la jeune fille avançant telle une somnambule parmi la foule est de nature à plaire aux cinéastes' (the image of the young woman making her way through the crowd is the kind of thing that pleases real filmmakers) (Champeaux 1932). Yet many critics expressed dismay at the insertion of an intermission halfway through the film, which ran just under two-and-a-half hours, and its stark juxtaposition of two distinct styles.

The first ninety minutes are consistently well balanced thanks to the judicious integration of theatrical studio scenes and documentary-like open-air sequences shot in Marseilles. As with Fanny's stunned march to Notre Dame de la Garde, the use of location shooting enhances characterisation and adds emotional punch. Panisse's joy at marrying Fanny is expressed in his jaunty stroll along the quay in top hat and tails to ask her hand, then in their wedding procession from city hall across the port aboard the ferry boat. Whereas the devastation, anger, and solitude that César initially feels after Marius' departure are captured in images of him walking forlornly along the port and resentfully accusing Escartefigue of cheating during a game of *pétanque* next to a tramway track, his recovery is highlighted in a sequence that shows him babysitting with Honorine in a sunny park next to Sainte-Marie-Majeure cathedral in the Joliette suburb of Marseilles. This location, adjacent to the city's new commercial docks several miles away from the Old Port, offers a topographic metaphor for César's emotional healing and social reintegration, his acceptance of the past and embrace of a new life as a godfather and de facto grandparent.

However, the film's final half-hour depicting Marius' return is utterly theatrical in form, dominated by a marathon twenty-four-minute sequence in which he confronts Fanny in her living room, learns about his son, and bitterly leaves after César and Panisse intervene. In sharp contrast both to the rest of the film and *Marius*, here there is little effort to enhance the acting or intensify emotion through visual technique: no expressionistic lighting, no close-ups or cut-aways to highlight reactions. Mid-range two- or three-shots dominate until Panisse arrives and the group sits around the dining table, necessitating the use of a few shot/counter-shot combinations to ensure that characters always face the camera while speaking. The men's entrances are also faithfully theatrical: Marius climbs through a window at the rear of the set after whistling to get Fanny's attention; César bursts through the main door just as Fanny is about to give herself to Marius; as Panisse arrives calmly a few moments later through the same door, Marius hides behind it.

Panning is used minimally, only to keep moving characters in frame, and is in several instances awkwardly replaced by quick cuts and repositioning the camera at a matching angle but a slightly different distance, thereby producing poor visual continuity. In addition, the editing is exceptionally slow, with the final 24 minutes spread over only 80 shots. At an average shot length (ASL) of 18 seconds, this sequence is substantially slower and more 'theatrical' than *Marius*, with an ASL of 10.5 seconds, the rest of *Fanny* (13.4 seconds), and the national mean for French films made between 1930 and 1939, which has been estimated at 12.1 seconds (O'Brien 2005: 83). The pace diminishes even within the sequence, with the final 6 minutes, 25 seconds spread over only four shots: César explaining to Marius that the love and care Panisse has invested give him a moral right to the baby (1 minute, 5 seconds); Fanny passionately expressing her love for Marius while supporting César's argument (2 minutes, 26 seconds); César telling Marius that his very presence in Marseilles would endanger the baby's future (2 minutes); and Marius confessing his love for Fanny then exiting in anguish (54 seconds).

With an ASL of 1 minute, 36 seconds, here the film's rendering is actually more theatrical than the original play, in which the monologues are shorter and less florid, interrupted twice as Panisse enters and leaves the room with a doctor who has come to examine the baby. Finally, the device used to remove Panisse from the scene – his claiming to hear the baby cough over their heated conversation, even though no cough is audible on the soundtrack – demonstrates a reliance on stage conventions and contradicts the principles articled in Pagnol's 1930 manifesto.

The stylistic disconnect between the first ninety minutes of the film and the final sequence, whose wilful theatricality and awkward use of cinematic technique are uncharacteristic of Allégret, suggests that Pagnol took the lead in directing and possibly even editing it. Whatever the case, it exemplifies the 'canning' of theatre for which critics would excoriate Pagnol throughout his career. 'On pense à un film tourné dans des studios en grève par un opérateur improvisé qui ne dispose que de quelques mètres carrés' (One imagines a film shot during a strike at the studio by an impromptu cameraman who has only a few square feet at his disposal), wrote an incredulous Georges Champeaux, while Jean Fayard concluded bluntly that 'ce *Fanny* n'est pas un film' (this *Fanny* is not a film) (Champeaux 1932; Fayard 1932). Even an otherwise glowing review in the fan magazine *Pour Vous* lamented 'l'asservissement du cinéma au texte' (the subjugation of cinema to text) in the final sequence (Bizet 1932).

By cultivating dramatic intensity through dialogue rather than camera movement, editing, or other visual means, the end of *Fanny* underscores Pagnol's emphasis on the social, performative value of the spoken word and its physical embodiment through acting. As Stephen Heath notes, this is:

> not a matter of reproducing a text (despite Pagnol's talk at times of recording theatre), but of having us *see* speech: speech in action in the image, working in the film. The characters, like us, live in and through their speech and it is the fact of 'living through' which is filmed in the trilogy, to give a representation – precisely a *talking picture* – of how speech performs. To Gilles Deleuze's categories of image-movement and image-time, we could add that of image-speech, the exploration of which might place Pagnol in a surprisingly modern perspective. (Heath 2004: 30)

Along the same lines, Christopher Faulkner adds that 'in its timbre, tempo, accent, tone and volume – in all the qualities of the voice, in other words – speech comprises a complex of desires, repressions, investments and projections which shape our attitudes, behaviours, beliefs and values. The film soundtrack is understood to be as much a discursive system for the formation of certain kinds of social and cultural knowledge as is the visual track' (Faulkner 1994: 166). Labelling Pagnol's style as 'literary', 'textual', or 'anti-cinematic', as so many critics have done since the 1930s, thus unfairly denies his role in expanding film's power to capture and reflect critically on the linguistic and psychological mechanisms that structure human interaction.

Taking Heath and Faulkner's observations a step further, Pagnol's cinema can be characterised as a web of speech acts – utterances positioning the speaker in a certain way affectively and socially with regard to his or her audience – that serve the same narrative functions as the manipulation of sight, space, or time in 'standard' cinematic practice. Though often complemented by visual elements, particularly in *Marius* and the first two-thirds of *Fanny*, nearly all comedy and pathos in Pagnol's work hinges on the performative dimension of speech, which takes precedence even in scenes that would be comprehensible without any soundtrack.

The best illustration is the famous card game in *Marius* pitting César and Escartefigue against Panisse and Monsieur Brun (see Figure 6). As a signal to his partner that Panisse will trump their hand by playing a heart (in French, 'couper à cœur', literally, 'to cut hearts'), César initially makes a slicing motion across his heart with his hand, then with his fingers in the shape of scissors, and winks. When the dim-witted ferry boat captain fails to understand and Panisse accuses César of cheating, César feigns offence and quietly says 'Tu me fends le cœur' (you're breaking my heart), then emphatically repeats the phrase several times with increasing volume and emphasis, first to Panisse then to Escartefigue: 'Ho! A moi, il me fend le cœur; à toi il ne te fait rien?' (Hey! He's breaking *my* heart; he's not doing anything to *you*?) Escartefigue finally catches on and plays a heart himself to thwart Panisse's trump attempt; the sail-maker immediately quits the game in outrage, to which César retorts: 'Si on ne peut pas tricher entre amis, c'est pas la peine de jouer aux cartes' (If we can't cheat among friends, there's no point in playing cards).

Paradoxically, in the social context of the bar, the speech act of cheating becomes a signifier of friendship; more generally, it highlights César's inability to express uncomfortable, 'vulnerable' sentiments directly and his instinctive sublimation of love, grief, and the need for emotional support into anger and indignant exasperation. This practise characterises virtually all of César's interactions, especially with regard to his son. In the open scene of *Marius* César reprimands him for drinking free coffee with Fanny, belittles the 22-year-old as 'un enfant qui doit obéir à son père (a child who must obey his father), 'un ingrat' (an ingrate), and comments bitterly that 'les enfants, ça vous empoisonne l'existence' (children poison your existence). Moments later, in the middle of reproaching Marius for letting liquor dribble down the sides of the bar bottles, César notices that the sticky labels make them 'plus faciles à prendre qu'à lâcher' (easier to pick up than to put down), and starts to laugh along with his son in a moment of spontaneous affection, but quickly catches himself and reasserts his patriarchal authority by saying 'mais moi, je ris de ma patience' (but me, I'm laughing at my patience).

In *Fanny*, after Marius' departure, César stubbornly represses his intense loneliness and sense of abandonment, resisting his friends' entreaties to open up and claiming that he has no interest in 'ce navigateur dénaturé' (that unnatural navigator) despite anxiously awaiting the postman every day in the hope of receiving a letter. When he finally does give voice to his true feelings, it is only indirectly, under the pretext of denying them and 'rectifying' neighbourhood gossip that he cries alone at night, heartbroken, in his big, empty house. 'Non, je n'attends pas le facteur', he emphatically tells Escartefigue, Panisse and Monsieur Brun, 'parce que quand un garçon a eu le courage d'abandonner son vieux père, et de ne pas lui écrire même une seule fois depuis vingt-neuf jours, il n'y a guère d'espoir qu'il lui écrive le trentième'.[3]

Upon learning from Monsieur Brun that it would take at least thirty days for any mail to reach Marseilles from Marius' ship, César launches into a similar performance of bravado that betrays his deep sense of relief and newfound hope through denial of those emotions. After giddily imagining aloud that he will soon receive a month's worth of letters all at once – un paquet de trios kilos, de quoi lire toute la nuit, en les relisant trois fois chacune (a 3-kilogram stack of letters, enough to read through the night, rereading each one three times) – César catches himself and concludes: 'Je prendrais le paquet, je le foutrais sous le comptoir, et je ne l'ouvrirais pas, parce que ça ne m'intéresse pas!' (I would take the stack, I would shove it under the counter, and I wouldn't open it, because it doesn't interest me!).

By dramatising the distinction between the ostensible, surface meaning of speech (César's disingenuous assertion that he no longer cares about Marius), its actual, semantic meaning (César's expression of his emotional suffering because he loves Marius so much), and its social/psychological impact on the speaker (providing César relief) and listeners (reinforcing their friendship and affection for César), Pagnol provides an incisive illustration of the locutionary, illocutionary, and perlocutionary aspects of speech long before these terms were formally defined in the 1950s and 1960s. In so doing, the Trilogy concurrently articulates a philosophy of sociolinguistics that weighs the ethical implications of not being able to always tell the truth completely and transparently; in other words, to maintain

---

[3] No, I'm not waiting for the postman, because when a boy has the courage to abandon his aged father, and not to write him a single time in twenty-nine days, there is not much hope that he will write on the thirtieth.

perfect harmony between the locutionary and illocutionary dimensions of one's utterances.

This position, which implicitly rejects Immanuel Kant's 'categorical imperative' that one's acts be a forthright means of pursuing a desired result, underscores the affinity between Pagnol and Nietzsche by justifying an aesthetics predicated on the articulation of profound social and moral critique through seemingly superficial narrative forms – banal family melodrama and comic sketches. Here again the Trilogy is ahead of its time, anticipating Jürgen Habermas' theory of 'communicative rationality', which holds that the ethics of speech and speech acts are not absolute, but context dependent and evershifting. Thus, in certain circumstances lying may fulfil a positive social function and be morally preferable to telling the truth (Cooke 1994; Habermas 1988).

Virtually all the characters in the Trilogy dissimulate or lie in some fashion, but without ever being fundamentally immoral or unethical and only as a result of social taboos and psychological pressures. Thus cheating at cards functions as a powerful bond of friendship; César's exasperated accusation that Marius 'poisons his existence' is in fact an expression of the deep love and weight of responsibility he feels as a long-time single parent. Just prior to the scene in which César unburdens himself, Escartefigue and Panisse exchange tall tales about men whose brains ostensibly softened and shrank from excessive grief, to the point of audibly rattling around in their skulls as they walked. 'Mon histoire est aussi vraie que la tienne' (my story is just as true as yours), Panisse chides the captain, 'naturellement, je te prends pour un menteur' (of course I take you for a liar). After momentarily feigning offence, Escartefigue responds: 'Honoré, j'ai l'honneur de te dire que tu as absolument raison. A la tienne!' (Honoré, I have the honour of telling you that you're absolutely right. To your health!), and the two men touch their glasses in a toast. Lying thus accomplishes both the illocutionary goal of allowing the worried friends to express their concern for César without appearing emotionally 'soft' and the perlocutionary function of reaffirming their mutual respect for each other and shared commitment to help their troubled friend.

Even the most potentially cruel, gratuitous instance of deception – Escartefigue and his stoker's placing a large paving stone under a bowler hat on the sidewalk in front of the bar so that they can watch passersby break their toes kicking it – is redeemed by comedy and its morally redemptive function within the plot of *César*. The man who takes the bait is Marius' business partner Fernand, who earlier in the film convinced Césariot that he and Marius were using their garage as a front for prostitution and opium smuggling, prompting the gullible young man to condemn his biological father as a 'voyou' (hoodlum) and question Fanny's morals as well. The pain that Fernand suffers from kicking the concealed stone is thus not the senseless result of other people's sadism, but rather a morally just, self-inflicted punishment for his callous lying and attempt to destroy what rightfully belongs to another person (the presumably lost hat and Marius' potential for a relationship with his son).

The scene is the perfect illustration of Nietzschean laughter, for it allows both the characters on-screen (especially Monsieur Brun, who initially objected to the game as 'grotesque') and the audience 'to gloat [*sein schadenfroh*], but with a clear conscience' (Nietzsche 1974: 207). The fact that Fernand does not injure himself seriously, only bruising a sensitive callus on his toe, underscores the deeper philosophical and ethical dimensions of what at first glance seems a frivolous comic sketch. After sitting down on the terrace to recover, he converses with César's friends, realises the harm he has done to the family by misleading Césariot, and immediately sets things right by confessing the truth to César.

As Heath astutely points out, Pagnol consistently distinguishes between two different modes of lying: on the one hand, a 'sociable', usually comedic variety associated with male camaraderie; on the other, 'serious, structuring deviations from the truth that impel the drama' and without which 'there would be no revelation, no drama, no films' (Heath 2004: 48–9). The seminal deceptions are of course the failure to inform Marius of Fanny's pregnancy and the public affirmation of Panisse as the baby's father following their expedient marriage. Marius learns of his son's existence only upon his impromptu return to Marseilles after a year at sea, and Césariot of his real father's identity only at the age of 20. Just as their ignorance gives *Fanny* and *César* emotionally climactic endings, it is the other main characters' knowledge of the truth and the tacit pact they share to conceal it from those outside the family circle (Monsieur Brun, Escartefigue) that maintains the psychological tension throughout the films. Naturally, the complicity between César, Panisse, Fanny, and Honorine requires them to lie, to accept a permanent disjuncture between the locutionary and illocutionary aspects of their speech, raising the possibility that any one of them could crack at any moment.

Pagnol paints a nuanced portrait of lying as a socio-linguistic practice, highlighting the role played by gender, age, and environment. Whereas men tend to dissimulate proactively through verbal excess, women do so passively, through silence and omission. Critics have often asserted that Honorine functions as a female equivalent of César, but this is not quite accurate, for while she is easily excitable and often verbose, her outbursts always express her feelings honestly. Upon learning of Fanny's pregnancy, she immediately cries: 'Va-t-en, fille malhonnête, fille perdue! A la rue, fille des rues! Je ne veux plus te voir. Va dans ta chambre, fais tes paquets, et file!' (Get out, dishonest girl, fallen girl! Into the street, streetwalker. I don't want to see you again. Go to your room, pack your bags and march!). Honorine lies only by not telling the truth: she pressures Fanny to marry Panisse without telling him about the pregnancy, claiming that 'une femme n'est jamais malhonnête avec un homme. Si nous sommes dans cette misère, c'est à un homme que nous le devons. Eh bien, faisons payer la faute par un homme' (a woman can never be dishonest with a man. If we're in this miserable situation, we owe it to a man. So let's make a man pay for it). Fanny, however, finds her mother's attitude 'abominable', resolutely states that she will not accept 'd'être malhonnête à ce point-là' (being dishonest to that extreme) and confesses everything to Panisse – thereby suggesting moral progress between generations. The difference is one of degree rather than an abrupt break, for Fanny does of course refrain from informing him about the baby, either by letter when she has the opportunity, or in person, when he returns at the end of the film. The same shift characterises César and Marius' use of language to mask their feelings. In the days preceding his departure, Marius professes his commitment to staying with Fanny, even telling her that he no longer wants to sail. Yet unlike his father, Marius is capable of expressing uncomfortable emotions candidly: just before leaving Fanny he openly confesses his true desire d'épouser la mer' (to marry the sea) and he tearfully tells César 'je t'aime bien papa, tu sais' (you know, I really love you dad) – a speech act that César cannot reciprocate in kind. In a characteristically tragic example of sublimation, the best he can do is to mutter 'moi aussi, grand imbécile' (me too, you big fool).

It is also worth noting that regardless of gender or generation, instances of truth-telling occur exclusively in private spaces behind closed doors, especially kitchens and bedrooms, while lying is a social phenomenon reserved for the public sphere of the quay, cafés and bars, or the street. Finally, lying is presented as a marker of regional identity differentiating natives of Marseilles from outsiders: Monsieur Brun the Lyonnais never lies, socially or otherwise, nor does Césariot, who is culturally Parisian, having always attended school there.

Pagnol exploits the dramatic tension between honesty and deception to the fullest in a trio of memorable scenes that use language to deftly blend humour and pathos. In *Fanny*, César dictates to Fanny his response to Marius' first letter, comically expressing his love and concern by warning him to avoid contact with sailors who might be infected with bubonic plague. While doing so fills the irascible patriarch with joy, it accentuates his inability to express himself directly and intensifies Fanny's suffering by preventing her from communicating with Marius on her own terms.

Later in the film, just prior to Marius' return, César and Honorine engage in a richly performative conversation while babysitting. Responding to her self-satisfied comment that Fanny hardly ever mentions Marius any more and that Panisse, who always seemed 'si calme, si mou' (so passive, so limp) could father such a handsome child, César says slyly that the baby would not be any more handsome if Marius were his father. Honorine agrees, adding emphatically 'ça, on peut le dire' (that we can say), to which César retorts: 'Ah, oui. Ça, on peut le dire. On peut le dire, surtout quand y a personne. (Ah, yes. *That* we can say, especially when nobody else is around).

As in all the best moments of Pagnol's cinema, the dialogue is enhanced by location shooting (a sunny park next to Marseilles's new port in the suburb of La Joliette, metaphorically showing that César and Honorine have 'moved on' with their lives since Marius' departure) and the actors' physical performance. Here Raimu and Alida Rouffe reveal the real meaning and impact behind their characters' words by using vocal inflection, facial expressions, and glances. At the beginning of the sequence, Honorine is unsure whether César knows the truth about the baby and cannot allow herself to divulge it – as indicated by the tight pursing of her lips and looking away from César while asserting that Panisse is the father. Conversely, César wants to let her know that he knows without stating so outright, instead looking at her and grimacing when he agrees that the child belongs to Panisse. Eyes still turned away, she misses the sign but understands a moment later as they share a laugh and knowing look over the 'limp', middle-aged sailmaker ostensibly fathering a child. Their bond is definitively sealed by César's final quip, delivered with a broad smile while leaning towards Honorine. Realising that César's knowledge gives him the power to expose her family to public humiliation and claim Fanny and his grandson should Marius return, she again glances down at her knitting and purses her lips tightly (see Figure 7).

Absent from the original stage play, this brief scene sets up the final cathartic confrontation in which Fanny and César send Marius away to protect the baby's future and their family reputations, thereby reaffirming the collective, social good over their own personal desires. Ironically, this act of repression is justified through an exceptionally candid, emotionally crushing use of language that contains no trace of dissimulation. As Fanny says:

> Toi, Marius, tu étais le père d'un petit bâtard, un désastre pour une famille, le père un enfant sans nom porté par une pauvre fille dans la honte et le désespoir. Où est-il, cet enfant? Il n'existe pas. Ce n'est pas le mien. Le mien, il est né dans un grand lit de toile fine, entre la grand-mère et les tantes. Cet enfant, tu ne l'auras pas. Il est planté en haut d'une famille comme une croix sur un clocher.[4]

César supports her without hesitation, adding quietly:

> Cet enfant, quand il est venu au monde, il pesait quatre kilos, quatre kilos de la chair de sa mère. Maintenant il pèse neuf kilos. Ces cinq kilos de plus, tu sais ce que c'est? C'est de l'amour. Et pourtant, c'est léger, l'amour. Il en faut pour faire cinq kilos. Moi, j'ai donné ma part, elle aussi. Mais c'est lui qui a donné le plus, lui, Panisse. Et toi qu'est-ce que tu as donné? Non, Marius, cet enfant, tu ne l'as pas voulu. Le père, c'est celui qui aime.[5]

[4] Marius, you were the father of an illegitimate son, a disaster for a family, the father of a child without a name carried by a wretched girl in shame and despair. Where is that child? He doesn't exist. He's not mine. Mine was born in a big bed with fine linen, between his grandmother and his aunts. You won't get this child. He is planted at the top of a family like a cross on a church tower.
[5] When that child came into the world, he weighed 4 kilos, 4 kilos of his mother's flesh. Now he weighs 9 kilos. Those five extra kilos, do you know what they are? They're love. And yet love is light. It takes a lot to make five kilos. Me, I gave my share, she too. But it's he who gave the most, him, Panisse. And you, what have you given? No, Marius, you didn't want that child. The father is the one who loves.

The scene is exceptional not only for its thick situational drama, but César's substituting calm, forthright speech for his usual sublimation of grief into a tirade of anger. As an example of utterly honest emotional expression, this monologue represents a breakthrough for him and inaugurates a gradual embrace of vulnerability and candour that in *César* will transform him from a social liability who instigates conflict and requires constant pacification into an attentive caregiver and astute mediator who maintains family cohesion through a series of traumas: Panisse's death, Césariot's realisation that Marius is his father, and Marius' reluctant return to the family. In the end it is César who single-handedly dissipates Marius and Fanny's mutual trepidation about whether they really belong together and the possible social stigma of reuniting so soon after Panisse's death.

Despite its appearance of superficiality, this happy ending has an unusually strong appeal because it relieves basic Oedipal anxieties. César's consistent infantilisation of Marius, his overdetermined efforts to claim Fanny and the baby as his own after Marius' initial departure, and his refutation of Marius' claim to baby and wife at the end of *Fanny* all suggest a deep patriarchal fear of usurpation. Towards the end of *César* Marius reproaches his father for exactly this, noting bitterly that 'j'aurais eu l'autorité sur le petit, tandis qu'avec Honoré tu l'avais belle pour satisfaire ta manie de commander' (I would have had power over the boy, whereas with Honoré you had it all to satisfy your mania for control). In the end César willingly cedes his alpha-male role to Marius, but only after family honour and fortune (which in the end includes the combined assets of the bar and the late Panisse's shop) are secure – thanks of course to his actions. The Trilogy thus offers a happy melodramatic resolution to archetypal father–son confrontation, replacing Sophocles' irreparable violence and trauma with just enough conflict and suffering to make the final family reunion both realistic and satisfying.

The depth of César's transformation becomes clear mid-way through the film when he explains his relationship with Marius to Césariot in a monologue of remarkably lucid self-analysis:

> Il a été toute ma vie, tout mon amour. C'était à cause de lui que je ne me suis pas remarié. J'étais son père. Quand sa mère est morte, j'étais sa mère. Evidemment, je disais pas des paroles de gentillesse.

Je n'osais pas. Je disais beaucoup de paroles d'engueulade. Tu sais, moi, ça me vient naturellement. Je croyais qu'il comprendrait. Il n'a pas compris.[6]

In addition to openly admitting the tender, 'feminine' side of his personality and regretting his speech acts of tough male bravado, the once-domineering patriarch cries on-screen for the first time in the Trilogy.

The general public and critics unanimously acknowledged the unique power of the richly performative dialogue and acting in the last two chapters of the Trilogy. Princess Astrid of Belgium reportedly wept during a gala screening of *Fanny* in Brussels (Chantal 1932); in Paris ticket sales reached 665,000 (Crisp 2002: 314) and the film was voted best of the year by readers of the cinema magazine *Pour Vous*, surpassing several of France's most respected directors: Raymond Bernard for *Les Croix de bois*, a reconstruction of trench life during the Great War; Jacques Feyder for the Saharan fantasy adventure *L'Atlantide*; and Julien Duvivier for his poignant family drama *Poil de Carotte* (Anon. 1933). According to co-producer Roger Richebé, *Fanny*'s box-office gross for the 1932–33 season totalled a whopping 38,000,000 francs yet cost less than two million to make (Richebé 1977: 95). At the start of the following yearly cycle in mid-November 1933, the film was playing at twenty-eight 'second-run' cinemas in and around Paris, reportedly outdrawing many new releases (Anon. 1933a). As a testament to its exceptionally durable appeal in the provinces, *Fanny* ranked first in a popularity poll conducted by the daily newspaper *La Dépêche de Toulouse* in January 1934. More surprising still, *Marius* placed third in the voting despite being over two years old (Crisp 2002: 302).

Public and critical response to *César* in 1936 was more favourable still. Citing César's confession to his grandson as 'un grand moment d'une qualité sans pair dans le cinéma contemporain' (a great moment of unmatched quality in contemporary cinema), Georges Champeaux praised *César* as 'du meilleur Pagnol et du plus savoureux Raimu. Parmi tant de films exsangues, pauvrement joués, on est heureux de retrouver, à nouveau réunis, l'auteur et l'acteur les plus richement

---

6 He was all my life, all my love. It was because of him that I never remarried. I was his father. When his mother died, I was his mother. Obviously, I didn't say many kind words. I didn't dare. I said lots of cross words. You know, that comes naturally to me. I thought he would understand. He didn't understand.

doués de ce temps' (Pagnol at his best and Raimu at his most delightful. Among so many lifeless, poorly acted films, we are happy to see reunited the most gifted author and actor of our time). Like most commentators, Champeaux chided Pagnol for this film's epic length (168 minutes) and verbosity but immediately pardoned him by noting that 'sa sincérité exaltée, son aptitude naturelle au pathétique nous tiennent en haleine jusqu'au bout' (his exalted sincerity, his natural gift for the pathetic keeps us holding our breath until the very end) (Champeaux 1936).

Released simultaneously at four cinemas in Paris, *César* sold an estimated 725,000 thousand tickets in its first four months (Crisp 2002: 333). On the Sunday following its premiere, spectators refused to vacate their seats after the first daily showing and clashed with those arriving for the second, necessitating police intervention and a public warning in several daily newspapers (Anon. 1936). In a survey conducted by the corporate weekly *La Cinématographie française*, the owners of France's 400 largest theatres identified it as the highest-grossing film of the year (Colin-Reval 1937). A poll of spectators in Toulouse ranked it 'best film of the year' by a landslide, outdistancing Marcel Herbier's *Veille d'armes* by over 4,000 votes (Anon. 1937). In some large provincial cities such as La Rochelle ticket sales equalled 25 or 30 per cent of the total population despite 'special' admission prices that were one or two francs higher than normal (Anon. 1937a). In order to meet demand, Pagnol's development laboratories worked overtime to produce extra screening prints. Whereas the industry average at the time fell between forty-five and fifty copies for major new releases, by February 1937 there were a whopping sixty-eight copies of *César* in circulation – fifty-eight in France and another ten in Switzerland and North Africa – representing some 250,000 metres of filmstock in all (Epardaud 1937; Bessy 1937).

A counter-model: Paramount's *Topaze*

While it was primarily the success of *Marius* and *Fanny* that convinced Pagnol to adopt a hybrid style blending the verbosity of theatre with the authenticity of location shooting, Paramount's 'hostile' screen adaptation of *Topaze* mid-1932 also played a crucial contributing role. After rebuffing Pagnol, the studio appointed consummate company man

Louis Gasnier as director. Though French-born, since 1914 Gasnier had worked in the United States churning out assembly-line comedies for a variety of producers including Pathé and Hal Roach. By the time he signed with Paramount in 1929, his work with silent stars Max Linder and Laurel and Hardy had made him one of the most reliably bankable foreign directors in Hollywood (Waldman 1998: 75–6, 86). Like René Clair, Gasnier conceived cinema as an art of vision and movement in which dialogue should play only a supplemental role, figuring in no more than 45 per cent of the film's shots (Anon. 1932). Needless to say, Gasnier's attachment to silent film aesthetics and denial of speech's narrative value made him incompatible with Pagnol, who disavowed the project so completely as to ignore friend Louis Jouvet's repeated requests to meet when the studio offered him the title role, his first as a screen actor (Jouvet 1932).

Gasnier was true to his word, cutting approximately forty-five minutes of dialogue with the assistance of writer Léopold Marchand, using quick editing with an ASL of 10.4 seconds, and 'opening up' the action by showing the audience events referred to only indirectly on stage: Topaze imagining that the street-sweeping trucks he has purchased for the city in order to pocket a large kickback are rhythmically whispering 'Tri-po-teur, tri-po-teur' (swindler) and 'To-paze l'es-roc, To-paze l'es-croc' (Topaze the crook) as he passes by; later on, Topaze's crooked mentor Castel-Bénac extorting money from café owners to have mobile public toilets removed from the street in front of their terraces.

While on the surface Gasnier's approach was similar to that employed in *Marius* and *Fanny*, its execution was uneven and fundamentally altered the tone of the original play. Rather than injecting authenticity into the theatrical, as Korda and Allégret had done so effectively through location shooting in Marseilles, the additions to *Topaze* were filmed on quickly assembled outdoor sets at Joinville and draw attention to their own artificiality, thereby undermining the credibility of the entire narrative. The supposedly revolutionary, state-of-the-art street sweepers are clearly everyday trucks whose bodies have been awkwardly covered in bright white cardboard, with painted black lines approximating metal welding seams and buttons for rivets; in addition, the circular brushes attached to the undercarriage barely spin and are oriented so that they could not possibly touch the ground. The effect is even more jarring in the toilet sequence, which features a quick shot/counter-shot showing two cafés supposedly across the street from each other. The first is a laughably immaculate cardboard set without real doors or windows and generically labelled 'La Grande Brasserie' with waiters languishing at empty tables; the second, stock footage of a real Paris brasserie, 'Le Bertillon', bustling with activity as cars pass by in the foreground.

Worse still, virtually all of Gasnier's modifications cultivate superficial comedy at the expense of the play's biting irony and philosophical message. For example, in the play Castel-Bénac's corruption is attributed to his lust for women, money, and power, which are exaggerated just enough to make the point; in the film he is reduced to a one-dimensional caricature from the outset: a close-up of a horse's rear in the street dissolves to a matched shot of actor Paul Pauley's rotund posterior splayed wide as he stoops to pick up a cigar. As for the cuts Marchand made to the dialogue, the removal of several key scenes from the first act illustrating Topaze's fervent belief in probity and altruism makes his eventual self-serving revolt against an inherently corrupt system less ethically compelling, and his closing promise to conduct business without disadvantaging others utterly unbelievable.

While lauding the actors' performances, especially Jouvet's, critics were quick to point out the film's narrative shortcomings in relation to the play. 'C'est de loin le plus mauvais des trois films qu'on a tirés des pièces de Pagnol, une bouffonnerie gaie qui n'a rien à voir avec la satire au théâtre et qui nous laisse indifférent' (It's by far the worst of the three films based on Pagnol's plays, an exercise in merry buffoonery that has nothing to do with the satire of the stage play and leaves us indifferent), wrote one disappointed reviewer (Wolff 1933). 'Une suite de sketches ne fait pas un film', objected another, 'c'est une pièce sans articulations' (a series of sketches does not constitute a film; it's a play without any structure) (Champeaux 1933). The movie did well at the box-office on the strength of Pagnol's reputation and the play's popularity, placing roughly tenth during the 1932–33 season, but well behind *Fanny* (Crisp 2002: 314). Pagnol, who was outraged at Paramount's 'massacre' (Pagnol 1995: I, 612), would twice attempt his own transpositions of *Topaze* as a point of honour, each time restoring his original stage dialogue almost word for word.

The first, made quickly in early 1936 to fill an open slot in his schedule before shooting *César*, had Topaze (played this time by

Antoine Arnaudy) gleefully relish rather than regret the irony of his transformation, thereby symbolically counterbalancing Gasnier's comic overkill with bitter social commentary. Released in late May as the annual moviegoing season wound down, Pagnol's remake was not widely seen and competed directly with Paramount's version, which the studio rereleased to assert its control over the material. Under the threat of mutual lawsuits for copyright infringement, both parties agreed to withdraw their films from circulation and agreed not to distribute them until a definitive settlement was reached. Pagnol's second adaptation of *Topaze*, made in 1950 and starring Fernandel in the lead role, was an exercise in nostalgia for a director nearing the end of his career. Scrupulously faithful to the play's original tone and text, it finally achieved Pagnol's elusive goal of preserving his career-making hit on celluloid thirty years after the fact.

New polemics: *cinématurgie* in theory and practice

By mid-1933 the ongoing popularity of *Fanny* and comparative failure of Gasnier's *Topaze* had given Pagnol the confidence necessary to realise his long-term ambition of directing films solo and founding his own production company. Officially created in early August, it was named 'Les Auteurs associés', an allusion to United Artists that made clear Pagnol's intention to transform the French film industry just as Douglas Fairbanks, Charlie Chaplin, and D.W. Griffith had shaped Hollywood during its early years (Harlé 1933). The enterprise was small, operating out of a modest townhouse in the seventeenth *arrondissement* of Paris, but like UA and Paramount prioritised efficiency through vertical concentration. The team of colleagues Pagnol recruited was composed primarily of old friends from Marseilles – former stage actor Charles Corbessas as accountant and business manager; former *Fortunio* board members Marcel Gras and Arno-Charles Brun, as production and script managers, respectively; and caricaturist Antoine Toé as advertising director. To assist with advertising and secure an outlet for publishing his screenplays, Pagnol also brought aboard Charles Fasquelle, whose father's press had made bestsellers of his *Topaze, Marius,* and *Fanny* scripts. Logistically, the only elements missing were a studio and development laboratories, which Richebé agreed to furnish until Pagnol could acquire his own.

The production strategy of Les Auteurs associés was straightforward and meant to vindicate its owner's vision of talking cinema: to transpose popular stage plays, keeping the original dialogue unchanged while amplifying its dramatic effect through the use of basic visual technique and adding a leavening of realism through location shooting (Gorel 1933). The two plays Pagnol chose to adapt were Emile Augier and Jules Sandeau's *Le Gendre de Monsieur Poirier* (1854), a satire contrasting the ambitious commercial bourgeoisie against the decadent remnants of hereditary aristocracy, and Jean Sarment's *Léopold le bien-aimé* (1927), a romantic melodrama recounting a young man's exile from his native town, return home after a military career, and subsequent reconciliation with his first love. Pagnol wrote the screenplay for both, but chose to direct only *Monsieur Poirier*, delegating *Léopold* to Arno-Charles Brun.

Released in mid-December 1933, *Monsieur Poirier* was an inauspicious debut that fell far short of Pagnol's aspirations and failed to apply the lessons of his apprenticeship under Korda and Allégret. Despite good performances from a cast of talented stage actors, including Fernand Charpin, Jean Debucourt, Annie Ducaux, and Léon Bernard, long-time star of the Comédie Française, in the title role, the film uses cinematic technique minimally and in the most rudimentary way, capturing dialogue in static mid-range two- or three-shots only rarely interrupted by shot/counter-shot sequences. Shifts in shooting angle or distance are often awkward and abrupt, disrupting the flow of the dialogue and visual continuity. There is almost no variation in lighting and no use of transitional devices to link different sequences; theatrical entrances and exits are preserved unmodified, with scene changes handled by fade-outs to black. In sharp contrast to *Marius*, *Fanny*, and Pagnol's own 1930 manifesto, there are almost no close-ups or cut-aways shots to enhance psychological or emotional depth, except for the bizarre attempt that occurs in the final frame: a zoom into Poirier's face that stops abruptly with only his nose and mouth in frame as he loudly proclaims his ambition to serve in the national legislature.

The editing is exceptionally slow as well. With only 313 shots spread over 89 minutes, its ASL of 17.1 seconds far exceeds that of *Marius* (10.5 seconds) and the first two-thirds of *Fanny* (13.4 seconds), but replicates the languid pace of the latter film's final half-hour, whose ASL of 18 seconds offers further evidence that Pagnol himself rather than

Allégret directed it. The only improvement Pagnol made to Augier and Sandeau's *Poirier* lies in the addition of several outdoor scenes recorded at a manor house adjoining Pagnol's estate in the Sarthe. A horseback conversation between the Marquis de Presles and Antoinette is nicely captured through tracking, as is Poirier's outraged promenade to confront the couple for squandering her wedding dowry. Even so, the film overwhelmingly justifies characterising Pagnol's cinema as a mechanical reproduction of theatre generated by placing a camera in the prompter's box.

Emile Vuillermoz seized the opportunity in his weekly column for *Le Temps*, withholding even the bits of praise he had previously offered *Marius* and *Fanny*.

> Il faut désapprouver les metteurs en scène qui s'imaginent, dans une œuvre exclusivement théâtrale, être en règle avec leur conscience cinégraphique parce qu'ils introduisent un morceau de forêt ou un lopin de terre. Le 'montage' ici n'est que juxtaposition. Ces visions se succèdent comme les illustrations d'un livre, sans lien visuel. Que le théâtre ait l'honnêteté de séparer sa cause de celle d'un mode d'expression pour lequel il manifeste son dédain. Cette version phono-photographiée du *Gendre de Monsieur Poirier* peut prétendre à la faveur du public, mais ce n'est pas du cinéma.[7] (Vuillermoz 1933)

Another critic went a step further, adding that 'selon son propre enseignement, Pagnol a commis un crime de lèse-théâtre, car en y introduisant des changements de décors il rompt l'harmonie du dialogue et les plus beaux effets dramatiques' (according to his own teachings, Pagnol has committed a crime against the theatre, for his introduction of multiple settings disrupts the harmony of the dialogue and the best dramatic effects) (Reusse 1934). Even André Antoine, Pagnol's most ardent defender, wrote that the film 'm'a infligé une vive désillusion' (left me deeply disillusioned), reproaching his former protégé for spoiling good writing and acting with

---

[7] One must disapprove of directors whose work is purely theatrical yet convince themselves that they do justice to cinema by inserting a bit of forest or a patch of earth. The so-called 'montage' used here is no more than juxtaposition. These images follow each other like the illustrations in a book, without any visual links. Let theatre be honest enough to distinguish between its impetus and that of an alternative mode of expression for which it shows disdain. This phono-photographed version of *Le Gendre de Monsieur Poirier* may carry favour with the public, but it's not cinema.

un étonnant manque d'ingéniosité et d'imagination dans l'ordonnance des tableaux et des personnages de sorte que le mouvement du texte et les répliques les plus significatives se perdent ... Vraiment, la déception est grande entre ce que Pagnol nous avait promis et ce qu'il nous a donné.[8] (Antoine 1933)

The film's box-office performance offered no vindication either. A reporter for the fan magazine *Pour Vous* noted that 'les mêmes répliques qui déchaînent encore des applaudissements nourris à la Comédie Française laissent le public du cinéma, d'abord attentif, parfaitement froid et sans réactions' (the same lines that prompt hearty applause on stage at the Comédie Française leave cinema audiences, who are initially attentive, utterly cold and unresponsive (Lehmann 1933). *Monsieur Poirier* was an unqualified flop, playing at only two Parisian theatres for a total of three weeks before being pulled from circulation, never to be rereleased in France.

Pagnol anticipated the criticism and pre-emptively defended himself in the pages of his newly founded magazine *Les Cahiers du film*, a 'revue mensuelle de doctrine cinématographique' (a monthly journal of cinematic doctrine) printed by Fasquelle whose purpose was to justify its financier's approach to filmmaking and promote the first contingent of pictures released by Les Auteurs associés. The inaugural issue, which appeared just after the release of *Monsieur Poirier*, contained numerous publicity photos, a review column by Pagnol's long-time friend Gabriel d'Aubarède heralding the film as 'une œuvre audacieuse et impertinente au milieu du désordre de la production contemporaine' (a bold and provocative work amidst the disorder of contemporary production) and a three-thousand word manifesto by Pagnol himself titled 'Cinématurgie de Paris'. The title was a rather pretentious, though justifiable reference to *Hamburgische Dramaturgie*, the revolutionary series of articles that Gotthold Lessing published between 1767 and 1769 while serving as creative consultant and publicist for Germany's first national theatre troupe (Luckhurst 2006: 24–44).

Pagnol's rejection of the prevailing theatrical and cinematic conventions of his era echoed Lessing's argument that classical

---

8 A surprising lack of ingenuity and imagination in arranging the scenes and choreographing the actors, so that the rhythm of the text and the most crucial lines are lost ... The difference between what Pagnol promised us and what he delivered is wide and truly disappointing.

French tragedy, as exemplified by Racine and Corneille, had stifled the development of dramatic art by following the ancient Greek model too strictly, removing theatre from its contemporary context and rendering it inaccessible to the masses. Lessing urged playwrights to instead draw inspiration from Shakespeare and to cultivate easily recognisable, socially relevant 'bourgeois realism' – a phrase that applies perfectly to Pagnol's populist aesthetic. Lessing also believed in the creative dominance of playwright, viewing acting and *mise en scène* as important only insofar as they gave life to the script. This position was as divisive in the late eighteenth century as it was in the early 1930s and drew widespread protests from actors, directors, and critics. In a final point of convergence, Lessing shared several key personal characteristics with Pagnol. Both men came from educated yet financially modest families (Lessing's father was a Protestant pastor), had a reputation for conviviality mixed with a hot temper, and achieved success through perseverance and hard work rather than patronage, even self-financing the publication of their respective manifestoes (Gerould 2000: 236–47).

In his article Pagnol radicalised the argument he had initially presented in 1930, reaffirming his view of authorship and the primacy of speech over image through a baldly commercial, populist logic that referred implicitly to the box-office success of *Marius* and *Fanny*:

> Un art, pour réaliser ses œuvres d'abord et pour les répandre ensuite, a besoin d'être nourri par un commerce. Pour faire plaisir aux idéalistes, disons que ce commerce est le fumier qui nourrit la fleur ... Lorsque j'écris: le muet est mort, le théâtre est à l'agonie, je veux dire que le commerce qui nourrissait le muet est mort, que le commerce du théâtre est près de la faillite. A la place de ces deux commerces est né le commerce du film parlant, qui a dévoré les deux autres: la prosperité de ce nouveau commerce nourrit abondamment un nouvel art, et prouve que ce nouvel art a conquis l'intérêt du public.[9] (Pagnol 1933: 3)

---

9 An art, from its initial creation to its subsequent dissemination, needs to be fed by a business. For the sake of idealists, let's say that this business is the manure that feeds the flower ... When I write that silent film is dead and that theatre is dying, I mean that the business which fed silent film is dead and that the theatre business is nearly bankrupt. The business of talking pictures has replaced the other two, devoured them; the prosperity of this new business is already richly supporting a new art and proves that it has won over the public.

He arrogantly proclaimed that 'pour écrire du dialogue, il faut UN DON special' (writing dialogue requires a special gift) and denounced filmmakers 'incapables d'écrire une pièce' (incapable of writing a play) who 'défigurent les œuvres des autres' (disfigure the work of others) by replacing dialogue with 'la technique désuète du film muet, née d'une infirmité; cette technique, qui avait pour but de remplacer la parole humaine, n'a désormais plus aucun but' (the outdated techniques of silent film, born of an infirmity; these techniques, whose goal was to replace human speech, no longer serve any purpose) (Pagnol 1933: 6–7).

Pagnol attempted to justify his position with a tendentious history of sound cinema that denigrated the *film sonore* as 'une sorte de monstre ridicule, parlant sans paroles, réticent, orné de bruits' (a kind of ridiculous monster, speaking without words, hesitant, adorned with noises), paid homage to *Jean de la Lune* (1931), Georges Marret's faithful adaptation of Marcel Achard's stage hit, as the first film ever to exploit the dramatic potential of speech, and construed Charlie Chaplin's silent masterpiece *City Lights* (1931) as 'le Waterloo du film muet' (the Waterloo of silent cinema). Whereas Chaplin cleverly used various synchronised sounds – of non-diegetic kazoos and of a diegetic whistle the Little Tramp swallows – to replace dialogue, mock the often poor quality of recorded speech at the outset of the sound era, and prove that cinema could do without the new technology, Pagnol simplistically asserted that the film marked:

> la victoire décisive du parlant, car cette parodie puisait toute sa force comique dans la bande de son. Les deux grands effets comiques, dûs au son et à la voix humaine, firent le plus grand tort aux gags visuels de *City Lights*. Nous avions l'impression que ce n'était plus aussi drôle, que ce n'était plus très drôle, que ce n'était plus drôle du tout. Et malgré l'immense génie de Charlot, les pauvres 'Lumières de la ville' ne clignotèrent pas longtemps sur les écrans du monde entier.[10]
> (Pagnol 1933: 5–6)

10 The decisive victory of talkies since this parody drew its comic power from the soundtrack. The two great comic effects, dependent on sound and the human voice, completely undermined the visual gags in *City Lights*. We felt that they were not as funny, no longer funny, not funny at all. And despite Chaplin's immense genius, despite the genuine love that people felt for his intelligent, moving little figure, the poor 'lights of the city' did not flicker very long on screens across the world.

Oblivious to the counterfactual nature of his assertions (*City Lights* was a bona fide international hit and French spectators would subsequently make Chaplin's last silent film, *Modern Times*, the sixth-highest-grossing picture of 1936), Pagnol concluded with a set of outrageously reductive, didactic aphorisms:

1. Le film muet était l'art d'imprimer, de fixer, et de diffuser la pantomime. (Silent film was the art of recording, giving definitive form to, and disseminating pantomime.
2. De même que l'invention de l'imprimerie eut une grande influence sur la littérature, l'invention du film muet eut une grande influence sur la pantomime. Charlot, Gance, Griffith, René Clair ont ré-inventé la pantomime. (Just as the invention of the printing press had a great influence on literature, the invention of silent film had a great influence on pantomime. Chaplin, Gance, Griffith, and René Clair reinvented pantomime.)
3. Le film parlant est l'art d'imprimer, de fixer et de diffuser le théâtre. (Talking film is the art of recording, giving definitive form to, and disseminating theatre.)
4. Le film parlant, qui apporte au théâtre des ressources nouvelles, doit ré-inventer le théâtre. (Talking film, which brings new resources to theatre, must reinvent theatre.) (Pagnol 1933: 8)

The article sparked a national controversy whose magnitude and vitriol in the French film and theatre world echoed the famous literary *querelles* surrounding Corneille's *Le Cid* in the seventeenth century and Hugo's *Hernani* in the nineteenth. The press books Pagnol compiled contain over five hundred newspaper and journal articles related to the incident, including withering ripostes by most of France's prominent cinema critics. While fully acknowledging the dramatic power of speech, Emile Vuillermoz objected that Pagnol's contemptuous equation of visual technique with pantomime stripped cinema of 'son instantanéité miraculeuse dans l'expression de nos pensées et nos sentiments', 'une puissance et une universalité très supérieures à la parole qui se modifie à toutes les frontières', and its identity as 'un art *plastique*, un art des rythmes, l'art d'apercevoir, entre des objets ou de êtres vivants, des rapports insoupçonnés que ni la peinture, ni la littérature, ni la musique n'avaient jamais devinés'[11]

---

11 The miraculous instantaneity with which it expresses our thoughts and feelings; a power and accessibility much greater than the spoken word, which changes at

(Vuillermoz 1933a). René Bizet and Lucien Wahl made the same point more directly, citing *Monsieur Poirier* as 'une erreur capitale, fondamentale qui fait bien voir celle de son système' (a major, fundamental error that reveals the error of his system) (Bizet 1934) and as a devastating illustration of Pagnol's own assertion that 'tout film qui porte à l'écran une pièce de théâtre et qui n'ajoute rien à l'expression de celle-ci est une très mauvais film parlant' (any talking film that brings a play to the screen and adds nothing to its expression is a very bad talking film) (Wahl 1933).

Perhaps the most trenchant indictment of Pagnol's commercially motivated populism came from Sacha Guitry, an accomplished stage author and actor who in early 1931 had commissioned an adaptation of his hit play *Le Blanc et le noir*. Like *Fanny*, the film was produced by Braunberger–Richebé and co-directed by Marc Allégret after the man initially hired to do the job, Robert Florey, resigned over conflicts with Guitry and leading man Raimu (Richebé 1977: 67–71). Despite favourable reviews and a good box-office take, the film left Guitry bitterly opposed to 'théâtre en conserve' (canned theatre) – an expression he coined to express his disgust (Knapp 1981: 69–70). In 'Pour le théâtre et contre le cinéma', a public lecture delivered and published several times between 1932 and 1934, Guitry denounced talkies as a vulgar mass commodity that catered to the lowest common denominator: 'le théâtre, c'est le dessin, l'aquarelle; le cinéma, c'est la lithographie' (theatre is sketching and watercolour; cinema is lithography) (Guitry 1977: 59). Though in agreement about the primacy of speech as a narrative tool, the creative dominance of the writer over the director, and the inferior quality of both silent and most talking films, Guitry contended that talking cinema would always remain an inferior form of expression because it was a mechanical, second-order copy of performance that eliminated the living, symbiotic interaction between author, actor, and audience. For him cinema represented nothing less than an intellectual and affective contagion whose effects mimicked malnutrition:

> Le cinéma n'est même pas du réchauffé, c'est du refroidi, c'est de la conserve. Et malheureusement, le public s'en contente. Vous perdez

---

every border; its identity as a *plastic* art, an art of rhythms, the art of perceiving, between objects and living beings, new relationships that neither painting, nor literature, nor music had ever suggested.

l'habitude d'applaudir, vous perdez l'habitude d'être ému. Il se passe exactement pour votre cœur ce qui se passe pour votre estomac – à force de manger des petits pois en conserve, vous ne voyez plus la différence qu'il y a entre eux et les petits pois frais. Or, les conserves sont dépourvues de vitamines. Si vous ne mangiez que des conserves, vous seriez atteints rapidement de scorbut![12] (Guitry 1977: 72)

As for Pagnol's contention that talkies would ensure the definitive realisation of the writer's vision, Guitry responded that 'canning' theatre undermined the author's ability to reinvent his text as tastes and society evolved (Guitry 1977: 68).

Pagnol counter-attacked in the second issue of *Les Cahiers du film* with an article defiantly entitled 'Le cinéma en conserve'. He answered the charge of undervaluing cinematic technique and simply photographing theatre by claiming that anything more than recording a play from the prompter's box with a single, immobile camera qualified as cinema. Reiterating the ways in which cinema improved upon theatre, he argued that talking film achieved 'l'unité de la salle' by standardising the viewing experience for all spectators; 'le bon marché de la représentation' by making tickets more affordable to a mass audience; and 'la fixité de la représentation' by preserving the performances of great actors for posterity. In an astute response to Guitry, Pagnol claimed that depriving spectators' of the actors' physical presence had the potential to enhance realism by amplifying the emotional and psychological appeal of their performance:

Ombre parmi les ombres, image parmi les images, l'acteur devient exactement aussi faux et aussi vrai que le décor. Sa voix n'est plus la voix d'un homme, elle est celle d'un personnage, d'un personnage qui vivra en dehors de l'acteur, affranchi des misères et des variations humaines. Voilà pourquoi, au lieu de dire que le film a perdu la présence des acteurs, je dirai que la pièce A GAGNÉ LEUR ABSENCE.[13] (Pagnol 1934: 6)

12 Cinema is not even reheated, it's gone cold, it's canned. And unfortunately, the public is satisfied with it. You get out of the habit of applauding, of being moved. Exactly the same thing happens to your heart as to your stomach – after eating so many canned peas, you no longer see the difference between them and fresh peas. Yet canned food lacks vitamins. If you eat only canned food, you will quickly fall prey to scurvy!
13 A shadow among shadows, an image among images, the actors become precisely as false or true as the setting. Their voices are no longer the voices of living people, but of characters who live outside the actors, liberated from

In support of this point, Pagnol stressed the value of location shooting, but only of 'les extérieurs qui QUI SONT COMMANDÉS PAR L'ACTION ... pour compléter un personnage qui en est l'âme, à la différence des belles photos de paysages qui ne veulent plus rien dire, dès que l'histoire qu'ils entourent n'est pas intéressante'[14] (Pagnol 1934: 11).

The polemic in the press ran nearly unabated for two months, culminating with a new exchange between Pagnol and René Clair that reignited their quarrel from 1930. Responding to an article in which Pagnol classified cinema as 'un art mineur' (a minor art) and 'un appareil de réalisation' (a production tool) that supported the 'superior' art of drama in the same way that the manufacture of violins or saxophones supported music and printmaking supported literature (Pagnol 1934a), Clair again dismissed his rival as a venal opportunist – 'le bonimenteur de sa propre marchandise qu'il vante avec un bagou parfois séduisant mais souvent comique' (the huckster of his own merchandise, which he vaunts with a glibness that is at times compelling but often comical) – and his theories as 'une plaisanterie' (a joke) that demonstrated:

> une étonnante ignorance du cinéma, son passé, ses moyens actuels, son essence même ... Pour Pagnol, l'heure des manifestes et des théories est passée. Il faut qu'il fasse un film, un vrai film. Qu'il apprenne ce métier qui est nouveau pour lui et où ses dons peuvent faire merveille s'il ne se contente pas de solutions toutes faites.[15] (Clair 1934)

As Christopher Faulkner has pointed out, the conflict between Clair and Pagnol ran deeper than the question of authorship or narrative technique; it was about the social dimension of speech, the value of realism, and the proper relation of cinema to the lived experience of spectators. Clinging to his surrealist background and silent-film aesthetics, Clair accepted speech only as a subcategory

---

human misery and vicissitudes. This is why, rather than saying that film has lost the presence of actors, I will say that the play gained their absence.

14 Locations THAT ARE JUSTIFIED BY THE ACTION ... to complement a character who is its soul, in contrast to lovely photos of landscapes that lose all their meaning as soon as the story they frame is no longer interesting.

15 An astounding ignorance of cinema, its history, its methods, its very essence ... For Pagnol, the time of manifestos and theories has passed. He must make a film, a real film. Let him learn his new profession, in which his talents may produce marvellous results if he does not settle for ready-made solutions.

of the soundtrack and a minor supplement to image and music in constructing an escapist, dream-like vision of the world for 'an ideal, universal, and trans-historical spectator whereas Pagnol's spectator has a local, particular and material existence' (Faulkner 1994: 164). In so doing, Pagnol invites audiences to construct their own subjectivities in relation to those presented on-screen and 'opens up the possibility of audience pleasure through the recognition of voices which, quite apart from actual meanings, speak a truth about one's own class, gender or region' (Faulkner 1994: 164–5).

Yet Pagnol's effectiveness in revealing such truths depends only in part on his masterful use of performative, socially authentic speech. His tempering of realism with elements of melodrama, satire, and vaudevillian comedy is just as crucial, for the incorporation of these genres allowed him to reach an audience far wider than strict social realism ever could. The deeply populist character of Pagnol's aesthetic explains not only the reaction of Clair and his fellow defenders of cinema as 'high' art, but the abiding admiration that André Antoine had felt since seeing *Topaze* on stage. Despite his disappointment in *Monsieur Poirier*, Antoine defended Pagnol's theory of *cinématurgie* in the strongest possible terms. Responding to a scathingly negative article by Jean Fayard in *Je Suis Partout*, Antoine issued a proclamation that reproduced the tone and content of Pagnol's own writings.

> [Louis] Delluc et les autres esthètes ont inutilement compliqué naguère le problème du cinéma. Les metteurs en scène se sont crus trop malins; ils ont voulu tout faire par eux-mêmes. Ils se sont cassé le nez. Voyez [Abel] Gance, voyez René Clair. Mais Pagnol! Voilà le succès, le chemin de l'avenir. Le cinéma va drainer de plus en plus toutes les forces, tous les capitaux, tous les talents. Le cinéma, c'est bien la nouvelle forme toute puissante de l'art dramatique. Avant quinze ans, il y aura dans Paris quatre ou cinq théâtres au plus.[16] (Antoine 1934)

Despite the rancorous tone of their public exchanges and very real differences in their conception of film aesthetics, in private Pagnol

---

16 Years ago [Louis] Delluc and the other aesthetes needlessly complicated the problem of cinema. Directors thought they were so clever; they wanted to do everything by themselves. They cut off their own noses. Look at [Abel] Gance, look at René Clair. But Pagnol! That's success, the way of the future. Cinema is progressively going to draw in all available resources, capital, and talent. Cinema is definitely the new, all powerful form of dramatic art. Fifteen years from now, there will be at most four or five theatres in Paris.

and Clair felt a shared sense of mutual respect. Having first met sometime in 1931, they played cards and fished together while on vacation at St Tropez, even sending each other advance copies of their polemic articles (Clair 1934a). Just prior to the publication of *Les Cahiers du film* in December 1933, Clair wrote to Pagnol that 'j'attends avec impatience le numéro 1 de ta revue afin de te traiter de tous les noms. Si tu me fais la rosserie d'y dire du bien de moi, je suis perdu, je le sais. Mais on continuera à se disputer quand même (Clair 1933).'[17]

Cinema at last

Though Pagnol never admitted so publicly, the failure of *Monsieur Poirier* and mediocre box-office performance of the other films produced by Les Auteurs associés marked a turning point in his career as a filmmaker, prompting him to abandon the strategy of adapting classic plays and to reprise the formula that had worked so well in *Marius* and *Fanny*. In April 1934 he suspended publication of *Les Cahiers du film* after only three issues, dissolved Les Auteurs associés, whose capital was reinvested in La Société des Films Marcel Pagnol after an amicable division of assets with Richebé, and began transforming an abandoned saw mill on the eastern edge of Marseilles into a small studio and development laboratory. The acquisition marked the final step in his drive to establish a fully independent, self-sufficient system for making movies and provided him the final tools needed to meet Clair's challenge of making 'real' films that drew their power from images as well as speech.

As a solo director Pagnol's work would always remain verbose and would never rival the visual complexity and deftness demonstrated by Korda or other exceptionally gifted directors of the era such as Jean Vigo, Jean Renoir, and Marcel Carné. Yet over time Pagnol did develop a level of technical competence equalling that of Allégret and the majority of his peers in the French film industry. From mid-1934 on, Pagnol used straightforward, effective cinematography to complement performative dialogue, inscribe his characters in authentic, minimally staged environments, and highlight the consistently strong

17 I am impatiently awaiting the first issue of your journal in order to call you every name under the sun. If you are lousy enough to say anything nice about me, I am lost, I know that. But we will continue arguing with each other anyway.

performances of his actors, thereby forging a signature style and a unique genre of melodrama that balanced realism with emotional and psychological potency.

The decisive step in this maturation process was Pagnol's decision to write original screenplays set in the contemporary social context – as exemplified in *César*, *Le Schpountz*, *La Fille du puisatier*, and *Manon des sources* – rather than recycling stage dialogue from stage hits of the nineteenth and early twentieth centuries. While he did continue to draw inspiration from literary sources (*Jofroi*, *Angèle*, *Regain*, and *La Femme du boulanger* were based on short stories and novels by Jean Giono, *Naïs* on a short story by Emile Zola), in each case Pagnol made the work his own through modifications to tone and content. Writing directly for the screen, with shooting locations already in mind, transformed his filmmaking by prompting him to reconceive dramatic art in concrete visual terms rather than as an abstract construct of acting and dialogue; this in turn made physical space an integral part of characterisation and the creation of an emotionally evocative, richly authentic atmosphere.

Pagnol first tested this approach in *Merlusse*, an hour-long *moyen métrage* about a group of high-school students sequestered during Christmas vacation under the supervision of a teacher despised for his glass eye, wild beard, and strict manner. When confronted with the deep sadness that the boarders feel at being separated from their families, Merlusse reveals an abiding kindness he had previously hidden for fear of losing control over the boys. After he secretly leaves personalised gifts in their stockings while they sleep, they reciprocate by each offering him a prized possession of their own. In recognition of his achievement, the headmaster offers Merlusse the promotion he has long sought.

Though it has been overlooked by film historians and on the surface might seem little more than a banal pastiche of Charles Dickens, whose work Pagnol admired and taught during his time as an English professor, the picture deserves to be remembered for the brilliant performance of Henri Poupon in the lead role, the casting of real students from Marseilles as secondary characters, and above all its exceptional poignancy of place. Written in mid-1934 and filmed on site at the Lycée Thiers in Marseilles during the Christmas holidays, then partially reshot the following summer because parts of the dialogue track turned out garbled, *Merlusse* effectively captures the melancholy, austere atmosphere of a nearly deserted school, then transforms it through a warm, redeeming human drama that reflects Pagnol's experience as a teacher who prided himself on flouting pedagogical conventions and cultivating friendly relationships with his students.

The movie is technically solid throughout and maintains a good balance of lively action sequences with longer dialogue shots, yielding an average shot length of 12.5 seconds, one-and-a half seconds faster than *Fanny* and four-and-a-half seconds faster than *Monsieur Poirier*. The shift in Pagnol's approach to cinematography and editing is clear in the film's opening sequence, a quick montage of shots from various angles and distances showing students being picked up by their parents at the school's main entrance while those obliged to stay mill about in an empty courtyard without toys or sports equipment of any kind. Prevented even from playing leapfrog by their despised teacher, the youngest languish in rows on the concrete steps, talking quietly about their dislike for the man and the school as the older students smoke in the shadows. The school bears a striking resemblance to a prison and the students to inmates hoping to be paroled, a parallel made explicit in a brief shot of them through the bars of the iron fence that surrounds the grounds.

Good use is also made of the school's long, shadowy hallways in a pair of contrasting shots. The first shows a student whose parents have arrived at the last moment running joyfully from the darkness at the end of the hall towards the brightly illuminated foreground; the second, in a perfect match of distance and angle, follows another student, who has just been informed that his parents will not keep their promise to pick him up, walking forlornly away from the camera from the light into the shadows, where he leans against the wall and begins to cry. Such moments are complemented by effective shot/counter-shot montage in dialogue sequences, as well as occasional close-ups and cut-aways to reveal the characters' repressed emotions, as in the scene where we see Merlusse's foot tapping furiously under his desk while he monitors detention and pretends to ignore a cruelly mocking song improvised by students already safe outside the school gates.

The film was widely praised by critics, many of whom marvelled at the contrast with *Monsieur Poirier*. As a columnist for *Comœdia* wrote approvingly:

> C'est fichtrement épatant lorsque tout se rencontre à la fois sur l'écran comme dans ce film magistral: réalisme cruel, sentimentalité exquise, types humains saisis en profondeur aussi bien que selon l'apparence, paroles significatives, et images bien rythmées. Sans hésiter on peut qualifier *Merlusse* de chef-d'œuvre. (Reboux 1935)[18]

André Antoine published two articles in less than a week welcoming Pagnol's 'heureuse transformation' (happy transformation) and the benefits of his new approach to filmmaking.

> Voici une production dont personne ne pourra contester la valeur psychologique et morale, pas plus que la perfection technique ... C'est un parfait exemple d'une formule nouvelle, élaborée en face de l'ancienne esthétique du 'théâtre filmé', une démonstration que le cinéma et la scène tendent à une jonction qui enrichira l'art dramatique et haussera l'écran à un plan supérieur.[19] (Antoine 1935)

While Antoine and his fellow reviewers likened *Merlusse* to two other highly regarded realist dramas featuring children – Julien Duvivier's *Poil de carotte* (1932) and Jean Benoît-Lévy/Marie Epstein's *La Maternelle* (1933) – from today's perspective the film recalls Jean Vigo's *Zéro de conduite* (1933). Banned by censors and not released commercially at the time, that film also depicts the plight of students stifled by draconian adult authority and raises the possibility of reconciliation between the two groups by introducing a non-conformist teacher named Huguet who provides the children freedom and stimulates their creativity. Yet in contrast to Pagnol's school, where the adults are fundamentally kind and well intentioned, Huguet is surrounded by loathsome, irredeemable colleagues. Instead of resolving the teacher–student conflict in a flourish of mutual reform and newfound respect, as does *Merlusse*, Vigo opts for a triumphant, anarchistic rebellion during which the children openly denounce the school's headmaster by telling him 'Merde!' ('Shit!'), tie their most

---

18 It's really great when everything comes together on-screen as in this magnificent film: cruel realism, exquisite sentimentality, human characters developed through depth and surface appearance, meaningful dialogue, and nicely paced images. Without hesitation *Merlusse* can be described as a masterpiece.

19 No one will be able to contest the psychological and moral merit of this production, any more than its technical perfection ... It's a perfect example of a new formula developed in contrast to the old aesthetic of 'filmed theatre', proof that the screen and the stage are coming together in a way that will enrich dramatic art and raise cinema to a higher level.

hated tormentor, Pète-Sec, to his bed in a crucifixion-style pose, and throw trash on a group of local notables assembled in the courtyard for the school's annual fair.

Stylistically as well, *Zéro* is very different from *Merlusse*, with Vigo and cameraman Boris Kaufman drawing on the playful visual techniques and anarchistic spirit of surrealism, especially in the celebrated slow-motion sequence where the students rip open their pillows and frolic amidst a blizzard of white feathers, thereby transforming the austere, repressive dormitory into a utopian paradise ruled by children (Temple 2005: 74–7). In its earnest realism and straightforward cinematography, *Merlusse* is closer to François Truffaut's new-wave masterpiece *Les 400 coups* (1959), which also opens with a courtyard recess scene to underscore the repressive, prison-like atmosphere of French schools. Truffaut, who like Vigo was a rebellious child, loved *Zéro de conduite* and cited it as a major influence, subscribing to its militant critique of the educational system. He identified Pagnol as an 'important' director who was 'sous-estimé' (underestimated) by cinema historians (Truffaut 1975: 39–40), and though it is unclear whether he saw and absorbed elements from *Merlusse* specifically, Truffaut's voracious cinephilia during the 1940s and 1950s meant that he probably did encounter the film at some point in a ciné-club retrospective.

Whatever the case, Truffaut's recruitment of newcomer Jean-Pierre Léaud to play the role of Antoine Doinel directly echoed Pagnol's casting of untrained teenage actors, many of them actual students at the Lycée Thiers. The authenticity of their performance drew widespread praise. A reviewer for *Comœdia* wrote that 'on regrette que le programme ne mentionne pas leurs noms. Il faudrait les louer individuellement. Tous s'expriment et agissent avec le plus vif naturel et spontanéité' (one regrets that the credits do not mention their names. They all speak and act with superb naturalness and spontaneity) (Reboux 1935). Especially noteworthy among the older boys was Jean Castan, a teenager from the nearby village of La Treille whom Pagnol had discovered in mid-1934 while shooting *Angèle*. Initially noticed for his resemblance to star Fernandel, Castan appeared in every film Pagnol made between 1935 and 1938. Most of the time his demeanour and thick southern accent simply add a dash of comedy and authenticity: as a restaurant manager-in-training in *Cigalon*, a slow but studious pupil in the second version of *Topaze*, an altar boy with adenoids in *César*, and a shepherd in *Regain*. However, as the leader of the sequestered boys in *Merlusse*, his character has significant screen time and is integral to the story. After initially terrorising the younger students with tales of the one-eyed teacher's cruelty, he articulates their guilt after receiving unexpected Christmas gifts and inspires them to reciprocate Merlusse's kindness. Likewise, in *Le Schpountz* he is the sole member of his small-town, petty bourgeois family to support older brother Irénée (Fernandel)'s dream of moving to Paris and becoming a movie star.

In *Merlusse* Castan perfectly complemented lead actor Henri Poupon, whom Pagnol had previously used to good effect in *Jofroi* and *Angèle*. Poupon gave the performance of his career, showcasing his capacity for vulnerability and kindness as well as for anger and intimidation. Antoine described him as 'prodigieux de naturel et de simplicité' (tremendously natural and unaffected) (Antoine 1935a); others saw 'un artiste complet et brillant qui atteint au sommet du pathétique' (a complete, brilliant artist who reaches the height of pathos) (Anon. 1936a), noting that 'ses gestes, ses silences obsèdent la mémoire' (his gestures, his moments of silence haunt one's memory) (Reboux 1935). It was Pagnol himself who paid Poupon the highest possible compliment, calling him 'un très grand comédien, comparable à Raimu' (a truly great actor, comparable to Raimu) (Pagnol 1995: II, 257).

If Pagnol's emphasis on authentic casting foreshadowed that of the French new wave and Italian neo-realism, so too did his spontaneous approach to working with his actors on set. In a continuation of his work as a playwright, he afforded them the opportunity to modify dialogue spontaneously without worrying about the multiple takes, wasted filmstock, and extra cost that such experimentation incurred, telling his actors: 'Ne vous en faites pas, la pellicule, c'est de la merde' (Don't worry about it; celluloid is shit) (Blavette 1961: 57). When performers caught up in the moment forgot their blocking or wandered out of frame, Pagnol let them continue until the scene was complete; on other occasions he filmed rehearsals without their knowledge. If the final result was good, he reshot after making the necessary camera adjustments or simply integrated the best bits into the final montage (Fieschi et al. 1965: 58; Labarthe 1966). That philosophy was reassuring for amateur actors, but sometimes frustrated disciplined professionals with busy schedules such as Pierre Fresnay, who described the shooting of *César* as 'décousu' (disjointed) and 'assez déroutant' (rather disconcerting), but 'agréable' (pleasant) because of the creative freedom and the convivial, collaborative working atmosphere it offered (Fresnay 1975: 43).

Pagnol applied the same improvisational approach to the technical aspects of filmmaking, assembling a production team that would remain with him from 1933 until the end of his career. His primary cinematographer was Russian-born Willy Faktorovitch, an experienced professional who had worked steadily in Paris since the early 1920s and already had thirty films to his credit by the time he signed with Les Auteurs associés in mid-1933. On the rare occasions when Willy was unavailable, he was replaced by Albert Assouad, a former highschool classmate of Pagnol's from Marseilles and trained chemical engineer who became director of his old friend's development laboratory when it opened in late 1934. Significantly, the disparity in Faktorovich and Assouad's backgrounds is not visible in the visual style or quality of their respective films, with each man signing unimaginative, mundane flops (for Willy, *Monsieur Poirier*; for Assouad, the 1936 version of *Topaze*) as well as consistently solid, at times innovative successes (for Willy, *Angèle*, *César*, *Regain*, *Le Schpountz*, and *Manon des sources*; for Assouad, *Merlusse*). Rather than reflecting the respective skill of his cameramen, this pattern manifests Pagnol's own growing attention to visual technique and demonstrates that he assumed primary responsibility for cinematography.

Even so, he continued to prioritise dialogue as the cornerstone of moviemaking and always used the highest quality sound equipment available regardless of cost. In mid-1934 just prior to shooting *Angèle* he purchased a custom-made mobile system from Philips that included a truck with generators and recording equipment, microphones equipped with special preamplifiers, and several hundred metres of cable. Later that year he installed a Western Electric 'noiseless' system in his small Marseilles studio, ensuring proper maintenance by hiring a technician from the company to live on the premises (Guégan et al. 1965: 27). Sound engineer Jean LeCoq and lead editor Suzanne de Troye reported that Pagnol always prepared shots in advance with his technicians once on set, but that his shooting scripts contained almost no visual guidelines and that during filming he typically listened in the recording booth or truck rather than watching the action (Fieschi et al. 1965: 57–8). Jean Renoir, who visited Pagnol during the making of *La Femme du boulanger* in August 1938, noted the same eccentricities, but defended them as integral to the unique appeal of Pagnol's work.

> Pendant les prises de vue, Marcel Pagnol disparaît. Il ne veut à aucun prix influencer personne. Il s'en voudrait de contrarier les idées personnelles du plus humble de ses collaborateurs. Certains s'en plaignent et préféreraient une direction plus ferme. Mais je crois que, quelle que soit la méthode, seul le résultat compte. Et il est un fait avéré, c'est que les films de Marcel ne ressemblent à aucun autre. Autant la production d'un quelconque auteur de films peut sembler banale et semblable à toutes les autres productions du monde, autant celle de Marcel Pagnol se signale par une parfaite originalité. Il a raison de travailler comme cela, puisqu'il réussit.[20] (Renoir 1938)

Though certainly unusual, and perhaps unique to Pagnol, this practice was not as extreme as it might first appear, for in the context of the 1930s it reflected a characteristically French approach to the aesthetic function of sound. Whereas American films tended to conceive sound as one of many interdependent, malleable narrative elements whose importance varied according to montage, French cinema emphasised the accurate reproduction of dialogue and diegetic song as part of a performance staged specifically for recording (O'Brien 2005: 87–8). In France even directors who saw cinema as a visual art, René Clair and Jean Renoir chief among them, largely subscribed to this approach, thus differentiating their work from foreign peers such as Fritz Lang and Sergei Eisenstein.

To capture just the right vocal inflection while maintaining image quality and variety, Pagnol took to shooting key scenes several times from beginning to end with lenses of increasing magnification: a first run-through at 25 millimetres captured establishing shots; a second and third, at 40 and 50 millimetres, respectively, mid-range shots; finally, a fourth at 75 millimetres, close-ups and cut-aways. Because Pagnol rarely used multiple cameras, doing so only by necessity

---

20 During shooting, Marcel Pagnol disappears. He does not want at any cost to contradict the ideas of even the least prominent members of his team. Some complain and would prefer firmer directing. But I think that, whatever the method, only the result counts. And it is an indisputable fact that Marcel's films do not look like any other. While the work of another filmmaker may seem hackneyed and similar to all the other productions in the world, Marcel Pagnol's work distinguishes itself through its utter originality. His success proves that he is right to work like that.

in outdoor settings when time and light were limited, the shot/counter-shot footage crucial to effective dialogue sequences had to be gathered by repeating the middle- and close-range passes of the cycle from a different angle (Fieschi et al. 1965: 57–8, 61; Blavette 1961: 57–8). This system was outrageously inefficient and expensive, but satisfied Pagnol's ear and compensated for his lack of proficiency as a visual artist by generating a mass of heterogeneous footage from which to select the best segments. As Fresnay dryly commented in his memoirs: 'Intinctivement, Pagnol n'était pas du tout un technicien du cinéma, mais il l'est devenu plus ou moins' (Instinctively, Pagnol was not at all a cinematic technician, but he more or less became one) (Fresnay 1975: 60).

Though sometimes maddening for de Troye and her assistants, the editing process generally produced good results on-screen. Unfortunately, Pagnol's preoccupation with dialogue occasionally led him to join shots recorded at different distances or angles, thereby introducing poor visual continuity. While the effect is usually a momentary awkwardness that passes almost unnoticed in a flood of performative speech, there are also more jarring examples that disrupt the narrative. One of the worst occurs in *César* when Marius' son learns the truth and bitterly reproaches his grandfather for not telling him the truth. During their conversation the pair is initially framed in a mid-range, left-to-right pan moving slowly towards the end of the bar counter. Before they reach it, the camera suddenly cuts to Raimu in close-up leaning back against the middle of the bar just as he retorts that Césariot has 'le cœur gâté' (a rotten heart). Rather than enhancing emotional and psychological realism of performance, here the editing undermines it.

On the whole, such serious errors in continuity are rare, more than counterbalanced by moments when comedy and pathos are expressed visually through cinematography and open-air location shooting, with little or no support from speech. The extensive tracking shots in *César* are particularly effective in this regard, capturing César's breathless climb to the cathedral in search of a priest to give the dying Panisse last rights; the sight gag in Panisse's funeral procession when César, who has unwittingly exchanged his bowler with that of a much smaller mourner at the church, must wear it anyway to escape the blazing sun; Césariot leaving aboard a boat to secretly search for Marius; finally, in a striking parallel with the endings of both Chaplin's *Modern Times*

(1936) and Renoir's *Les Bas-Fonds* (1936), Marius and Fanny walking down a country lane together, away from the camera, in the final shot. Beyond indicating a new spirit of generosity and respect towards his peers in the industry, this dual homage offers compelling evidence that Pagnol had finally become a cinephile, acting on Clair's advice 'qu'il aille voir des films' (that he go see some films) (Clair 1934) to enrich his own work rather than summarily dismissing all competitors.

While Pagnol's approach to filming was often laborious and wasteful, he and his crew were also capable of exceptional efficiency when circumstances dictated. The funeral procession for Panisse in *César*, a series of reverse tracking shots on La Canebière in Marseilles, was captured in a single take using a strategy that foreshadowed the early work of Godard, Rivettte, and Truffaut on the streets of Paris. In order to maximise authenticity and to avoid the security-related complications of barricading a section of Marseilles' busiest thoroughfare, Pagnol assembled two unmarked equipment vans followed by twenty taxis carrying his actors. When they arrived at the appropriate spot, the convoy suddenly stopped, with technicians and performers quickly taking their places. The taxis blocked traffic from the rear as camera rolled, and the scene was completed without incident in less than five minutes (Régent 1936). The result on-screen, whose full impact can be appreciated only by viewing the uncut print preserved at the Cinémathèque de Toulouse, is a masterful blend of the scripted with the real: on the one hand, Pagnol's dialogue, close-ups of key actors, and wider shots of the entire procession; on the other, the inimitable sights and ambient background noise of a busy city street on a Sunday afternoon – tramway bells dinging, car horns honking, buses humming, and sidewalks filled with curious pedestrians stopped to watch the procession.

This fusion of innovative cinematography with performative speech and poignant acting recurs more powerfully later in the film when Escartefigue, César, and Monsieur Brun pay homage to Panisse by reprising the card game from *Marius*. The dead man's absence is represented by an empty chair at the table and beautifully registered at the outset of the sequence in an overhead establishing shot (see Figure 8). As the men are swept up in the pleasure of their game and conversation, which involves César comically attempting to convince Monsieur Brun that alcoholic drinks 'ne peuvent pas attaquer le foie parce qu'il sonts faits avec des plantes qui n'ont jamais vu de foie, qui ne savent pas ce que c'est qu'un foie' (cannot attack the liver because they are made with plants that never saw a liver, that don't know what a liver is), they forget that Panisse is missing. César, laughing heartily, turns towards the dead man's spot and abruptly falls silent, his smile draining away in a quick series of shot/counter-shot between the three friends' faces and the empty chair. 'Cette fois, il est mort', César observes, 'C'est seulement maintenant que j'ai compris' (This time he's dead. It's only now that I realised). As the camera cuts to a medium close-up of the chair, Monsieur Brun recites from Parnassian poet Sully Prudhomme's poem 'Le dernier adieu' (1869): 'C'est aux premiers regards portés / En famille, autour de la table / Sur les sièges plus écartés / Que se fait l'adieu véritable' (It's at the first glances exchanged / With family, around the table / Upon chairs spaced farther apart / That the true farewell is bid). Next they joyfully play out the hand Monsieur Brun instinctively dealt Panisse, praising the skill of his moves and declaring him the winner. While César lays down the final cards, Panisse declares placidly in voice-over: 'Mes enfants, tout le reste est à moi' (Kids, all the rest are mine). Answering the doctor's observation that 'c'est la première fois que j'ai vu jouer à la manille avec un mort' (this is the first time I've seen anybody play cards with a dead man), César replies in the sequence's final shot: 'Oui, c'est la première fois qu'on n'a pas triché et on a perdu' (Yes, this is the first time we didn't cheat, and we lost).

Composed of 37 shots spanning 4 minutes, 30 seconds, the sequence boasts nearly perfect visual continuity and maintains a lively pace (average shot length = 7.3 seconds) despite its verbosity and emphatically 'literary' dimension underscored by the poem citation. Image and dialogue complement each other perfectly: Panisse's voice-over retrospectively transforms the establishing overhead shot, which initially appears generic and omniscient, into a subjective representation of Panisse's gaze as he looks down on the game from heaven. The card game is especially bittersweet because of its richly meta-cinematic function: for Pagnol and his actors, paying tribute to a colleague (Fernand Charpin) for whom they all had deep, genuine affection; for spectators, bidding farewell to a character and a story that had been part of their lives for the past five years. In so doing, the sequence constitutes the single best illustration of Pagnol's view that 'la véritable technique consiste à donner du movement avec des gens qui ne bougent pas. L'écran est petit, fait pour le gros plan d'une lèvre, d'un œil, d'un beau regard' (true technique consists of creating a sense of movement with actors who do not move about. The screen is small, made for close-ups of a lip, an eye, a significant glance) (Bessy 1938).

Even critics who still harboured a grudge against Pagnol over the *cinématurgie* scandal concurred. Georges Champeaux described the card game as 'un grand moment d'une qualité sans pair' (a great moment of unequalled quality) (Champeaux 1936); Emile Vuillermoz as 'un chef-d'œuvre de prestidigitation' (a masterpiece of magic) and 'la seule véritable scène de cinéma dans toute la pièce' (the only truly cinematic scene in the entire play) (Vuillermoz 1936). Even while dismissing the film in general as 'un mélodrame exécrable' (an atrocious melodrama), Jean Fayard characterised the sequence as 'un morceau de bravoure étourdissant' (a stunning bit of bravura) (Fayard 1936). Predictably, the most lavish praise came from André Antoine, who by 1936 was in declining health and at the age of 78 was having difficulty maintaining his weekly review column for *Le Journal*. He put special effort into his evaluation of *César*, launching a passionate vindication of Pagnol's 'cinématurgie' as the perfect blend of screenwriting and acting, speech and image, melodrama and realism.

> L'auteur administre de nouveau la preuve que le cinéma parlant, libéré des règles arbitraries et singulièrement étroites avaient retardé l'évolution d'un art de plus en plus goûté par le public, permettra aux auteurs la création d'un répertoire d'œuvres qui élargiront singulièrement l'intérêt des spectacles de chez nous. Le dialogue ne diffère plus en rien du théâtre, et le drame s'élargit de tout ce que l'écran peut lui apporter de vie, de mouvement, et de vérité humaine. La puissance, l'émotion, la vérité du dialogue de Pagnol classent cette œuvre parmi les plus belles, les plus fortes du cinéma contemporain. Une interprétation sans égale de la part de Raimu et de Pierre Fresnay, Charpin, et surtout Orane Demazis forment un ensemble tout à fait exceptionnel.[21] (Antoine 1936)

21 Once again the author proves that talking film, liberated from the arbitrary, extraordinarily constrictive rules that had held back the evolution of an art increasingly appreciated by the public, will allow authors to create a repertoire of work that will substantially broaden the appeal of French-made entertainment. The dialogue is in no way different from that of the theatre, and the drama is enriched by all the life, the movement, and the human truth that the screen can offer. The power, the emotion, the truth of Pagnol's dialogue places this film among the strongest and most beautiful in contemporary cinema. The unequalled acting of Raimu and Pierre Fresnay, Charpin, and especially Orane Demazis make for a truly exceptional team.

Pagnol was touched by the homage and thanked his 'cher maître et ami' (dear mentor and friend) in a long, heartfelt letter that read in part:

> Si j'ai tenu bon dans cette bagarre du parlant qui dure depuis 1931, c'est à *vous* que je le dois, comme c'est à vous que je dois mes premiers succès au théâtre. Sans eux je n'aurais pas eu l'argent qui m'a été indispensable pour réaliser des films *librement*, sans commanditaires qui arrangent le scénario, sans metteur en scène qui pour trouver le fameux rythme détruit tout ce qui faisait la valeur de l'œuvre. (Pagnol 1936)[22]

'Pagnol was right'

The making of *César* in mid-1936 inaugurated a two-year period of exceptional creativity that generated a series of box-office hits confirming Pagnol's status as France's most popular filmmaker. More important, *Regain*, *Le Schpountz*, and *La Femme du boulanger* earned him the widespread critical respect he had sought since entering the profession, despite his clinging defiantly to the position that 'il n'y a rien de plus bête que la technique. N'importe qui peut filmer à l'aide d'un appareil électrique qui marche tout seul. Il suffit d'appuyer sur le bouton' (there is nothing dumber than technique. Anybody can film with an electric camera that runs by itself. It suffices to press the button). Seasoned cinema journalist Maurice Bessy rightfully dismissed that claim as yet another exercise in provocation, assuring readers that in fact Pagnol 'a compris, il ne néglige plus l'image et il fait même un gros effort de technique' (has understood, he no longer neglects the visual and he even pays close attention to technique) (Bessy 1938).

By that time, nearly everyone in the French film industry had accepted the irresistible economic logic of Pagnol's method as talking film progressively drained box-office receipts from theatre and every other live performance genre. Lured by increased fortune and celebrity, in 1935 Sacha Guitry followed Pagnol's lead and began adapting his

---

22 If I have held out in this brawl over talking cinema that began in 1931, I owe it to *you*, just as I owe my first successes on stage to you. Without them, I would not have had the money that has been indispensable in allowing me to make films *freely*, without investors who alter the screenplay, without a director who in attempting to create the much-vaunted rhythm destroys everything that gives the work value.

own plays for the screen, directing or co-directing and starring in eleven feature films over the next four years. Though film historians have often grouped the two men together under the rubric of 'theatrical' or 'literary' filmmaking, their approaches to cinema encompass as many differences as similarities, and the contrast between them is essential for appreciating the uniqueness of Pagnol's achievement.

In characteristically paradoxical fashion, Guitry justified his conversion to cinema via an argument he had initially used to discredit it: its 'caractère purement américain' (purely American character) (Guitry 1977: 71), with all the usual negative connotations of economic and cultural imperialism, soulless industrial standardisation, and poor quality. Following Pagnol's lead, Guitry made it his mission to craft a uniquely French brand of cinema prioritising high-quality dialogue and the actors' performances while dismissing visual technique as unnecessary (Guitry 1977a: 81). Yet Guitry disdained traditional melodrama and 'Anglo-Saxon' comedy in favour of cultivating verbal and dramatic irony, which he regarded as distinctively Gallic and a 'diapason pour déceler ce qui sonne faux' (a tuning fork for discening what rings false) (Guitry 1977b: 83). At the same time, he wilfully retained theatrical artifice and unlike Pagnol made little effort to 'open up' his plays through location shooting, casting untrained actors, or adding other elements of realism, relying instead on self-reflexive narrative devices (rejection of linear chronology, frequent temporal ellipses, double identities, abandoned plot threads, *mise en abyme* of performance) that highlight both the ultimate creative control of the writer-actor-director and the inherently contrived nature of his enterprise (Keit 1999: 63–79).

The most prominent of these techniques – deployed in *Le Roman d'un tricheur* (1936), *Les Perles de la couronne* (1937), *Remontons les Champs-Elysées* (1938) and *Ils étaient neuf célibataires* (1939) – is omniscient voice-over narration by the author himself, who addresses the spectator directly while sardonically commenting on and controlling the action (Knapp 1981: 117–30; Andrew 1995: 127–8). Whereas the appeal of Pagnol's cinema hinged on creating a wholly believable illusion of reality embellished just enough to reliably evoke comedy and pathos, Guitry's consisted of forging complicity with his audience through shared detachment, which afforded both author and spectators an even deeper enjoyment of the spectacle played out on-screen. In this sense, Guitry's films remain true to the self-reflexive, avant-garde variety of modern theatre pioneered by Luigi Pirandello's *Sei personaggi in cerca d'autore* (1921) – a narrative style that Pagnol scorned from the outset of his career as a playwright.

Eventually Pagnol also reconciled publicly with René Clair. In an April 1946 article published shortly after his election to the Académie Française, Pagnol acknowledged their longstanding friendship by looking back on their venomous exchanges from the 1930s with gratitude and nostalgia.

> Sans l'avouer, nous nous sommes mutuellement convaincus. Il s'est mis à faire des films parlants qui parlent. J'ai cherché, à cause de lui, à réaliser des images. Si notre querelle continue, et je crois qu'elle durera aussi longtemps que notre amitié, qui est parfaitement indestructible, je finirai par tourner des films muets, pendant qu'il fera du charme à la radio.[23] (Pagnol 1946)

Clair echoed that sentiment five years later in his memoirs, recanting his earlier denunciation of Pagnol as an arrogant, ignorant opportunist.

> Face à face, on ne résiste pas au charme de cet extraordinaire personnage qui se lança dans le cinéma avec l'enthousiasme juvénile qu'il apporte à toutes ses entreprises ... Ce caractère du 19e siècle balzacien, tombé par erreur dans le nôtre et qui s'y meut avec l'aisance que lui donnent ses talents et son goût de la vie, fut sans doute un des premiers à oublier que selon sa propre formule, 'le film parlant est l'art d'imprimer, de fixer et de diffuser le théâtre', ou s'il ne l'oublia tout à fait, il fit prevue d'une distraction des plus heureuses quand il composa des films commes *Angèle* ou *La Femme du boulanger*.[24] (Clair 1951: 197–8).

---

23 Without admitting it, we mutually convinced each other. He started to make talking films that talk. Because of him, I tried to cultivate images. If our dispute continues, and I think it will last as long as our friendship, which is utterly indestructible, I will end up making silent films, while he will charm listeners on the radio.

24 Face to face one cannot resist the charm of this extraordinary character who launched himself into cinema with the youthful enthusiasm he brings to all his endeavours ... This personality out of Balzac's nineteenth century, who landed in ours by mistake and moves about with an ease born of his talents and taste for life, was one of the first to forget that, in his own words, 'talking film is the art of recording, giving definitive form to, and disseminating theatre'; or if he didn't forget so entirely, he digressed in the most fortunate way when he made films such as *Angèle* and *La Femme du boulanger*.

Pagnol subsequently nominated Clair for the Académie in 1960 and personally saw to his election by defeating the objections of 'literary' members initially opposed to accepting a 'pure' filmmaker. Clair reciprocated in 1974 by serving as the Académie's official representative at Pagnol's funeral, where he delivered a eulogy wistfully noting that the departed would have savoured the irony of the occasion.

Yet for Pagnol the most satisfying vindication had already come in early 1953 with the release of *Manon des sources*, arguably the fullest expression of his unique approach to cinema. Unlike Claude Berri's two-part remake released in 1986, the original version almost totally elides the heart-wrenching back story of Jean de Florette, his wife, and daughter Manon. Except for a few brief, dreamlike flashbacks representing Manon's childhood memories, the film does not show the young family's move to rural Provence from the city, torturous struggle to irrigate their crops in the arid countryside, cruel exclusion from the surrounding community, and the family's disintegration after Jean dies from exhaustion. Instead, Pagnol recounts the story indirectly through long retrospective conversations among members of the village and eventually Manon herself as she takes her revenge on the community by blocking off its water supply.

The result is a fragmentary, often contradictory narrative in which performative speech, or more precisely, the filming of performative speech in an irreproachably authentic social and physical milieu (the village of La Treille and its environs), takes over the function traditionally filled by images and visual technique. The terrible truth surrounding Jean's death – that there was a spring on his property dissimulated by the village patriarch – is thus revealed slowly in a complex web of silences, half-truths, and outright lies, thereby maintaining a tantalising moral ambiguity throughout the film's three-and-a-half hours.

Manon drew nearly unanimous critical acclaim, including special attention from André Bazin, who published a long theoretical essay heralding the film as the triumphant culmination of Pagnol's career-long battle to reinvent the seventh art.

> La prédominance de l'expression verbale sur l'action visuelle ne saurait nullement définir le théâtre par rapport au cinéma. La parole théâtrale est abstraite, le résultat de la conversion de l'action en verbe; la parole cinématographique est au contraire un fait concret, elle existe par et pour elle-même; c'est l'action qui la prolonge et qui, presque, la

dégrade ... Aussi le cinéma de Pagnol est-il tout le contraire de théâtral, il s'insère par l'intermédiaire du verbe dans la spécificité réaliste du film. Pagnol n'est pas un auteur dramatique converti au cinéma, mais le plus grand auteur de films parlants.[25] (Bazin 1953)

Two weeks later *Cahiers du cinéma* ran a review fleshing out Bazin's remarks. Emphatically entitled 'Pagnol avait raison' (Pagnol was right), it described *Manon* as 'un cas limite du cinéma parlant' (a case that tests the limits of talking cinema') and 'un emploi nouveau de la parole' (a new use of the spoken word).

> Cette nouveauté est si profonde que *Manon des sources* peut être considérée comme le premier exemple d'un genre cinématographique particulier. Marcel Pagnol rompt avec le théâtre filmé et le théâtre tout court ... Dans l'art du récit oral, le choix de mots parlés importe moins que le ton et l'accent, la suite de l'histoire est inséparable de la voix du conteur et du cadre dans lequel se fait le récit. Dans *Manon* les mots et les phrases du texte sont inséparables de la silhouette des personnages, du soleil qui baigne le film et de l'atmosphère provençale évoquée par la terrasse du petit café ou par les vues sur le paysage rocailleux et grillé.[26] (Tallenay 1953: 51–2)

The film remained a touchstone for Bazin over the next two years, serving as the centrepiece of his attempt to define the relationship between cinema and the other arts. His appreciation for *Manon* grew with time, peaking in late 1954.

> C'est au travers d'une assimilation malheureuse au théâtre filmé que Marcel Pagnol avait cependant raison de ne considérer dans le cinéma

25 The predominance of verbal expression over visual action is utterly insufficient to differentiate theatre from cinema. Theatrical speech is abstract, the result of converting actions into words; on the contrary, cinematic speech is a tangible fact; it exists by and for itself; actions are what stretch it out and in a sense erode it ... Pagnol's films are thus precisely the opposite of theatrical; his use of language inscribes them within the specific reality of cinema. Pagnol is not a dramatic author converted to cinema, but the greatest author of talking films.

26 This originality runs so deep that *Manon des sources* can be considered the first example of a special film genre. Marcel Pagnol breaks away from filmed theatre and theatre altogether ... In the art of oral storytelling, the choice of the words spoken is less important than the tone and the accent; the story's development is inseparable from the voice of the storyteller and the context in which the story is told. In *Manon* the words and sentences in the script are inseparable from the physiognomy of the characters, from the sun that drenches the film, and the southern atmosphere created by the terrace of the little café or by the shots of the rocky, scorched landscape.

qu'un nouveau moyen d'expression littéraire: l'instrument moderne du conteur ... Pagnol renoue d'abord avec la tradition orale. Ses personnages n'agissent pas par la parole comme les acteurs de théâtre: ils se racontent l'un l'autre et le cinéma leur offre l'aire concrète de ce récit, il lui conserve son indispensable enracinement terrestre et lui assure en même temps la seule audience à la mesure de son inspiration: l'innombrable auditoire des cinémas. Car un film de Pagnol n'est pas un spectacle, mais simplement une forme moderne, orale, et populaire de la littérature.[27] (Bazin 1954)

The affinity Bazin felt for Pagnol's populism and ethnographic filming of speech was a product of his own anti-elitism, identification with the working classes, and respect for mass culture – values that led him to embrace cinema as a means of educating and involving the public in socio-political debate (Andrew 1978: 132–7).

Yet as a Christian democrat wary of capitalism and committed to progressive social reform, Bazin was instinctively wary of the aggressively commercial dimension of Pagnol's work, his Nietzschean will to individual glory and creative superiority, and his contemptuous disdain for other directors' contributions to the seventh art. These traits invariably skewed the otherwise astute critic's assessment of Pagnol's career as a whole, blinding him to the importance of key early pictures and their fundamental continuity with *Manon*. Bazin went so far as to characterise the Trilogy as a stylistic regression, writing that '*Fanny* ne valait déjà plus *Marius*; *César* 'ne mérite que l'oubli' (*Fanny* was already inferior to *Marius*; *César* deserves only to be forgotten) and dismissed *Merlusse* as 'ignoble' (vile), yet defended Pagnol's mediocre screen adaptation of Alphonse Daudet's *Les Lettres de mon moulin* against overwhelmingly negative reviews and comparatively poor box-office figures (Bazin 1954).

Subsequent generations of scholars have echoed Bazin's conflicted attitude by tending to identify either with his strong admiration for or disappointment in Pagnol. In a 1957 article naming France's sixty

---

27 Despite his unfortunate affair with filmed theatre, Marcel Pagnol was right to seize upon cinema as a new means of literary expression: the modern tool of the storyteller ... Above all, Pagnol revives the oral tradition. His characters do not use speech in the same way as theatre actors: they narrate themselves to each other, and cinema gives their account a material context, keeps it vitally anchored in the soil, and at the same time guarantees the only audience commensurate with its inspiration: the movie theatres' countless listeners. For a Pagnol film is not a visual spectacle, but simply a modern, oral, and popular form of literature.

most influential living directors, *Cahiers du cinéma* presented the two views as insoluble: 'Très souvent insupportable, misérabiliste et bâcleur, Pagnol surpend favorablement au moment où nous y attendions le moins. A vrai dire, on ne sait qu'en penser' (Very often intolerable, dwelling on misery, and given to technical incompetence, Pagnol surprises us pleasantly when we least expected it. One really doesn't know what to think of him) (Anon. 1957: 61). The critical rehabilitation that followed Pagnol's death in 1974, led by cinema historian Claude Beylie and supported by the filmmaker's friends, unfortunately swung the pendulum too far in the opposite direction, turning excessive disdain into hagiography. A dispassionate assessment from today's perspective yields a more balanced conclusion: Pagnol's glaring personal and intellectual shortcomings were inseparable from his brilliant capacity for innovation and integral to the seminal role he played in the aesthetic and commercial development of French cinema from the advent of sound through the birth of the new wave.

References

Agay, Philippe (1932), 'La société des films Pagnol annonce sa première production: *Fanny*', *Cinémonde*, 16 June.
Andrew, Dudley (1978), *André Bazin*, Oxford and New York, Oxford University Press.
Andrew, Dudley (1995), *Mists of Regret: Culture and Sensibility in Classic French Film*, Princeton, Princeton University Press.
Anon. (1932), 'Louis Gasnier nous parle de *Topaze* à l'écran', *Express Midi*, 22 June.
Anon. (1933), '*Fanny* est le meilleur film français de 1932', *Pour Vous*, 26 January.
Anon. (1933a), '*Fanny* de Marcel Pagnol: un chef-d'œuvre de l'écran', *Paris-Soir*, 17 November.
Anon. (1936), 'Les nouveaux films: les interprètes de *Merlusse* sont des lycéens marseillais', *Comœdia*, 16 February.
Anon. (1936), 'Le scandale de *César*', *Le Journal*, 21 November.
Anon. (1937), 'Les dix meilleurs films de 1936', *La Dépêche de Toulouse*, 2 April.
Anon. (1937a), '*César* au Théâtre Municipal', *Le Courrier de La Rochelle*, 10 March.
Anon. (1957), 'Soixante metteurs en scène français', *Cahiers du cinéma* no. 71, May, 47–67.
Antoine, André (1933), 'Les premières de l'écran', *Le Journal*, 22 December.
Antoine, André (1934), 'Le plateau et l'écran: Antoine parle', *Je Suis Partout*, 1 December.

Antoine, André (1935), 'Absurdité des règles', *Le Journal*, 13 December.
Antoine, André (1935a), 'Le film du jour: *Merlusse*', *Le Journal*, 18 December.
Antoine, André (1936), 'Le succès de *César* confirme l'effort de Marcel Pagnol', *Le Journal*, 20 November.
Bazin, André (1953), '*Manon des sources*', *France Observateur*, 29 January.
Bazin, André (1954), '*Les Lettres de mon moulin* et le cas Pagnol', *France Observateur*, 18 November.
Bessy, Maurice (1937), 'Marcel Pagnol tout joyeux', *Cinémonde*, 26 March.
Bessy, Maurice (1938), '"Il n'y a rien de plus bête que la technique", déclare Marcel Pagnol', *Cinémonde*, 6 October.
Bizet, René (1932), 'Parmi les nouveaux films de la semaine: *Fanny*', *Pour Vous*, 3 November.
Bizet, René (1934), '*Le Gendre de Monsieur Poirier* et les théories de M. Pagnol', *L'Antenne*, 7 January.
Blavette, Charles (1961), *Ma Provence en cuisine*, Paris, Editions France Empire.
Champeaux, Georges (1932), '*Fanny*', *Gringoire*, 4 November.
Champeaux, Georges (1933), '*Topaze*', *Gringoire*, 13 January.
Champeaux, Georges (1936), '*César*', *Gringoire*, 13 September.
Chantal, Suzanne (1932), 'J'ai vu pleurer la princesse Astrid en assistant au film *Fanny*', *Cinémonde*, 3 November.
Clair, René (1933), Letter to Pagnol, Archives of the Compagnie Méditerranéenne de Film, 15 December.
Clair, René (1934), 'Le sens du cinéma: à propos des théories de Marcel Pagnol', *Candide*, 22 February.
Clair, René (1934a), Letter to Pagnol, Archives de la Compagnie Méditerranéenne de Film, 19 February.
Clair, René (1951), *Réflexion faite: notes pour servir à l'histoire de l'art cinématographique de 1920 à 1950*, Paris, Gallimard.
Colin-Reval, Marcel (1937), 'Les films champions de 1936', *La Cinématographie française*, 26 March.
Cooke, Maeve (1994), *Language and Reason: A Study of Habermas's Pragmatics*, Cambridge, MA, MIT Press.
Crisp, Colin (2002), *Genre, Myth, and Convention in the French Cinema, 1929–1939*, Bloomington, Indiana University Press.
Epardaud, Edmond (1937), '*César* en province: 58 copies en circulation', *La Cinématographie française*, 21 January.
Faulkner, Chistopher (1994), 'René Clair, Marcel Pagnol, and the Social Dimension of Speech', *Screen*, no. 2, 157–70.
Fayard, Jean (1932), '*Fanny*', *Candide*, 3 November.
Fayard, Jean (1936), '*César*', *Candide*, 19 November.
Fieschi, Jean-André et al. (1965), 'Pagnol au travail par ses collaborateurs: rencontres avec Marius Brouquier, Suzanne de Troye, Jean LeCoq, et Charles Blavette', *Cahiers du cinéma* no. 173, December, 56–62.
Fresnay, Pierre and François Possot (1975), *Pierre Fresnay*, Paris, La Table ronde.
Gerould, Daniel (2000), *Theatre, Theory, Theatre: the Major Theoretical Texts from Aristotle and Zeami to Soyinka and Havel*, New York, Applause Books.
Gorel, Michel (1933), '"Je n'ai pas changé de métier", nous déclare Marcel

Pagnol', *Cinémonde*, 17 August.
Guégan, Gérard, Jean-André Fieschi and Jacques Rivette (1965), 'Une aventure de la parole: entretien avec Marcel Pagnol', *Cahiers du cinéma* no. 173, December, 24–37.
Guitry, Sacha (1977), 'Pour le cinéma et contre le théâtre', in André Bernard and Claude Gauteur (eds), *Sacha Guitry: le cinéma et moi*, Paris, Editions Ramsay, 54–76.
Guitry, Sacha (1977a), 'Non, le cinéma n'est pas un jeu!', in André Bernard and Claude Gauteur (eds), *Sacha Guitry: le cinéma et moi*, 79–81, reprinted from *Paris-Soir*, 9 May 1936.
Guitry, Sacha (1977b), 'L'ironie au cinéma', in André Bernard and Claude Gauteur (eds), *Sacha Guitry: le cinéma et moi*, 82–84, reprinted from *Paris-Soir*, 20 September 1936.
Habermas, Jürgen (1988), 'Actions, Speech Acts, Linguistically Mediated Interactions, and the Lifeworld', in Maeve Cooke (ed.), *On the Pragmatics of Communication*, Cambridge, MA, MIT Press, 1998, 215–55.
Harlé, Pierre (1930), 'Braunberger–Richebé, spécialistes du parlant', *La Cinématographie française*, 21 June.
Harlé, Pierre (1933), 'Les projets de Marcel Pagnol, qui vient de fonder "Les Artistes associés"', *La Critique cinématographique*, 12 August.
Heath, Stephen (2004), *César*, London, British Film Institute.
Jouvet, Louis (1932), Letters to Pagnol, Bibliothèque Nationale de France, Département des Arts du Spectacle, Archives Louis Jouvet, MS-229, 18 May, 20 May, 1 June
Keit, Alain (1999), *Le Cinéma de Sacha Guitry: vérités, représentations, simulacres*, Liège, Editions du CEFAL.
Knapp, Bettina (1981), *Sacha Guitry*, Boston, Twayne Publishers.
Labarthe, André (1966), *Marcel Pagnol, ou le cinéma tel qu'on le parle*, French television documentary broadcast on Antenne 2, 5 and 12 May. Archived at the Inathèque de France.
Lasky, Jesse (1932), Memo to A.M. Botsford, Margaret Herrick Library, Special Collections, Paramount Pictures Scripts, Production File no. 1131, 21 April.
Lehmann, René (1932), 'Marcel Pagnol à l'écran: *Fanny*', *L'Intransigeant*, 5 November.
Lehmann, René (1933), '*Le Gendre de Monsieur Poirier*', *Pour Vous*, 21 December.
Luckhurst, Mary (2006), *Dramaturgy: A Revolution in Theatre*, Cambridge, Cambridge University Press.
Nietzsche, Friedrich (1974), *The Gay Science*, trans. and ed. Walter Kaufmann, New York, Random House.
O'Brien, Charles (2005), Cinema's Conversion to Sound: Technology and Film Style in France *and the US*, Bloomington, Indiana University Press.
Pagnol, Marcel (1932), 'Marcel Pagnol nous parle de *Fanny* qu'il vient tourner à Marseilles', *Le Petit Provençal*, 18 June.
Pagnol, Marcel (1933), 'Cinématurgie de Paris', *Les Cahiers du film* no. 1, December, 3–8.
Pagnol, Marcel (1934), 'Cinématurgie de Paris: le théâtre en conserve', *Les Cahiers du film* no. 2, 15 January, 3–13.

Pagnol, Marcel (1934a), 'Le cinéma est un art mineur', *Candide*, 8 February.
Pagnol, Marcel (1936), Undated letter to André Antoine, Bibliothèque Nationale de France, Département des Arts du Spectacle, MS-78 [late November/early December].
Pagnol, Marcel (1946), 'Mon ami René Clair', *Cinémonde*, 23 April.
Pagnol, Marcel (1995), *Œuvres complètes*, 3 vols, Paris, Fallois.
Reboux, Paul (1935), '*Merlusse*', *Comœdia*, 8 December.
Régent, Roger (1936), 'J'ai suivi sur la Canebière le convoi funèbre de Maître Panisse', *L'Intransigeant*, 15 August.
Renoir, Jean (1938), 'Une journée avec Marcel Pagnol', *Regards*, 4 August.
Reusse, André de (1934), 'Pagnol le cinématurge', *Hebdo-Film*, 13 January.
Richebé, Roger (1977), *Au-delà de l'écran: 70 ans de la vie d'un cinéaste*, Monte Carlo, Editions Pastorelly.
Tallenay, Jean-Louis (1953), 'Pagnol avait raison', *Cahiers du cinéma* no. 20, February, 51–4.
Temple, Michael (2005), *Jean Vigo*, Manchester, Manchester University Press.
Truffaut, François (1975), *Les Films de ma vie*, Paris, Flammarion.
Vermorel, Claude (1933), 'En laissant parler Marcel Pagnol à l'heure du dessert', *Pour Vous*, 2 February.
Vidal, Jean (1932), 'Un jeune metteur en scène: Marc Allégret', *Pour Vous*, 24 November.
Vuillermoz, Emile (1933), '*Le Gendre de Monsieur Poirier*', *Le Temps*, 23 December.
Vuillermoz, Emile (1936), '*César*', 21 November.
Wahl, Lucien (1933), 'Réponse à Monsieur Pagnol', *Pour Vous*, 4 January.
Waldman, Harry (1998), *Paramount in Paris: 300 Films Produced at the Joinville Studios, 1930–1933*, London, Scarecrow Press.
Wolff, Pierre (1933), 'La critique des films: *Topaze*', *Paris-Soir*, 13 January.

1 'Keep rolling! Having struck the mother lode, Marcel Pagnol continues to mine it. His next film will be *César* (and there will be sequels).' Caricature published in *Mon Ciné*, 21 February 1935

2 An apprentice filmmaker: Pagnol at the Joinville complex with (from right to left) Alexander Korda, Paramount executive Jacob Karol and two unidentified Paramount employees, 1931

137

3 A love triangle: Marius (Pierre Fresnay) longs for the sea while Fanny (Orane Demazis) longs for Marius

4 Seduction by jealousy: Fanny savours Marius' hostility towards Panisse (Fernand Charpin)

5 Shadows of temptation: Piquoiseau (Alexandre Mihalesco) tries to lure Marius away from Fanny to the sea

6 Performing friendship: César (Raimu) and Escartefigue (Paul Dullac) cheat Panisse and Monsieur Brun (Robert Vattier) at cards

7 Unspoken truths: César (Raimu) and Honorine (Alida Rouffe) acknowledge their grandson's paternity

8 A heavenly view: the late Panisse looks down at his friends playing cards

9 Decadence redeemed: Saturnin (Fernandel) comforts Angèle (Orane Demazis) in the Marseilles brothel

10 Constructed ruins: the village of Aubignane, Pagnol's most elaborate outdoor set

11 Familial bliss: Angèle, Albin (Jean Servais), and baby atop a sunny hill in Provence

12 Adulterous chemistry: Aurélie (Ginette Leclerc) seduces the shepherd (Charles Moulin) in the bakery

13 Domesticity regained: Aimable (Raimu) reaffirms his love for Aurélie with a heart-shaped loaf

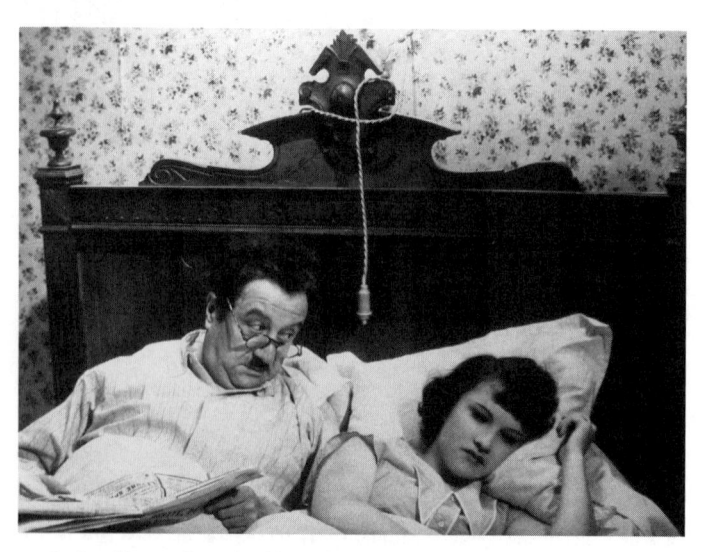

14 Conjugal frustration: Aimable neglects Aurélie's needs

15 Comedic pathos: Jofroi (Vincent Scotto) threatens Fonse (Henri Poupon) with a shotgun

16 Filmmaking *à la marseillaise*: a game of *pétanque* during the shooting of *Angèle*. Participants (from right to left) include actor Edouard Delmont, an extra, Pagnol, actress Annie Toinon, star Fernandel, head cameraman Willy Faktorovitch, and actor Andrex

17 Atmospheric angst: *Fanny* advertising poster by Henri Cerutti, 1932

18 An economy of gazes: *Angèle* advertising poster by Henri Cerutti, 1934

19 Saturation marketing: a billboard for *Regain* in the Paris subway, 1937

20 Stardom by caricature: *Le Schpountz* advertising poster by Toé, 1938

21 Human comedy on the Old Port: *César* advertising poster by Albert Dubout, 1936

4

Another poetic realism

While Pagnol battled to defend and perfect his signature brand of *cinématurgie*, he simultaneously pursued an alternative production model that rejected both theatrical convention and contemporary film industry practice by shooting feature-length pictures on site in the Provençal countryside. This was an expensive and logistically complicated proposition, but one that paid substantial dividends aesthetically and financially. Beyond providing the authenticity that Pagnol had always craved since the beginning of his career, outdoor filming prompted him to recognise that cinematic narration was not simply a matter of creating effective dialogue, story, and characters, but the art of using images to inscribe these elements in a compelling physical and social setting.

Perhaps most important, Pagnol's rural melodramas moved him closer to writing directly for the screen by drawing inspiration from literary sources rather than transposing pre-existing plays. While his first cycle of rural films – *Jofroi* (1933), *Angèle* (1934), and *Regain* (1937) – were largely faithful adaptations of texts by popular Provençal writer Jean Giono, in each case they incorporated elements specific to Pagnol, especially performative speech and comedy, that made the work inimitably his own. This evolution is apparent not only in his original screenplays for *Merlusse* and *César*, but *La Femme du boulanger* (1938), a final adaptation of Giono that reproduces only the broadest lines of the original short story. In addition to winning over reviewers who had previously dismissed Pagnol's work as canned theatre, these films occupied a unique place within the style known as poetic realism and appealed strongly to Depression-era spectators as an antidote to France's perceived cultural decadence.

Pagnol was of course not the first filmmaker to shoot extensively on location in the countryside. By the 1910s a number of European directors were already experimenting with real landscapes and natural light to enhance the authenticity, visual depth, and psychological intensity of their work. Among the first were Victor Sjöstrom and Mauritz Stiller, who used the stark terrain of rural Sweden to craft tales of hardship, passion, and madness (Idestam-Almquist 1952). A similar movement retrospectively labelled 'provincial realism' or 'pictorialist naturalism' emerged in France immediately after the First World War. Exemplified by the work of Jacques de Baroncelli, Léon Poirier, Louis Mercanton, and Pagnol's mentor André Antoine, it dramatised the struggles of peasants, fishermen, and artisans by drawing on a range of literary and painting styles, from the lyrical romanticism of Victor Hugo, Alphonse Lamartine, and Jean-François Millet to the socially critical realism of Emile Zola, Pierre Loti, and Gustave Courbet. Whereas Poirier and Baroncelli worked primarily in the former mode, and Mercanton in the latter, Antoine successfully bridged the two. After filming an adaptation of Hugo's *Les Travailleurs de la mer* on the Breton coast in 1917, he made Zola's *La Terre* two years later in the Beauce region, followed by *L'Hirondelle et la mésange* along the barge canals of Flanders (Abel 1984: 94–120; Williams 1992: 112–20).

A forgotten classic

While Pagnol's aversion to silent cinema suggests that he probably did not see any of these films and was aware of them only indirectly through his contact with Antoine, the production of *Marius* and *Fanny* had sensitised him to the value of using location shooting to enhance the theatrical approach he instinctively favoured. He implemented that approach for the first time in the otherwise disastrous *Le Gendre de Monsieur Poirier*, whose outdoor scenes were shot on an elaborate set that required clearing several acres of forest on Pagnol's estate in the Sarthe, transplanting forty mature trees to create a classic French garden, and constructing the façade of a mid-nineteenth-century bourgeois country villa (Anon. 1933). When pressed to make a short film for distribution with *Poirier*, Pagnol decided to take the experiment a step further by adapting *Jofroi de la Maussan*, a ten-page story by Giono to which he had purchased the rights a year earlier. Whereas Giono's original text underscores the pathos of an elderly Provençal peasant who sells his orchard of decrepit olive trees to a neighbour and stubbornly preserves them by threatening to kill himself if they are uprooted to plant wheat, Pagnol creates a tragi-comic tone by depicting Jofroï's suicide attempts as a passionate expression of his love for the soil, a clever charade to win public sympathy, and a means of reasserting the relevance of purportedly 'unproductive' persons and objects for the life of their communities.

Apart from a few interior sequences later added at the Natan-Pathé studios in Joinville, the picture was shot in and around the hamlet of La Treille (located between Marseilles and Aubagne) in November 1933 without any set construction whatsoever. It ran only 52 minutes but would prove seminal in the development of Pagnol's career, establishing his work as an echo of pictorialist naturalism and a precursor of Italian neo-realism. Unlike his predecessors in silent cinema and the immediate post-war work of Roberto Rossellini and Vittorio De Sica, Pagnol was not limited by technical or financial constraints and insisted on synchronous sound recording because of his preoccupation with authentic dialogue.

He rented a mobile RCA audio truck from Pathé and had to battle strong gusts of the Mistral during filming (Blavette 1961: 55–7), but the result on-screen was worth the effort and expense. In addition to faithfully reproducing the inimitable regional grain of the actors' speech, the soundtrack captures a wide range of ambient noises in the background, from the singing of cicadas to the snorting of horses, cracking of tree branches, and rustling of long grass – all of which remain audible even on the VHS edition of the film. These qualities drew widespread praise, especially from those who panned *Monsieur Poirier*. As one reviewer noted approvingly: 'Nous voilà loin du théâtre filmé. Le réalisateur a confié le dialogue au micro et a remplacé les descriptions par des images mouvantes' (Here we are far from filmed theatre. The director entrusted his dialogue to the microphone and replaced descriptions with moving images) (Anon. 1933a). A special screening held for the Parisian press was reportedly interrupted several times by 'des applaudissements prolongés et des exclamations admiratives' (sustained applause and admiring exclamations) and drew a chorus of bravos at its conclusion (Anon 1933b).

A second crucial feature that distinguished *Jofroi* was the use of non-professionals in both leading and secondary roles. That practice was already familiar to him from the shooting of *Marius*. Shortly after the production crew arrived on the Old Port, the actor supposed to play the ferry boat's stoker, Marcel Maupi, withdrew because of illness. While scanning the crowd of curious onlookers, Raimu spotted a teenager named Vincent di Giovanni who was working at the port as a delivery boy (Anon. 1931). With his thick southern accent and mischievous enthusiasm, a soot-smudged di Giovanni makes a memorable appearance in the film's first comic scene by blowing the steam whistle of the ferry boat repeatedly and forcing the lazy, rotund Escartefigue to waddle quickly to the dock from his comfortable chair in the shade.

To play Jofroi Pagnol cast Vincent Scotto, a popular composer with no prior acting experience who had provided the music for *Fanny* and *Monsieur Poirier*. Painfully self-conscious about appearing on camera, Scotto accepted the role despite himself and proved difficult to direct. His refusal to deliver several long tirades and to reshoot certain scenes 'a tourné Pagnol en bourrique' (drove Pagnol up the wall), but that stubborn antagonism fit perfectly with his on-screen persona and gave his performance a rare degree of authenticity (Scotto 1947: 168). It was Scotto's first and only screen role, lauded by critics as 'étonnant' (stunning) and 'remarquable' (remarkable) (Anon. 1933; Liausu 1933).

The film also marked the screen debuts of two unknown locals from Provence in supporting roles. The first was Charles Blavette, owner of a small tinworks in Marseilles and a regular patron of Pagnol's favourite bar (Blavette 1961: 53–4). As a townsperson who helps prevent Jofroi from killing himself, Blavette complemented Scotto by providing realism and local colour. He subsequently became a key figure in the 'troupe' of loyal actors and technicians who would surround Pagnol until the end of his career. Equally important, Blavette served as the unofficial cook on each of the shoots, producing home-style Provençal cuisine whose succulence eventually launched him on a second career as a chef (Blavette 1961). On-screen his salt-of-the-earth charisma earned him work with a range of high-profile directors including Jean Grémillon, Henri-Georges Clouzot, and Jean Renoir.

Pagnol's second casting coup in *Jofroi* was selecting Henri Poupon to play Fonse, the frustrated neighbour who buys the orchard but cannot legally obtain a refund or morally bring himself to plough over its decrepit trees lest the old man actually carry out his suicide threat. Poupon, a song lyricist and friend of Scotto's from Bandol, had previously dabbled in acting without much success, yet this time drew acclaim as 'tour à tour violent et craintif, exprimant avec beaucoup de finesse les divers sentiments qui l'agitent' (alternatively outraged and fearful, expressing with great subtlety the various emotions that move him) (Anon. 1933a). Working with Pagnol made him a regular in the French film industry, launching a career that would span twenty years and more than thirty roles, including the critically acclaimed lead in *Merlusse* and the tormented, self-destructive patriarchs in *Angèle*, *Naïs*, and *Manon des sources*.

Though still slow-paced, with an average shot length of over 18 seconds, in technical terms *Jofroi* largely eliminated the numerous theatrical contrivances that marred *Monsieur Poirier*: jarringly abrupt cuts between and within scenes; nearly exclusive reliance on mid-range group shots; and the actors' predictably artificial entrances and exits. Moreover, the incorporation of numerous outdoor tracking shots evokes both the rugged physical beauty of the Provencal landscape and the flavour of life in a rural village. As one reviewer exclaimed: 'Ici, pas de décor au pistolet. On nous donne de la campagne, des champs qui fument, des branches qui pendent. Avant tout, l'accent des gens chante' (Here there are no spray-painted sets. We are given the countryside, steaming fields, bending branches. Above all, there is the song-like accent of the people) (Brunet 1934). The film also effectively uses close-ups, shot/counter-shot montage, and a variety of camera angles to capture Pagnol's signature blend of pathos and humour. An especially memorable sequence alternates tilt-up shots of Jofroi, who has climbed atop a roof in the village square and is threatening to jump unless Fonse pledges publicly not to 'assassinate' his trees, with tilt-down views of the horrified blackmail victim on the ground below surrounded by curious onlookers, who scurry back and forth holding a mattress to break Jofroï's fall.

In recognition of such flourishes, *La Cinématographie française* cited the film as a model for others to follow: 'En somme, la mise en scène est très souple et la photographie excellente, de toute beauté, avec un choix d'images judicieux. Il faut voir ce film, l'entendre, il faut en rire, en être ému par l'humanité mêlée de cocasserie formidable. Un film de cette qualité relève le niveau de la production française, qui a besoin de semblable leçon"[1] (Anon. 1933a). Yet because of its brevity and pairing with the disastrous *Monsieur Poirier*, *Jofroi* was not widely seen or appreciated in 1933–34. Its importance for the development of European realism was eventually acknowledged only after being distributed in the United States alongside two complementary short dramas: Renoir's *Partie de campagne* (1936) and Rossellini's *Il miracolo* (1948). The three films shared the 1950 New York Film Critics' award for best foreign-language picture, with several voters lobbying to recognise *Jofroi* individually (Anon. 1950).

Ethnographic melodrama

Despite its limited initial exposure, the film was crucially important in Pagnol's search for a production model that would afford him total creative and financial independence. Location shooting not only distinguished his work stylistically and galvanised his identity as a non-conformist auteur; it also satisfied his business ambitions by allowing him to avoid the expense of renting studios and the aggravation of working on other people's timetables. During the summer of 1934 Pagnol implemented that approach by filming *Angèle*, his adaptation of Giono's 1929 novel *Un de Baumugnes*, at an isolated farm he had purchased in the Marcellin valley near La Treille. A local stone mason and childhood friend named Marius Brouquier rebuilt and enlarged the crumbling house and barn, each with strategically placed holes in the roof and walls to accommodate a variety of camera placements. To maximise audio recording quality, the walls of the house were lined with velum (Godefroy 1934; Chantal 1934). Because the site was served by a single unpaved road that snaked through steep hills, it was originally inaccessible to trucks carrying the seven tons of electric generators, sound and lighting equipment that Pagnol required (Blavette 1961: 65–7). The only solution was to carve a wider path out of the rock cliffs with dynamite – a dangerous and expensive endeavour that drew substantial publicity in the national press (Anon. 1934; D'Aubarède 1934; Raoul 1934; Régent 1934).

1 The direction is very flexible and the photography excellent, quite lovely indeed, with judiciously chosen images. One must see this film, hear it, laugh at it, be moved by its humanity mixed with wonderful funniness. A film of this quality raises the level of French production, which needs just such a lesson.

The authenticity of the sets was enhanced by an array of accessories – horses, tools, tractors, carts, and furniture – borrowed from neighbours living in and around La Treille, as well as numerous long takes that inscribe characters within the ruggedly beautiful landscape. The combined effectiveness of these elements is particularly striking in several sequences depicting various forms of agricultural labour such as cutting hay, chopping wood, ploughing fields, threshing wheat, and storing grain in a barn to protect it from a sudden rainstorm. Filming outdoors presented significant logistical challenges: laying rails for tracking shots across rocky, uneven terrain, enduring scorching heat that threatened to melt film inside the camera, transporting massive cisterns of water to cool the electric generators, wrangling kilometres of electric cables, and improvising covers to protect microphones from strong gusts of wind.

The shoot required nearly twice as long as planned, but the result was impressive: a 'documentaire romancé' (fictionalised documentary) – as an anonymous critic from Nantes put it – whose ethnographic feel enhances the believability and poignancy of its melodramatic plot: 'Toutes les images sont justes et belles. C'est la campagne dans toute sa simplicité et sa splendeur. Les travaux des champs sont si bien rendus qu'on y croit sans réfléchir'[2] (Anon. 1934a). In Paris, a reviewer for *Comœdia* added: 'On pourrait aisément taquiner Pagnol sur une certaine facilité d'émotion à laquelle il fait appel en spéculant une fois de plus sur le cas d'une fille-mère, mais l'histoire d'Angèle demeure émouvante par son ton de vérité et de naturel. Parfumé d'un plaisant goût de terroir et d'optimisme, le "tout s'arrange" semble surgir du sol même' (Rey 1934).[3]

Though in many ways reminiscent of provincial realism from the silent era, *Angèle* achieved a new level of authenticity thanks to Pagnol's rich dialogue, direct sound recording, and convincing performances by both leading and supporting actors. Orane Demazis' multiple transformations in the title role – from naïve, dissatisfied

2 All the images are accurate and beautiful. It's the countryside in all its simplicity and grandeur. The farm work is so well rendered that one automatically believes in its authenticity.

3 One could easily chide Pagnol for once again exploiting the theme of a young, unwed mother for its emotional appeal, but Angèle's story remains moving thanks to its truthful, naturalistic tone. Complemented by a pleasingly earthy atmosphere and optimism, the 'all ends well' seems to emerge organically from the soil itself.

farm girl to debauched, self-loathing urban prostitute, then honourable mother and wife – surpassed her previous work as Fanny in the first two chapters of the Marseilles Trilogy. Henri Poupon turned in an equally powerful performance as her father consumed by anger and grief. A pair of experienced recruits trained on the Marseilles music hall circuit, Andrex and Edouard Delmont, brought gritty authenticity to their respective roles as a pimp who seduces Angèle and a hired farm hand who orchestrates the redemptive meeting with her eventual husband.

Yet the film's greatest revelation was Fernand Contadin, better known to film audiences as Fernandel, a vaudevillian famous for his buffoonish roles in the military farce genre that was so popular at the time. Playing Saturnin, a simple-minded orphan who has worked for Angèle's family since childhood, gave Fernandel his first opportunity to balance comedy with pathos. The two elements complement each other when Saturnin, acting on a tip from a friend, seeks out Angèle in Marseilles. In a long tracking sequence echoing *Fanny*, the camera records him walking from the St Charles train station down the busy Canebière to a brothel near the Old Port (in reality, a small hotel that Pagnol rented for the shoot). Blithely unaware that Angèle is a prostitute, despite being propositioned by another woman in the entryway, Saturnin comprehends the truth only after his adoptive sister emphatically confesses in an outpouring of suicidal despair. He responds with one of the most poignant speeches in 1930s French cinema (see Figure 9).

> Ecoute, ce qui t'arrive, voilà comment je me le comprends. Si on me disait brusquement 'Angèle est tombée dans le fumier', je te prendrais et je te laverais en bien m'appliquant. Je te passerais des bois d'allumette sous les ongles, et je te tremperais les cheveux dans l'eau de lavande pour que tu n'aies pas une paille, pas une tache, pas une ombre, rien. Je te ferais propre comme de l'eau. Et tu serais aussi belle qu'avant. Parce que, tu sais, l'amitié, ça rapproprie tout.[4]

---

4 Listen, here's how I see what's happening to you. If somebody suddenly told me 'Angèle has fallen into the manure pile', I'd take you and wash you really carefully. I'd run matchsticks under your nails and soak your hair in lavender water so that you wouldn't have a piece of straw, a stain, even a shadow on you, nothing. I'd make you as clean as water. And you'd be just as beautiful as before. Because you know, friendship makes everything clean again.

In addition to offering moral redemption, Saturnin also protects Angèle from her pimp and the wrath of her father once they return home – selfless, risky gestures that make him the film's unlikely hero.

Absent from Giono's novel, which omits the circumstances of Angèle's homecoming, the brothel sequence was added by Pagnol specifically to display Fernandel's dramatic potential and his ability to match the proven skills of Orane Demazis. That strategy earned the previously one-dimensional comedian instant critical respect and legitimate stardom, transforming him from 'un vulgaire grimacier' (a vulgar grimacer) into 'un acteur inoubliable, de très grande classe' (an unforgettable actor of the highest order) (Vuillermoz 1934). It also began a long, fruitful relationship with Pagnol, to whom Fernandel addressed a heartfelt letter shortly after the film's Parisian premiere: 'Laissez-moi vous dire la joie que j'ai éprouvée devant le succès d'*Angèle* et que si mon évocation de Saturnin vous a donné pleine satisfaction, c'est à votre dialogue que je le dois. Je ne l'oublierai pas' (Let me tell you that I took joy in seeing the success of *Angèle* and that if you were happy with my performance as Saturnin, I owe it to your dialogue. I will not forget that) (Contadin 1934). Over the next fifteen years, they would collaborate on five additional films, successfully recycling variations on the Saturnin character in both *La Fille du puisatier* and *Naïs*.

As the first French feature film since the advent of sound to be shot entirely outside the studio, *Angèle* drew substantial attention from industry professionals, who lauded the picture as evidence that France could maintain a distinctive production style and aesthetic originality that would enable it to compete with a deluge of Hollywood imports. Reversing his scathing assessment of *Monsieur Poirier* a year earlier, André Antoine wrote that 'Pagnol est celui qui a vu le plus clair dans l'avenir du cinéma. Son nouveau film est tout bonnement un chef-d'œuvre, une date dans l'évolution du cinéma. Aucune production française n'a été mise en scène avec plus de perfection' (It was Pagnol who most clearly foresaw the future of cinema. His new film is quite simply a masterpiece, a crucial date in the evolution of cinema. No French production has been more perfectly directed) (Antoine 1934). In reality, the direction is far from perfect, showing occasional lapses in continuity between shots, awkward framing of certain close-ups, and uneven sound quality. Yet as part of Pagnol's innovative blend of ethnographic realism and melodrama, these flaws went largely unnoticed and even became assets. One of his toughest critics, Jean Fayard, noted that 'Pagnol n'aura jamais le sens du mouvement cinématographique, mais on lui pardonne à peu près tout pour la sincère honnêteté de ses intentions. Il sait admirablement rendre plausibles les situations les plus excessives, les plus sentimentales. Jamais encore l'on n'avait vu à l'écran français des paysans d'une pareille vérité' (Fayard 1934).[5]

Arguably the greatest admirer of *Angèle* was Jean Renoir, who almost immediately after the film's release in October 1934 borrowed Pagnol's equipment and technicians to shoot an ethnographic melodrama of his own entitled *Toni* (1935), the story of a Piedmontese quarry worker caught in a murderous love triangle. Inspired by a real crime committed in Martigues several years earlier, it was shot entirely on site using synchronous sound and a cast led by Charles Blavette and Edouard Delmont, with numerous non-professionals from the area in supporting roles. In the last issue of Pagnol's magazine *Les Cahiers du film*, Renoir excitedly wrote of capturing on film 'une réalité si dépouillée et tellement stylisée qu'elle me fournit des personnages taillés dans la matière même' (a reality so raw and so stylised that it provided me characters chiselled out of matter itself) and 'l'occasion d'apporter ma modeste part à la transfusion de sang que le cinéma français cherche en se dirigeant vers le plein air et le travail sur nature' (the opportunity to make my own modest contribution to the blood transfusion that French cinema is seeking in the open air and working with life unadorned) (Renoir 1934). Looking back four years later after a period of exceptional productivity that generated *Le Crime de Mr. Lange*, *Les Bas-fonds*, *La Grande Illusion*, and *La Bête humaine*, he credited the experience as a turning point in his career.

> Je faisais de rares et pauvres films jusqu'au moment où Marcel Pagnol me permit de tourner *Toni*. C'était pour moi la possibilité de tourner réellement, de sortir de ce conformisme imbécile qui est celui de tellement de gens qui dirigent notre industrie. Ce film m'a communiqué le courage nécessaire pour tenter de nouvelles choses dans des directions différentes. (Renoir 1938: 285)[6]

---

5 Pagnol will never have a feel for cinematic movement, but one can forgive him for virtually anything thanks to the sincere honesty of his intentions. He has an admirable knack for making the most excessive, sentimental situations plausible. Never before had French cinema shown peasants so truthfully.

6 I made a few weak films until Marcel Pagnol allowed me to shoot *Toni*. For

The only serious criticism levelled against *Angèle* was its run time of 163 minutes – twice that of the average French feature. While critics lamented the slow narrative pace, distributors and theatre owners disliked having to reduce their number of daily showings by half and to divide screenings into two parts separated by an intermission. Initially resistant to compromising his work, Pagnol released the full version in Marseilles on 27 September 1934 (Anon. 1934a), but shortly after the film's Parisian premiere in late October he agreed to remove twenty-three minutes of episodic digressions (Thierry 1934).

In the capital *Angèle* benefited from simultaneous, unusually long exclusive runs of fifteen, seven, and seven weeks, respectively, at the Ciné-Opéra, Agriculteurs, and Bonaparte cinemas (Anon. 1935). Nearly all period sources ranked it as the top-grossing production of the 1934–35 season. Many theatre owners in the provinces reported that it surpassed attendance records set by *Marius* and *Fanny*, with one estimate suggesting that between 15 and 20 per cent of the population (6 to 8 million spectators) in metropolitan France purchased tickets (Anon. 1935a). Pagnol's distributor in French North Africa reported that the film performed even better there, having reached 24 per cent of Europeans living in Casablanca and 30 per cent of those in Algiers (Lamy 1935). Demand to see the picture was so strong that it was rereleased twice nationally: the short version in September 1935 at the outset of the new fiscal year, and the long version from June to September 1937.

The success of *Angèle* transformed Pagnol's conception of 'cinématurgie' by prompting him not only to abandon the transposition of plays and write directly for the screen, but to incorporate substantial location shooting into nearly all his subsequent films – an evolution visible in *Merlusse*, *Cigalon*, and most strikingly in *César*. Whereas *Marius* and *Fanny* incorporate only a few travelling shots along the Old Port and its environs, the third chapter of the Trilogy features extensive footage recorded in Marseilles, Toulon, aboard Césariot's boat along the coast, and the countryside near Les Lecques. Doing so marked the definitive opening up of Pagnol's theatrically inspired cinema and his maturation from dramatic author into bona fide screen director. Exemplified mid-way through the film in consecutive

---

me *Toni* represented the opportunity to shoot realistically, to leave behind the moronic conformism that characterises so many of those who run our industry. That film gave me the courage necessary to try new things in different directions.

point-of-view shots where Honorine throws open the shutters of her bedroom to see Césariot off and he waves goodbye while motoring away from the dock, that evolution is confirmed in the picture's long closing sequence, which has Marius and Fanny reconcile at an isolated stone cottage in the countryside, then walk away from the camera together down a picturesque lane in an unmistakable homage to Chaplin's *Modern Times*.

Poetic realism, *autrement*

In late 1936 Pagnol took his aesthetic of ethnographic melodrama to new heights by adapting Giono's novel *Regain*, an elemental parable of civilisation-from-savagery in which an isolated man and woman come together to rebuild a crumbling rural village. He initially considered shooting on location at Redortiers, the isolated hamlet in the foothills of the Alps that had inspired Giono, but abandoned the idea after scouting revealed that during autumn and winter the site received only enough natural light to allow two or three hours of filming a day. Pagnol instead decided to construct Giono's fictionalised village, Aubignane, atop a 400-metre cliff overlooking the farm where he had filmed *Angèle* (Pagnol 1995: II, 495–7). Working full-time under the supervision of master stone mason Marius Brouquier, a team of sixty men needed almost four months to complete the project since mules and a specially engineered cableway provided the only conveyance from the valley below. It was the most elaborate and expensive outdoor set in the history of French cinema, boasting several houses, a forge, a windmill, a bakery, a well, and a church with a 20-metre bell tower – all carefully crafted to give the appearance of age and neglect (Epardaud 1936; Rohl 1937) (see Figure 10). In order to capture visually the annual cycle of death and rebirth that structures Giono's narrative, Pagnol filmed the autumn and winter sequences between February and May 1937, then returned in July and August to get the spring and summer shots that conclude the story (Rohl 1937a).

If in a sense the principles of production and set design that Pagnol employed were unique in 1930s French cinema for insisting on outdoor, *in situ* construction, his approach also had much in common with other practitioners of poetic realism who preferred to create an illusion of reality in the studio. Like *Angèle* and *Regain*, the urban milieus crafted by René Clair, Jean Renoir, Julien Duvivier, and Marcel Carné were irreproachably authentic in their concrete details and relatable to spectators' lived experience, yet carefully stylised to create an intensity of atmosphere, thereby infusing the familiar with a special emotional and psychological depth. Thanks in large part to art director Lazare Meerson, Clair successfully evoked the melancholy tribulations and small joys of urban working-class life in *Sous les toits de Paris* (1930), *Le Million* (1931), and *Quatorze juillet* (1932). The mood grew progressively darker as the decade and the Great Depression wore on – moving towards pessimism in *Le Crime de Monsieur Lange* (Renoir, 1935), *Les Bas-fonds* (Renoir, 1936) and *La Belle Equipe* (Duvivier, 1936), then sinking into an irresistible fatalism that pervades Duvivier's *Pépé le Moko* (1937), *La Bête humaine* (Renoir, 1938), and Carné's morose trilogy *Le Quai des brumes* (1938), *Hôtel du nord* (1938), and *Le Jour se lève* (1939).

This 'tragic populism', as period observers sometimes labelled it, took place in a labyrinthine cityscape of shadowy staircases, foggy alleyways, and claustrophobic bedrooms which owed their ambiance to elaborate sets designed by Eugène Lourié (for Renoir), Jacques Krauss (for Duvivier), and above all Alexandre Trauner (for Carné). It also depended on the socially authentic dialogue of Jacques Prévert, Charles Spaak, and Henri Jeanson – writers who like Pagnol had an ear for performative language and popular dialects – and on the ritualistic sacrifice of beleaguered working-class characters brought to life by iconic actors such as Louis Jouvet, Arletty, and Jean Gabin. The cumulative effect was to create a 'fantastique social', as Carné preferred to call it – an oneiric representation of society that registered the injustice of class hierarchy, expressed the disappointment many lower-middle-class French moviegoers felt in the wake of the failed Popular Front, and provided them a means of collectively working through their anxieties in the public space of the movie theatre (Andrew 1995: 177–88, 260–71).

Even commentators impressed by the emotive power of this style and favourably disposed towards its leftist political overtones were often dismayed by its crushing malaise. As Pierre Bost, chief film reviewer for the Popular Front's official weekly newspaper, wrote of *Les Bas-fonds*:

> La pauvreté, la maladie, et le crime sont évoqués avec tant de force qu'il exige l'admiration. Mais vraiment, nous ne pouvons pas échapper

de ces murs gluants où s'enferment les personnages du film, pris dans leur misère. Les extérieurs ont la tristesse pauvre des gazons du 20e arrondissement; le plein air lui-même ne peut pas apporter aux hommes des bas-fonds le vrai sens de la liberté, seulement son apparence.[7] (Bost 1936)

The corporate weekly *La Cinématographie française* took the same position towards *Le Quai des brumes*, hailing it as 'un témoignage de l'intelligence et de la technique françaises, admirablement réalisé, photographié, décoré, et joué' (a testament to French intelligence and technique, admirably directed, photographed, designed, and acted), yet concluded 'on déplore que tant de talent, de beauté, de sens artistique s'emploient à magnifier une aventure sordide qui respire le sang et la peur' (one abhors that so much talent, beauty, and artistry be invested in glorifying a sordid adventure pervaded by blood and fear) (Anon. 1938).

In contrast, Pagnol's poetic realism transported spectators away from sombre urban mists of regret and the wistful pleasures of commiseration to a world of open spaces, bright sunshine, human warmth, and redemptive happy endings. *La Cinématographie française* welcomed *Regain* as proof that 'le cinéma doit par moments s'évader des bureaux, des boîtes de nuit et des bouges pour nous élever, en pleine nature, sous le ciel et les nuages de Dieu' (cinema must sometimes escape from offices, nightclubs, and hovels in order to elevate us, in the middle of the countryside, under God's sky and clouds) (Anon. 1937). An anonymous bank teller from Paris added emphatically in a letter to the fan magazine *Pour Vous*:

Regain, c'est rudement beau et ça vous change des niaiseries habituelles. Pensez donc, pas de vamp à la noix, d'adultère, de blagues ou de drames cousus de grosses ficelles à toute épreuve. De la vie, de la nature, de la poésie, l'éternel drame de la terre et de l'homme, un magnifique amour fruste et solide, une sensibilité qui ne se paye pas de grimaces à la glycérine. C'est net, viril, et fort.[8] (Anon. 1937a).

7 Poverty, disease, and crime are so strongly evoked that it demands admiration. But truly, we cannot escape from the sticky walls where the film's characters sequester themselves, trapped in their misery. The outdoor shots have the same indigent sadness as the grass in the Paris' working-class districts; fresh air itself cannot bring the residents of the lower depths a true sense of freedom, only its appearance.
8 It's terribly beautiful and a change from the usual rubbish. Just think, no crummy vamps, adultery, jokes, or dramas with obvious, generic plots. There's

Bost found *Regain* far too long, uneven in its balance of comedy and pathos, and technically inferior to Renoir and Carné, but in the end he too was won over by the picture's scintillating atmosphere and social optimism. 'De beaux paysages, une admirable lumière éblouissante, des moments d'émotion simple à peine teintés de mélodrame, et par-dessus tout, beaucoup de probité et de dignité. C'est un film bien solide et habile dont les héros pleins de terre et de beaux sentiments inspirent l'amitié' (Lovely landscapes, admirable, dazzling light, moments of direct emotion barely tinged with melodrama, and above all lots of probity and dignity. It's a very solid and skilful film whose earthy heroes and lovely sentiments inspire friendship) (Bost 1937).

Genealogies of the rural

If the unique appeal of Pagnol's rural films depended in large part on outdoor cinematography, a hopeful tone, and an illusion of simplicity that belied painstaking stylisation, their resonance with preceding representations of peasants in French culture also played an important role. Whereas tragic populism drew its inspiration from resolutely avant-garde, twentieth-century art – in particular expressionist cinema and surrealist photography, which critics sometimes warily designated as 'foreign' in origin – Pagnol recycled quintessentially Gallic discourses from nineteenth-century literature and visual art. Following these traditions, he depicts country-dwellers in paradoxical fashion, as both simple-minded brutes and as virtuous, hard-working role models.

The former view, exemplified by Honoré de Balzac's *Les Paysans* (1845) and Emile Zola's *La Terre* (1887), applies particularly to Angèle's father Clarius, who menaces passers-by with his shotgun, berates his wife and employees, and locks his daughter and baby in the cellar after their return from Marseilles. Saturnin personifies peasant credulity by believing that Angèle's pimp is a respectable businessman, then dispassionately chopping off his head with a scythe after realising the truth. Similarly, in *Regain* Panturle clings with irrational tenacity to his abandoned village and dilapidated house, living on wild game that

---

life, nature, poetry, the timeless drama of man and the earth, a magnificent, primal, solid love, a sensibility that does not depend on glycerine-enhanced grimaces. It's plain, virile, and hardy.

he skins indoors without bothering to wash the blood from his hands or the floor afterwards. On-screen he is a lumbering mass whose sullen demeanour, wild beard, and filthy clothes make him look as much like a bear as a man. Giono likens him to 'un morceau de bois qui marche' (a walking chunk of wood) (Giono 1971: I, 329), echoing Balzac's belief that 'les paysans vivent d'une vie purement matérielle qui se rapproche de l'état sauvage' (peasants live a purely material existence that is close to a state of savagery) (Balzac 1976–81: IX, 91).

Yet both films temper these negative traits with the morality, selflessness, and courage attributed to peasants in classic texts such as Jules Michelet's historical essay *Le Peuple* (1846) and George Sand's pastoral novel *La Petite Fadette* (1851). Like Pagnol's flawed yet sympathetic urban protagonists – Topaze, Merlusse, and César in particular – the shortcomings and misdeeds of his rural protagonists do not ultimately define them, serving instead as a foil to their essential goodness and making their eventual rehabilitation all the more satisfying. Pagnol thus takes care to emphasise that Clarius' cruelty is a sublimation of the guilt and sorrow he feels at not having protected Angèle. At the end of the film, the irascible old farmer tearfully recants his bad behaviour and grants Albin's marriage proposal, thereby welcoming daughter and illegitimate grandson back into his life. In the context of the Great Depression, the film perfectly illustrates Sand's directive that 'dans les temps où le mal vient de ce que les hommes se détestent, la mission de l'artiste est de célébrer la douceur, la confiance, l'amitié et rappeler ainsi aux hommes découragés que les mœurs pures, les sentiments tendres, et l'équité primitive sont ou peuvent être encore dans le monde' (Sand 1979–80: XVII, 6).[9]

Similarly, Pagnol portrays Saturnin's murder of Louis the pimp as motivated by his unwavering devotion to protect the Barbaroux family from harm. The crime is framed as an act of self-defence, for it occurs only after Louis threatens to kill Angèle and burn down the farm. In the film's original montage, Pagnol scrupulously avoids showing the killing on-screen, having Saturnin mention it to Angèle in passing after the fact. The entire episode disappears from the version shortened to facilitate distribution, indicating that Pagnol heeded the advice of critics who objected to 'un fait-divers gratuit qui

---

9 In an era when hatred among men breeds evil, the artist's mission is to celebrate gentleness, trust, and friendship, thus reminding the disheartened that pure morals, delicate emotions, and basic fairness exist or can still exist in this world.

détruit entièrement l'harmonie et la signification du film en jetant une ombre sur les meilleurs personnages' (a gratuitous event that completely destroys the harmony and the meaning of the film by casting a shadow over the best characters) (Achard 1937). This change puts Saturnin on an equal footing with the other farm hands Amédée and Albin, who display great courage and tact in placating Clarius and convincing him to allow the redemptive marriage.

As for Panturle, during the course of *Regain* he transforms from a primal, solitary hunter-gatherer into a well-groomed, hard-working family farmer, raising a wheat crop that becomes the envy of the entire county. In so doing, he exemplifies Michelet's view that peasants accomplished 'l'œuvre sainte qui fait la force de la France: le mariage de l'homme et la terre' (the sacred work that constitutes the strength of France: the marriage of man and the soil) (Michelet 1974: 90) – a description that applies perfectly to the ploughing and wheat-sowing sequences that close the film.

Pagnol's portrait of the countryside and its inhabitants also drew liberally on pastoral painting, a genre that encompassed a range of styles, from the realism of Jean-François Millet, Jean-Baptiste Corot, and Rosa Bonheur to the impressionism of Camille Pissarro, Pierre-Auguste Renoir, and Claude Monet to the post-Impressionism of Vincent Van Gogh and Paul Cézanne. As the pace of industrialisation and migration to the cities accelerated during the 1920s and 1930s, their landscapes and scenes of peasant life became a *lieu de mémoire*, or site of collective memory 'où chacun pouvait retrouver des souvenirs visuels et son décor héréditaire' (in which viewers could find visual reminders of their family background) (Cachin 1997: 982–3), thereby symbolically safeguarding the rural foundation of French national identity against destruction.

The phenomenon coalesced around one touchstone image – 'un paysage légèrement vallonné où serpente une route, un clocher de village dans le fond, et un pré derrière un rideau d'arbres à demi tiré' (a gently rolling landscape with a road winding through it, a village church tower in the distance, and a meadow half hidden behind a curtain of trees) (Cachin 1997: 957) – whose constitutive elements pervade Pagnol's ethnographic melodramas. The shots of La Treille and its environs featured in *Jofroi* closely resemble Pissarro's *L'Entrée du village de Voisins* (1872), Cézanne's *Route tournante en Provence* (c.1866) and *La Maison du pendu* (1873). The rocky peak on which

Aubignane sits in *Regain* recalls Renoir's *Rochers à l'Estaque* (1882), while the Barbaroux's solitary farmhouse in the valley at the foot of the same cliff recalls the one captured in Cézanne's *La Montagne Sainte-Victoire* series (1882–1906). As for Panturle's crumbling house, it is nearly an exact copy of Cézanne's *La Maison aux murs lézardés* (1894).

Reflecting the notion that human mastery of nature defines a landscape as being quintessentially French (Cachin 1997: 982), agricultural labour occupies a central place in both the paintings and films. In this regard Pagnol owes a particular debt to the work of Millet. Like *Le Hameau de Cousin* (1873), *Jofroi* shows Fonse working in a field with his packhorse, while *Angèle* revisits the scenes of haymaking and grain threshing captured in *Le Vanneur* (1848) and *Les Faneurs* (1850). The most compelling parallel emerges at the end of *Regain*, which slowly zooms in from a wide-angle landscape shot to reveal Panturle and Arsule sowing wheat by hand in a field nestled between rugged hills. Recalling Millet's masterpiece *Le Semeur* (1850), the lyrical power of this sequence is amplified by several additional factors, the first being the link that Pagnol establishes between agricultural and human regeneration: as the camera approaches Arsule, she suddenly sinks to her knees, then rises to happily reassure her concerned husband that she is pregnant rather than sick.

Equally important is the accompanying music. Whereas Pagnol had previously regarded dialogue as the dominant element of the soundtrack and limited himself to short, one-or two-instrument arrangements by Vincent Scotto to enhance comic or dramatic effect, for *Regain* he planned numerous sequences without any dialogue to accommodate an orchestral score commissioned from Arthur Honegger (Pagnol 1995: II, 513). The renowned composer, who already enjoyed critical acclaim as 'the leader of modern film music in France' (London 1936: 234) for his contributions to *La Roue* (Abel Gance, 1922), *Napoléon* (Gance, 1927), *Les Misérables* (Raymond Bernard, 1934), and *Crime et châtiment* (Pierre Chenal, 1935), invested himself fully in the project. He made two trips to Aubignane during filming – two weeks in mid-July and two more in early September 1937 – to capture the spirit of the place, even helping workers carry heavy building materials up the cliff when he was not composing (Halbreich 1992: 176).

The result, recorded at Joinville Studios on 27–28 September, was a 35-minute composition divided into fifteen movements and requiring twenty-one musicians (Halbreich 1994: 844–8). Of these, five segments totalling approximately twelve-and-a-half minutes were actually used in the film. Honegger relished the opportunity to work collaboratively with Pagnol during shooting rather than composing 'artificially' for an already-finished film, as he had always previously done (Guégan et al. 1965: 32). Two notable pieces, 'Hiver' and 'Printemps', accompany panoramic landscape shots depicting those seasons. While the first expresses cold, windy desolation through brooding clarinets, the second evokes the slow, inevitable renewal of warmth through the addition of slowly rising alto saxophone. Similarly, 'Panturle' and 'Gédémus', are used to personify those characters during their first on-screen appearance. The physical mass and brutality of the former is suggested in a heavy, dissonant march, while the knife-grinder's comical dimension and profession appear in a light, circular melody (in reference to the rotating wheel of his grinding cart) punctuated by a bassoon that suggests his limp. The last arrangement, 'Regain', is a majestic, horn-rich leitmotif that surfaces in several variations during the film. In addition to playing over the opening credits and accompanying the first sight of Aubignane, it culminates in the final sequence showing Panturle and Arsule wheat planting while other families move back to the village.

Honegger was so pleased with the score that he took the unusual step of extracting a suite for live performance in Paris and distribution on record. Film critics sensitive to music unanimously shared that view and praised *Regain* as a model for other directors to follow. As one reviewer wrote: 'la musique a une telle puissance que les flots d'harmonie déversés sur les spectateurs sont impregnés tout à la fois des sentiments humains exprimés sur l'écran et des effluves parfumées et subtiles de notre chaude Provence (the music is so powerful that the waves of harmony washing over the spectators simultaneously encompass the fullness of human emotion expressed on the screen and the delicate, hot fragrances of Provence) (Déjan 1937). Swiss conductor-composer Adriano, who directed the Slovak Radio Symphony Orchestra's recording of the score in 1993, concurs that *Regain* is 'more inspired and more varied than most of Honegger's other film compositions, an attribute which makes it give way to the real and less pretentious demands of the screen' (Adriano 1993: 4). Looking back on Honegger's more than forty cinema-related scores, musicologist Harry Halbreich characterises his *Regain* as 'un chef-d'œuvre, l'une de ses quatre ou cinq musiques de film *capitales*. Aucune autre n'a cette saveur terrienne, cette santé pastorale' (a masterpiece, one of his four or five *capital* compositions for the cinema. None of the others has this earthy flavour, this pastoral vibrancy) (Halbreich 1994: 844–5).

For Pagnol, the incorporation of sequences featuring only music and image marked an important step in his maturation as a filmmaker and definitive proof that he had moved beyond a 'theatrical' reliance on dialogue as his primary means of creating dramatic effect. The judicious balance between the landscape photography, Honegger's score, and dialogue at the end of *Regain* marks a pinnacle not only in Pagnol's career as a director, but in poetic realism as a whole, constituting one of only a few worthy counterpoints to Carné and Renoir's darkest moments of urban despair. In the words of a columnist for *La Griffe cinématographique*:

> L'ensemencement de la terre nouvellement remuée, l'émotion joyeuse de la jeune mère qui sent son enfant remuer en elle, sont des choses merveilleuses. Il est des moments où l'on voudrait se lever et crier son enthousiasme. *Regain* est un chef-d'œuvre, un plaidoyer merveilleusement convaincant en faveur de la terre et de ses enfants, une véritable œuvre de régénération. (Chazal 1937)[10]

In addition to drawing on the 'high' arts of symphonic music and painting, Pagnol also perpetuated the popular iconographic tradition known as *images d'Epinal*. Founded in 1796 by a playing card maker from Lorraine named Jean-Charles Pellerin, the *Imagerie d'Epinal* was the most prolific of many regional print shops specialising in low-cost illustrations of popular legends, historical subjects, and traditional country life (Mistler 1961). Over the course of the nineteenth century *images d'Epinal* became famous throughout Europe and the expression itself became a general synonym of 'quelque chose d'emphatique, de traditionnel, qui montre le beau ou le bon côté des choses' (something emphatic and traditional that shows the lovely or good aspect of things) (Imbs 1971–94, IX, 1146). However, the popularity of Epinal prints declined steadily following the advent of modern photographic technology, which during the 1910s and 1920s

---

10 The sowing in freshly ploughed earth, the joyous emotion of the young mother who feels her baby moving inside her, are marvellous things. There are moments when one wants to stand up and cry out in enthusiasm. *Regain* is a masterpiece, a wonderfully convincing plea in favour of the earth and its children, a true work of regeneration.

became the primary means of bringing French folklore, peasant life, and landscapes to the urban masses.

Location shooting with synchronous sound constituted the next phase in this evolution, adding a new level of audio-visual realism to classic themes and representational conventions. Like the *images d'Epinal*, Pagnol's rural films were morality tales about love and family constructed around the binary oppositions of vice and virtue, fall and redemption, city and country. Visually, his landscapes and peasant characters were easily recognisable 'types' already ingrained in popular mentalities by the photos that adorned postcards, newspapers, and magazines. Reacting to the naturalistic performances of Henri Poupon and Edouard Delmont in *Angèle*, a perceptive commentator from Toulouse noted that

> le vieux paysan Clarius et l'ouvrier agricole Amédée sont tombés d'une carte postale ou bien d'un tableau de Cézanne. C'est la même barbe de huit jours, les mêmes vestons d'alpaga, les chemises qui bâillent. En prêtant aux acteurs les paroles, les reflexes, les attitudes exactes, Pagnol a fixé quelques apparences éternelles de la psychologie paysanne et française. (Anon. 1934b)[11]

Echoing his portrait of urban petty bourgeois life in the Marseilles Trilogy, Pagnol's depiction of peasant mentalities and social relations in his rural films is exceptionally rich in scope and subtle in its expression through dialogue and gesture. Using the motif of a land transaction gone bad, *Jofroi* emphasises both the instinctive mistrust that small farmers feel towards written contracts and notaries, as well as the prominent role that the local priest and schoolteacher play in mediating legal disputes between neighbours. Similarly, much of the pathos in *Angèle* hinges on the profound sense of familial disgrace that Angèle's father feels upon learning of her illegitimate child and the tortured resolution with which he sequesters them in the basement to keep that shame private. *Regain* highlights another aspect of peasant mentalities by having a farmer generously give Panturle an enormous loaf of unleavened homemade bread and wheat seed in a time of need, yet suddenly take offence at the suggestion of repayment in

[11] The old peasant Clarius and the farm worker Amédée fell out of a postcard or a Cézanne painting. They have the same eight-day beard, the same alpaca vests, and shirts wide open. By lending his actors the right words, reactions, and attitudes, Pagnol has captured some of the eternal features of peasant and French psychology.

cash rather than in kind. The ensuing dialogue and gesture of reverently crossing a loaf before cutting reminds viewers that rural culture traditionally views bread and the grain from which it comes as everyday sacraments above any vulgar monetary exchange value. The scene moved a critic for *Marianne* to observe that 'c'est avec ce qu'on pourrait appeler des "sentiments-matières-premières" que Pagnol fait ses admirables œuvres. Rien de plus "matière première" que le blé. Il dit sur le pain les plus jolies choses, les plus émouvantes, les plus poétiques. Et il parle du pain comme personne' (Achard 1937a).[12]

By bringing new life, depth, and immediacy to venerable iconographic traditions, Pagnol's films achieved the feat of overcoming what André Bazin identified as a fundamental insolubility between still images and cinema. Whereas the frame of a painting or photograph 'polarise l'espace vers le dedans' (polarises space inward) and offers a space of contemplation isolated from the world outside its borders, the motion picture screen preserves a slice of living reality 'qui est censé se prolonger indéfiniment dans l'univers' (which is meant to extend outward indefinitely into the universe) (Bazin 1958–62: II, 128). However, if the camera could enter the painting or photograph's frame, 'l'espace perdra son orientation et ses limites pour s'imposer à notre imagination comme indéfini' (the space will lose its inward orientation and limits, thereby becoming infinite in our imagination). Bazin credited Luciano Emmer's *Guerrieri* (1942) and Alain Renais' *Van Gogh* (1947) – documentaries that immerse viewers in a painted virtual universe through the innovative use of close-ups, tracking shots, and montage – with pioneering this feat, but audience response to Pagnol's ethnographic melodramas suggest that they produced a similar effect years earlier.

The voluminous dossiers of press clippings that he compiled attest to the unusual breadth of interest in and enthusiasm for his work, even from specialised publications that normally did not review films. A weekly paper devoted specifically to rural life noted that *Angèle* 'présente une sincérité émouvante en nous faisant pénétrer dans une petite exploitation familiale, les soucis du ménage, et de la récolte, les chagrins et les joies de l'existence paysanne, où rien n'est gaspillé'

12 Pagnol crafts his admirable films with what one might call 'elemental feelings'. Nothing more elemental than wheat. He says the most beautiful, the most moving, the most poetic things about bread. And he speaks about bread like nobody else.

(is movingly sincere by allowing us to enter a small family farm, to experience the worries of the household and the harvest, the sorrows and joys of peasant life, where nothing is wasted) (Anon. 1936), while the bimonthly magazine *La Revue de la famille* wrote of *Jofroi* that 'ces images vraies et directement humaines feront mieux connaître le visage de nos cultivateurs. Nous voulons croire qu'au sortir de la salle, tourneurs et comptables, ouvriers et employés se sentiront plus près de leurs frères de la terre' (these truthful, directly human images will help us better know our farmers. We want to believe that upon exiting the theatre, metal turners and accountants, factory workers and clerks will feel closer to their rural brothers) (Brunet 1934).

Cinema and national decadence

The suspension of disbelief that Pagnol's ethnographic melodramas might bridge the divide between rural and urban society – a nearly impossible task for any set of fiction films, no matter how popular – reflected an intensifying identity crisis that plagued France throughout the 1930s. Since the 1870s the school of sociology headed by Frédéric Le Play had linked urbanisation, industrialisation, and the disappearance of traditional peasant culture with national decadence and the disintegration of French cultural identity (Silver 1982), but it was only with the onset of the Great Depression that such arguments gained mass legitimacy and became a part of everyday public discourse under the influence of bestselling essays such as Georges Duhamel's *Scènes de la vie future* (1930), Daniel Halévy's *Décadence de la liberté* (1930), and Robert Aron's *Décadence de la nation française* (1931). Duhamel saw cinema as a particularly dangerous vehicle of intellectual and moral attrition – 'un divertissement d'ilotes, un passe-temps d'illettrés, de créatures misérables, ahuries par leur besogne et leurs soucis; un spectacle qui ne demande aucun effort, n'aborde sérieusement aucun problème, n'excite aucune espérance sinon celle, ridicule, d'être un jour "star" à Los Angeles' (Duhamel 1930: 58).[13]

13 A distraction for slaves, a pastime for illiterate, miserable creatures stupefied by their jobs and their worries; a spectacle that requires no effort, does not seriously address any problem, sparks no hope except the ridiculous one of being a star in Los Angeles.

Pagnol's peasant films constituted a striking exception to that view by dramatising the very issues that Duhamel and his peers emphasised. Jofroi pointedly denounces the dehumanising, socially destructive nature of modern capitalism by contending that the expenditure of time and labour, rather than money, confers ultimate possession and moral control over his orchard. As he incredulously tells Fonse, the new legal owner intent on removing the trees: 'Tu crois que l'argent paie tout? Parce qu'on a signé quatre mauvais papiers chez un notaire qui a une tête de rat, tu vas venir avec des haches et des picosses faire tout un carnage dans mon verger?' (You think that money buys everything? Because we signed four rotten papers in front of a rat-faced notary, you're going to come slaughter my orchard with axes and picks?)

Similarly, *Angèle* and *Regain* highlight the negative social and moral impact of migration from the countryside to large cities. The 1931 census had revealed that for the first time in the nation's history urbanites outnumbered peasants, with an additional 600,000 people deserting the countryside by 1938 (Sauvy 1984: II, 66). Both Angèle and her suitor Albin personify the reasons for and negative consequences of the so-called 'exode rural' (rural exodus). While he leaves his mountain hamlet for lack of family or work, and is obliged to eke out a living as an itinerant labourer, she flees her parents' farm to assert her independence, but instead finds only loneliness and suffering in Marseilles. *Regain* reinforces the lesson in its portrayal of two more 'déracinés' (displaced persons): the knife-grinder Gédémus, a Sisyphean figure condemned to drag his heavy cart from town to town through the rugged hills, and the travelling cabaret singer Arsule, who is systematically exploited by all the other men she encounters. In each case the protagonists find happiness only by returning to a stable family existence rooted firmly in the soil. Just as Angèle and Albin vow to revive his parents' farm, Arsule leaves behind Gédémus for Panturle, helping him grow a prize crop of wheat and draw others back to his previously abandoned native village. One of the returnees to Aubignane is a state railroad employee named Jasmin, who in a visually striking landscape sequence expresses his frustration with city life and removes his uniform jacket to plough a wheat field.

Pagnol's uplifting dramatisation of return to the earth complemented a wide range of state initiatives designed to battle moral and physical decline by reconnecting urbanites with the countryside.

Among the most prominent were the *colonies de vacances*, which placed city children with rural host families for stays of up to six weeks throughout the year, and the *auberges de jeunesse*, a network of youth centres that organised outdoor programmes for older children during school vacations. Both turn-of-the-century creations initially financed by private organisations, they multiplied rapidly during the 1930s thanks to government sponsorship and a substantial injection of public funding. By late 1937, there were some 350 *auberges* and 750 *colonies* in operation, together welcoming over a quarter million visitors annually (Ory 1994: 764–87).

The arrival of the Depression also sparked the institutional legitimisation of ethnography and folklore studies, which turned progressively away from the study of 'primitive' peoples outside Europe to document French rural patrimony before its imminent disappearance. The Popular Front played an especially crucial role in the movement. In addition to creating the country's first national folklore museum, Le Musée des Arts et Traditions Populaires, it sponsored the first annual meeting of the International Folklore Congress as part of the 1937 Paris International Exposition, whose centrepiece was an expansive 'Rural Centre' that highlighted peasant traditions as a counterweight to urban modernity (Peer 1998).

Yet France still lagged far behind its most menacing international rivals in the use of peasant culture and folklore to forge a sense of national strength and cohesion, particularly through the medium of cinema. Germany, Italy, and the Soviet Union produced a steady stream of documentaries and features about rural life that in each country earned recognition as a distinct genre: the *Blubofilme* ('blood and soil film' in reference to the Nazis' *Blut und Boden* ideology), *film strapaese* (or 'ultra-country films'), and *kolkhoznaia kino* (for its role in glorifying the *kolkhoz*, or state-run collective farms created by Stalin in 1929) (Petley 1979: 130–8; Hay 1987: 132–49; Kenez 1992: 101–57). In parallel to these works, Pagnol offered a compelling collective representation of French ethnic identity that emphasised peasant piety, honour, work ethic, family values, and attachment to the soil. As a reviewer for the arts magazine *Comœdia* wrote enthusiastically of *Angèle*:

> C'est un film où règne l'esprit du terroir, et qui anime la force de la Race, cette belle race du pays provençal. Dans ce pays merveilleux le soleil caresse tout le long du jour les êtres et les choses, les peines

semblent plus légères, le sens de la dignité et du devoir, le respect des gestes ancestraux restent ancrés profondément au cœur des habitants. L'œuvre s'appuie sur cette force incontestable qu'est la tradition. Il y a là une précieuse indication pour les metteurs en scène français. Notre histoire et notre folklore sont assez riches pour leur fournir ample moisson de sujets. Nous aurons alors des œuvres d'une parfaite unité et d'une force incontestable. *Angèle* en reçoit une grandeur simple, faite de vérité. La force de la race l'habite et la magnifie![14] (Proust 1934)

Yet such pleas went unheeded by other French directors. The few competing rural films made during the Depression presented a despairing view of life in the countryside. Renoir's *Toni*, shot on location near Marseilles using Pagnol's crew and equipment, recounted the ill-fated love affair between an Italian quarry worker and the wife of a brutal French foreman. When she murders her husband in self-defence, Toni takes the blame for the crime and is shot as he flees. Intended to expose the hardships facing immigrants to France, the film begins with a darkly ironic on-screen text noting that 'l'action se passe dans le midi de la France, en pays latin, là où la nature détruisant l'esprit de Babel, sait si bien opérer la fusion des races' (the action takes place in southern France, in a Latin region where nature has destroyed the spirit of Babel and so effectively merged different races). In Renoir's words, spectators reacted to *Toni* 'comme un cheveu sur la soupe' (like a hair in a bowl of soup) specifically 'parce qu'il venait tout de suite après *Angèle*' (because it came out immediately after *Angèle*') (Rivette and Truffaut 1957: 34). Equally pessimistic in tone were *La Terre qui meurt* (Jean Vallée, 1936), based on René Bazin's turn-of-the-century novel depicting the disappearance of agrarian traditions in the Vendée, and the screen adaptation of François Mauriac's *Les Anges noirs* (Willy Rozier, 1937), which painted a sinister portrait of peasant greed, murder, and infidelity in the swamps of the south-west coast.

14 It's a film steeped in the spirit of the soil which resuscitates the strength of the Race, that fine race of Provence. In this marvellous country the sun caresses both people and things all day long, life's troubles seem lighter, a sense of dignity and duty as well as respect for ancestral customs remains deeply anchored in the heart of its inhabitants. The film draws on the incontestable strength of tradition. That is a valuable lesson for French directors. Our history and our folklore are sufficiently rich to provide them an ample harvest of subjects, so that we might have films of perfect unity and unquestionable strength. In so doing, *Angèle* takes on a simple grandeur and truthfulness. The strength of the race pervades and amplifies it!

Like *Toni*, they too were commercial flops, highlighting the unique power of Pagnol's work as a symbolic antidote to national decadence.

Gender, maternity, and nation

Integral to this appeal was Pagnol's implicit endorsement of traditional gender roles and pro-natalism, which during the inter-war period gained currency not only as remedies to France's perceived decline, but as imperatives of national security and survival. While the birth rate in Germany and Italy increased during the 1930s, in France it continued to fall steadily despite a long-standing ban on abortion and contraception, the creation of state-subsidised family allowances, and a generous set of monetary prizes rewarding especially prolific couples (Thébaud 1986: 19–23). Throughout the decade France's leading pro-natalist organisation, the Alliance Nationale pour l'Accroissement de la Population Française (ANAPF), waged a tireless campaign framing procreation as the civic duty of all citizens and promoting female domesticity (Koos 1996). In particular, the ANAPF sought to combat the 'influence lamentable du cinéma' (lamentable influence of cinema), which its director Fernand Boverat accused of creating 'psychologie stérile' (sterile psychology) among young people by glamorising pre-marital sex, infidelity, and prostitution (Boverat 1936). While that denunciation did little to dissuade movie-goers, the idea that uncontrolled female sexuality posed a serious threat to the health of the nuclear family and to the nation as a whole, resonated across French society. As film historians have noted, these anxieties were played out obsessively in films where vamps played by Mireille Balin and Viviane Romance, among others, ruin the men who trust them (Crisp 2002: 107–19; Burch and Sellier 1996: 49–51).

Pagnol's rural melodramas incorporate that character type as well, but without the tragic ending and only as a prelude to the woman's eventual redemption. *Angèle* shows the destructive consequences of female individualism and promiscuity by dramatising her decision to leave the farm for an impetuous fling in the big city. Instead of love and excitement, her encounter with Louis bring only the misery and degradation of forced prostitution. As she tells Saturnin with tearful self-loathing in the brothel scene: 'Voilà ce que je suis: une fille des rues. Maintenant je suis une fille perdue!' (That's what I am: a streetwalker. Now I'm a lost girl!) Yet upon returning to the farm, Angèle regains her virtue and again becomes 'la demoiselle' (the maiden), as Saturnin calls her. This moral transformation is expressed visually through her physical appearance, which changes dramatically between the city and country. In Marseilles she wears heavy make-up, garish clothing, jewellery, and shiny spit curls, but on the farm she sheds all her artificial accoutrements, slipping back into a simple gingham dress, knitted shawl, and natural flowing hairstyle.

Significantly, Angèle's redemption is made possible only by submitting to male authority – first through a confession and apology to her father, then through marriage with her peasant suitor Albin to legitimise her bastard child. She does so with both contrition and joy, thereby turning her baby from a symbol of France's moral decadence into a source of national strength and renewal (see Figure 11). Not only is the baby a boy, a future soldier of the Republic and a procreator in his own right; as we learn in the film's closing sequence, he is only the first of many more children to come. As Albin reassures Angèle's father, who is worried that his grandson will forever bear the stigma of illegitimacy: 'Il aura des frères et des sœurs. Quand nous aurons fini de faire les nôtres, celui-là, on ne saura même plus lequel c'est' (He will have brothers and sisters. When we are finished having ours, people won't be able to tell them apart).

Regain takes on a similar allegorical value by showing Arsule's metamorphosis from an exploited, travelling cabaret singer into a loving housewife and expectant mother. In a publicity flyer distributed to cinema owners, Pagnol characterises her as 'une pauvre femme que le malheur a déracinée, un de ces êtres qui sont le jouet des vulgaires passion humaines et qui, dans la tourmente, reste toujours emplis de pureté. Elle est celle qui donnera un sens à la vie, la femme éternelle sans qui rien n'est possible' (Pagnol 1937).[15] Just as Panturle's love redeems her, she in turn motivates him to evolve from a savage, solitary poacher into a proud husband and gentleman farmer. The apotheosis of that symbiotic transformation occurs when she announces her pregnancy to him while they are sowing wheat together. Upon learning the news, he leads her back to their house to

15 A poor women uprooted by misfortune, one of those beings who are the toy of base human passions and who despite being tormented, remains forever full of purity. It is she who will give life meaning, the eternal woman without whom nothing is possible.

rest, telling her tenderly: 'Le blé, c'est ma graine. Toi, occupe-toi de la tienne' (Wheat is my seed. You take care of your own).

Released the following year, *La Femme du boulanger* specifically targets the socially destructive potential of female infidelity through the story of a middle-aged baker named Aimable whose young, sensuous wife Aurélie elopes with an Italian shepherd. Devastated by his loss and mocked publicly as a cuckold, the baker gets drunk and refuses to make bread until his wife returns, thereby jeopardising the very survival of his isolated mountain village. The townspeople mount a collective effort to return Aurélie to her conjugal duty, in the process resolving the many quarrels that previously divided them and emerging from the crisis with a renewed sense of community and mutual respect. The baker and his wife are reunited, the town's bread supply is restored, and the film ends with her contritely pledging her devotion to him. Raimu's performance as the baker was widely regarded as the best of his career, moving Orson Welles to praise him posthumously as 'the greatest actor in the world' (Pagnol 1995: I, 489). To play Aurélie Pagnol initially wanted to cast non-francophone American starlet Joan Crawford, writing her role with a maximum of physical sultriness and only 144 words of dialogue (Fieschi et al. 1965: 35). When Crawford withdrew late in pre-production because of previous contract obligations, she was replaced by relative newcomer Ginette Leclerc, whose provocative portrayal of the baker's wife would launch her to a successful career.

At the outset of the film, Aurélie perfectly embodies the destructive individualism of the modern woman denounced by the ANAPF. She wears heavy make-up, places her own pleasure above her marital duties, and aggressively seduces the shepherd on her first day in town (see Figure 12). Echoing pro-natalist propaganda that depicted the female body as representative of the French nation, Aurélie becomes a metaphor for the village's bread and well-being when the heartbroken Aimable refuses to bake after her departure. The motif of domesticating rampant female sexuality culminates powerfully in the film's final scene as the baker condemns his wife's conduct by proxy through their female cat, who has returned to her mate after a three-day absence and is contentedly lapping from his bowl of milk:

> Garce, salope, ordure, c'est maintenant que tu reviens? Et le pauvre Pompon, dis, qui s'est fait un mauvais sang d'encre pendant trois jours! Il tournait, il virait, il cherchait dans tous les coins. Il était plus

malheureux qu'une pierre. Et elle, pendant ce temps avec son chat des gouttières, un inconnu, un bon à rien, un passant de clair de lune. Et la tendresse, qu'est-ce que tu en fais? Dis, ton berger des gouttières, est-ce qu'il se réveillait la nuit pour te regarder dormir? Est-ce que si tu étais partie, il aurait laissé refroidir son four, s'il avait été boulanger? C'est pour ça que tu reviens? Parce que tu as eu faim et froid? Va, bois-lui son lait, ça lui fait plaisir. Mais est-ce qu'elle repartira encore?[16]

The tirade has its intended effect, for Aurélie responds tearfully: 'Non, elle ne repartira plus. Plus jamais' (No, she will never leave. Never again).

Allegorically the scene reduces Aurélie to the status of an animal motivated only by the base needs for sex, food, and shelter. She is quite literally 'une chatte', which in French slang denotes not only a female cat, but a loose woman and the female genitalia as well. The film ends with Aurélie relighting the oven that has lain cold in her absence – an obvious psycho-sexual analogy which in a Freudian perspective symbolises the biological act of insemination. Pagnol reinforces the effect visually by placing the camera inside the oven/womb so that we see Aimable and Aurélie performing the act together, their hands overlapping on the handle of the torch. This unmistakable image of marital fidelity and fertility leaves no doubt that the couple will henceforth take seriously their duty to each other and to their community.

Film historians have often retrospectively criticised Pagnol's representation of gender roles as archaic, hyper-conservative, and misogynistic. Referring to the sequence in *Regain* where Panturle pays Gédémus the price of a mule for having 'stolen' Arsule, Jean-Pierre Jeancolas describes the film's portrayal of women as 'même pas médiéval, mais néolithique; la femme n'est pas un objet, mais une marchandise' (not medieval, but Neolithic; women are not objects, but merchandise) (Jeancolas 1983: 267). Claudette Peyrusse regards the oven-relighting sequence in *La Femme du boulanger* as 'une régression utérine à rapprocher du rêve d'une société autarcique et involutive'

16 Slut, whore, piece of trash, now you come back? What about poor Pompon, who worried himself sick! He turned around in circles, wandered about, looked in every corner. He couldn't have been more miserable while she was out with her alley cat, a stranger, a good-for-nothing, a passer-by in the night. What about tenderness? Say, did your degenerate shepherd wake up during the night to watch you sleep? If he had been a baker and you'd left, would he have let his oven go cold? Is that why you came back? Because you're cold and hungry? Go ahead, drink his milk; it makes him happy. But will she leave again?

(a uterine regression linked to the dream of an autonomous society isolated from the outside world) (Peyrusse 1986: 122). For Jean-Marie Apostolidès, Aurélie has no identity of her own, 'sa présence étant transmise par le regard des autres parce qu'elle est l'expression de leur désir. C'est une image en creux que chacun vient remplir en y projetant ses rêves' (her being constituted by other people's gazes because she is the object of their desire. She is a hollow image filled by the projection of each individual's dreams) (Apostolidès 1987: 217). Noël Burch and Geneviève Sellier go yet a step further, denouncing *La Femme du boulanger* as 'une véritable apologie de l'ordre incestuo-patriarcal dont tout le monde sait qu'il est contre nature mais dont le maintien serait la condition de la paix civile et l'unité nationale' (a veritable apology for the incestuous, patriarchal social order which everybody knows is against nature but whose maintenance is a prerequisite to civil peace and national unity) (Burch and Sellier 1996: 43).

Yet in the context of the 1930s Pagnol's take on gender roles was not at odds with prevailing notions of French feminism. At the time the women's movement in France was dominated by 'relational' or 'maternalist' feminism, which in the tradition of Enlightenment philosophers Jean-Jacques Rousseau and Nicolas de Condorcet pursued the expansion of women's political rights by promoting their crucial contribution to the well-being of the nation – as wives and mothers in the private sphere; as care-givers and guardians of moral values in their work outside the home. There was also an individualist variety of feminism that rejected the notion of civic motherhood, stressed sexual emancipation from male authority, and lobbied for complete legal equality for women, but it attracted comparatively few followers prior to the Second World War (Bard 1995: 11–29, 209–26; Offen 2000: 50–76). As a study of the women's Depression-era magazines and newspapers shows, the vast majority of French women did not contest their roles as wives and mothers, identifying instead with the slogan of the women's weekly *Minerva*: 'nous sommes féministes à la manière de chez nous qui ne veut jamais séparer le féminisme de la fémininité' (we are feminists in the French way, never wanting to separate feminism from femininity) (Chevignard and Faure 1978: 48).

The spirit of relational feminism is expressed clearly in the overwhelmingly positive comments that Pagnol's rural films drew in women's magazines. Suzanne Chantal, a nationally known freelance cinema critic, published a review of *Angèle* in *Le Journal de la femme* that read in part:

> Nous regardons longuement avec le brave Saturnin la pièce misérable où Angèle moisit, cette pièce ornée d'éventails fanés, le lit avachi, et au milieu de tout ça, la 'demoiselle' en peignoir bâillant, avec des cheveux tristement frisés sur les yeux, une peau toute frottée de peinture, et un mauvais parfum trop fort. Quelle foudroyante scène de déchéance! (Chantal 1934a).[17]

Tellingly, the film contains no visual or auditory cues that Angèle is even wearing perfume. The nauseating fragrance to which Chantal referred was a creation of her olfactory imagination and a striking testament to the deep psychological resonance that the theme of female decadence, represented by the figure of the prostitute, held for the French spectators.

The disgust that Chantal felt at Angèle's fall triggered an equally strong feeling of satisfaction at her eventual redemption through marriage: 'Il y avait en Albin tant de force, de la paix, de l'indulgence, et la promesse de tant de joie! Il ne disait que des mots simples, les mots élémentaires qui justifiaient, qui absolvaient, qui purifiaient tout' (In Albin there was so much strength, peace, forgiveness, and the promise of so much joy! He spoke only simple words, elemental words that justified, absolved, purified everything') (Chantal 1934a). *Regain* drew similar praise three years later in the pages of *Minerva*, where a female reviewer closed with a rhetorical question that reads like a patriotic call to maternity:

> Qui d'entre nous n'est pas en mesure de s'imaginer à la place d'Arsule dans cette belle scène des semailles où elle sent dans son ventre les joyeux coups de pied de son enfant? Nous recommandons à toutes nos lectrices le nouveau film de Marcel Pagnol. C'est une œuvre émouvante, humaine, et de grande classe. (Airelle 1937)[18]

---

17 We gaze fixedly at the wretched room where Angèle moulders away, that room decorated with faded fans, a worn-out bed, and in the middle of it all, the 'maiden' in a half-open dressing gown, with her hair sadly curled over her eyes, her skin covered in make-up and cheap, overpowering perfume. What a devastating scene of degeneration!

18 Who among us is not is not able to imagine herself in Arsule's place during that lovely sowing scene where she feels the joyful kicking of the child in her belly? We recommend Marcel Pagnol's new film to all our readers. It is a moving, human work of great distinction.

If Aimable's tirade against Aurélie at the end of *La Femme du boulanger* is undeniably vicious and at first glance smacks of misogyny, a closer look at the overall plot structure reveals that the film indicts negligent husbands alongside adulterous wives. While drunk at the café Aimable acknowledges his own conjugal shortcomings by confiding to the priest: 'Ne me parlez pas d'enfants ! Si j'avais pu lui en faire un, le malheur ne serait pas arrivé' (Don't talk to me about children! If I had been able to give her one, this misfortune would never have occurred). Moreover, the baker's penance is in some ways more severe than Aurélie's. Whereas he endures cruel public humiliation during the search for her – most notably through a song mocking his cuckoldry and the gag gift of antlers, the latter of which pushes him to attempt suicide – she re-enters the village only after the streets have been cleared (at Aimable's request) in order to spare her the scornful glances of other women, having only to deal privately with Aimable. His respect of Aurélie's privacy constitutes a striking act of reform, since at the beginning of the film he explicitly flaunted her beauty to promote his business as well as to make the other men in town jealous of his wealth and presumed virility. Moreover, in preparation for his wife's return the baker performs the traditionally 'female' tasks of making the bed and cleaning the house, rejecting another man's indignant suggestion that he instead use his broom handle 'de lui foutre une danse qui lui persuadera la vertu' (to beat some virtue into her). In a final act of 'feminine' tenderness that counterbalances his vengeful tirade, he offers Aurélie a heart-shaped loaf of bread for dinner (see Figure 13). Like César in the Marseilles Trilogy, Aimable's anger is thus presented as a sublimation of the deep love he feels for those closest to him.

Following the precedent of his earlier films, Pagnol thus offers contradictory perspectives on gender roles and power without clearly endorsing either one. On the one hand, he legitimises women's socially transgressive sexual desire – Fanny's pre-marital relations, Angèle's fling with a seductive pimp, Aurélie's extra-marital affair – by linking these actions to a failure of masculinity in the form of emotional or physical neglect (see Figure 14). On the other, he underscores the negative consequences that sexual indiscretion can have for the women in the context of patriarchal society – specifically, the necessity of exchanging passion and freedom for companionship and financial security. In this perspective, the recurring figure of the fallen woman brought back to domesticity should be seen not as a hyper-reactionary expression of misogyny, but as a pragmatic assessment of 1930s French culture.

Women's reactions to *La Femme du boulanger* upon its release in late 1938 suggest that they understood the film in these exactly terms. Beyond receiving an endorsement from the Académie Féminine (Anon. 1939), the film earned wistful praise from Suzanne Chantal in *Le Journal de la femme*.

> Histoire simple, et belle justement pour cela, fondamentale et riche comme le pain, chaude et cruelle et douce comme l'amour. Ginette Leclerc, à la beauté provocante, est sensuelle et femelle jusqu'à l'impudeur. Son berger est viril, avec des yeux luisants, une médaille au cou, et de courtes dents carrées. C'est un couple qui évoque la volupté dans ce qu'elle a de plus direct et de plus vulgaire, de plus puissant aussi. Et Raimu, dans sa colère, ses larmes, ses inquiétudes et ses regrets, exprime la tendresse conjugale comme il a su, dans *Marius*, exprimer la tendresse paternelle. Lourd, candide, tendre et si profondément malheureux, il fait passer le mauvais goût des scènes grotesques par sa vulgarité saine, tranquille, émouvante. (Chantal 1938)[19]

A female typist echoed the sentiment in a letter to the fan magazine *Pour Vous*, noting that 'C'est le quatrième bon film de Pagnol après *Marius*, *Fanny*, et *Angèle*. Je préfère de loin *La Femme du boulanger* à *Regain*, qui m'a déçue. Il est un peu fort que la boulangère soit partie avec le berger qu'elle n'avait connu que le matin, mais sans cela le film n'aurait pas eu une si belle fin' (It's Pagnol's fourth good film after *Marius*, *Fanny*, and *Angèle*. I much prefer *La Femme du boulanger* to *Regain*, which disappointed me. It's a bit exaggerated that the baker's wife left with the shepherd after just meeting him the same morning, but without that the film would not have had such a lovely ending) (Anon. 1938).

---

19 A simple and thus beautiful story, elemental and rich as bread itself – hot, cruel, and sweet as love. The provocatively beautiful Ginette Leclerc is sensual and female to the point of immodesty. Her shepherd is virile, with twinkling eyes, a medallion dangling from his neck, and small, straight teeth. As a couple they exude the most direct, animalistic, and powerful form of carnal pleasure. And Raimu, in all his anger, tears, worries, and regrets, expresses the tenderness of marriage as he so movingly personified fatherly love in Marius. Heavy-hearted, ingenuous, caring, and so profoundly miserable, he redeems the bad taste of grotesque scenes through his salubrious, quiet, moving earthiness.

Like male commentators worried by the morally deleterious potential of 1930s French cinema, women thus appreciated Pagnol's optimistic twist on the *femme fatale* character so common in the dark variety of poetic realism. By dramatising her re-domestication, *La Femme du boulanger* cleverly played on audience expectations to articulate an age-old moral that had particular relevance in 1938–39 as France struggled to emerge from the Great Depression and braced for a new world war: men and women have a biological duty to each other and to the collective body of the nation that should be fulfilled in the framework of marriage.

Equally important in evaluating Pagnol's gender politics (and conspicuously absent from virtually all commentaries on the topic) is the decisive evolution that his female protagonists undergo in *Naïs* (1945) and *Manon des sources* (1952). Unlike Angèle, Arsule, Aurélie, and Patricia – all of whom submit to male authority and traditional gender norms, both Naïs and Manon are independent, wilful women who attain happiness by revolting violently against their patriarchal oppressors. In a striking reconfiguration of key plot elements and characters from *Angèle*, Naïs convinces her long-time friend and protector Toine (a variation on the Saturnin character played again by Fernandel) to dispose of her brutal peasant father in a rockslide after he has beaten her, twice attempted to kill her bourgeois lover Frédéric, and threatened her life as well. Naïs' proactive conduct on-screen also contrasts sharply with the 1884 short story by Emile Zola on which Pagnol based his script. Whereas the source text portrays her as a helpless victim of her class and gender by having her father die accidentally and Frédéric abandon her in the countryside to marry Toine by default, the film ends on a much happier note. Mutually in love, Naïs and Frédéric move to Aix-en-Provence to live with his wealthy family, while Toine stays behind as caretaker of the farm.

As for Manon, she takes revenge on César Soubeyran, the greedy patriarch who years earlier blocked the spring on her father's farm, waited patiently as he killed himself carrying water to sustain his crops, then bought the valuable land for next to nothing. In a striking condemnation of the same autarkic social model represented so favourably in *Jofroi*, *Regain*, and *La Femme du boulanger*, the entire village participates in the crime through inaction, refusing to help an 'outsider' such as her father in his labours and keeping secret the location of the blocked well. By subsequently cutting off their own water supply during a summer drought, Manon brings the village to the brink of ruin, forcing a collective confession and act of contrition that culminates in the suicide of Soubeyran's nephew Ugolin. Like Naïs, Manon finds happiness with an educated bourgeois (in this case, a schoolteacher) who admires her independent, proactive temperament and will join her in the continuing moral and social renovation of the village.

As a final testament to the feminist evolution of Pagnol's post-war heroines, it is worth noting that they do not suffer the negative social repercussions of pre-marital sex or unwanted pregnancy, instead controlling their own sexuality to achieve personal satisfaction. Manon flirts with and rejects Ugolin as part of her revenge, remaining free of all romantic complications until she and the teacher kiss in the film's final sequence. If at the end of *Naïs* there is a passing suggestion that she may be pregnant, that does not dissuade Madame Rostaing from taking the peasant girl with the family to Aix. On the contrary, as the bourgeois matriarch tells Toine, she regards accepting Naïs as a natural obligation since Frédéric genuinely loves her. The rigid, often crippling social distinctions and taboos that structure the action of the *Fanny*, *Angèle*, and *La Fille du puisatier* have thus dissipated almost entirely, replaced with a much more modern, liberal vision of class and familial relations.

Whether one persists in retrospectively viewing Pagnol's work from the 1930s as tainted with an apology for female domesticity and perhaps even misogyny, or simply as an expression of maternalist feminism, *Naïs* and *Manon* should be recognised as revising that position with a positive attitude towards women's post-war sexual and social liberation. Long mischaracterised by critics, Pagnol's gender politics end up surprisingly close to an endorsement of the individualist feminism that Simone de Beauvoir famously articulated in *Le Deuxième Sexe* (1949).

Pagnol, Giono, and the representation of peasant life

Pagnol's emphatic post-war critique of archaic, patriarchal communities also represented a definitive break from the work of Jean Giono, whose writings had provided the basis for *Jofroi*, *Angèle*, *Regain*, and *La Femme du boulanger*. Despite their ongoing friendship, shared love of the Provençal countryside, and a realist style seasoned with flashes of melodramatic lyricism, the two men had always held fundamentally different attitudes towards the peasantry. While Giono emphasised the austere, noble, and often tragic aspects of rural life, Pagnol consistently grafted comedy onto the source texts' pathos. The change of tone is usually accomplished by expanding a tersely narrated scene through humorous dialogue and physical comedy. Whereas Giono simply notes that Jofroi uses a shotgun to prevent Fonse from uprooting his olive trees, Pagnol has Jofroi chase the terrified buyer of his orchard around a tree several times with the gun in hand (see Figure 15).

Similarly, while Giono summarises Jofroi's three aborted suicide attempts in only a few lines through a narrator who underscores the old man's sense of anguish and worthlessness at no longer being able to care for his beloved olive trees, Pagnol transforms each episode into a long vaudevillian sketch. Jofroi's show of hanging himself in the centre of the village thus transforms from a desperate plea for compassion into a mischievous episode of public blackmail. When Fonse arrives to cut the rope, Jofroi gives him several sharp kicks, loudly denounces him as an 'assassin' to the gathering crowd, and even accuses him of strangulation as Fonse gently removes the noose. That dynamic is repeated when Jofroi threatens to jump from a rooftop as a crowd looks on, and again when he plays dead lying in the middle of the village's main road. In the first instance, he is talked down after duly humiliating Fonse and winning the sympathy of other villagers who run back and forth with a mattress to break his fall; in the second, he indignantly gives up the charade upon hearing a villager quip that 'il sent déjà mauvais' (he already smells bad) – an insult that he cannot bring himself to let go unchallenged.

Pagnol's success in lightening Giono's sober dramas with humour depended equally on writing sharp, witty dialogue and casting talented, versatile actors who had initially honed their skills in the demanding southern music-hall circuit anchored in Marseilles and Toulon. Just as the masterful tragic-comic performances of Vincent Scotto as Jofroi and Henri Poupon as Fonse earned them instant critical acclaim, Fernandel and Raimu achieved new high points in their already thriving careers – first individually, as Saturnin the farmhand and Aimable the cuckold baker, then collaboratively in *La Fille du puisatier*, one of the most successful films released in France during the Second World War.

The only partial misstep involves the Gédémus character in *Regain*. In deference to Fernandel, Pagnol attempted to transform Giono's knife-grinder, an invidious supporting character who uses the downtrodden Arsule to pull his heavy grinding cart, into a sympathetic protagonist plagued by a limp and comically detained by the police on murder charges after Arsule's secret elopement with Panturle. Far from producing 'un être fruste, un pauvre homme ridicule et touchant, pas très intelligent, mais plus égoïste encore que sot' (a wretched, ridiculous, and touching man, not very intelligent, but more selfish than stupid) (Pagnol 1937), as Pagnol initially intended, the result on-screen is a strangely artificial, contradictory role that disrupts an otherwise beautiful rendering of the clarity and elemental power of Giono's prose.

That incongruity divided the unanimous critical praise that greeted *Jofroi*, *Angèle*, and *La Femme du boulanger*. Georges Champeaux deplored 'l'erreur de coter moins haut le lyrisme de Giono que les gencives de Fernandel. Toutes les scènes où paraissait ce Gédémus ont été étriquées et surchargées. Aubignane est bien mort. Voici Fernandelopolis' (the mistake of valuing Giono's lyricism less than Fernandel's gums. All the scenes in which this Gédémus appears have been overloaded and stretched thin. Aubignane is dead and buried. Here we are in Fernandelopolis) (Champeaux 1937), while Jean Fayard took exactly the opposite view, arguing that the actor demonstrated 'une autorité, une intelligence, un naturel et un esprit qui l'égalent aux plus grands' (an authority, and intelligence, a naturalness and a wit that make him one of the greats) (Fayard 1937). Won over by Fernandel's sheer star power, average spectators concurred with Fayard and made the film a top-ten box-office hit.

French commentators have often explained Pagnol and Giono's contrasting sensibilities in terms of geography, with Pagnol supposedly personifying the relaxed, verbose temperament of coastal Provence and Giono the rugged, sober character of the foothills and valleys adjacent to the Alps. Another less deterministic explanation can be found in their differing conceptions of art's social function. Giono, who had joined the Marxist-inspired Association des Ecrivains et des Artistes Révolutionnaires in early 1934, portrayed peasants as alternatively brutish and civilised, virtuous, and vicious, but never as ridiculous or comical, for he conceived traditional rural culture as a final bulwark against the exploitative, dehumanising influences of capitalism, urbanisation, and modernity itself. Through his writing Giono tenaciously sought to promote social reform by remedying urbanites' misunderstanding of and contempt for the peasant way of life – a goal expressed most fervently in his 1936 novel *Les vraies richesses*. Two years later, as France began to prepare for a new war with Germany, he published a manifesto entitled *Lettre aux paysans sur la pauvreté et la paix* urging peasants to exercise their moral authority over the nation's politicians and force peace talks by withholding their harvests (Citron 1990: 290–2).

Having already renounced earnest socio-political engagement early in his career as a playwright, Pagnol saw his films not as a direct catalyst of reform or moral edification, but as mass-market entertainment that allowed spectators to feel solidarity in coping with the difficulties and injustices of modern life. Like Bergson and Nietzsche, Molière and Chaplin, Pagnol emphasised laughter's essential role in that process as a means of facilitating pathos. As he writes in the essay *Notes sur le rire* (1947):

> Avoir pitié, c'est se sentir égal à une autre créature humaine qui souffre, et dont nous redoutons le sort pour nous-mêmes ... Egoïste par ses causes, elle est belle et noble dans ses conséquences. Elle est, comme le rire, le propre de l'homme, et le rire s'arrête où la pitié commence. (Pagnol 1995: I, 1006–7)[20]

His view of the artist's social mission is expressed most clearly on-screen in *Le Schpountz* in a monologue delivered by Orane Demazis:

> Faire rire ceux qui rentrent des champs, avec leurs grandes mains tellement dures qu'ils ne peuvent plus les fermer; ceux qui sortent des bureaux avec leurs petites poitrines qui ne savent plus le goût de l'air; ceux qui reviennent de l'usine, la tête basse, les ongles cassées, avec de l'huile noire dans les coupures de leurs doigts: celui qui leur fait oublier un instant les misères – la fatigue, l'inquiétude, et la mort – celui qui fait rire des êtres qui ont tant de raisons de pleurer, celui-là leur donne la force de vivre, et l'on aime comme un bienfaiteur.[21] (Pagnol 1995: II, 727–8)

---

20 Feeling compassion means feeling equal to another human being who is suffering and whose fate we fear will befall us ... Selfish in its causes, compassion is lovely and noble in its consequences. Like laughter, it is uniquely human, and laughter stops where compassion begins.

21 Making laugh those who come in from the fields, with their large hands so callused that they can no longer close them; those who leave offices with their

Giono was deeply ambivalent towards Pagnol's adaptations, pleased that they exposed his writing to a mass audience, yet tormented by the feeling that they perverted his sense of his aesthetics and social responsibility. He perceived the comedic reinvention of Jofroi, Saturnin, and Gédémus as disrespectful towards the peasantry and an act of venal pandering to the prejudices of urban cinema audiences. Shortly after seeing *Angèle* in September 1934, Giono wrote to Louis Brun, his editor at Les Editions Grasset: 'j'ai été frappé par ce film comme d'un coup de bâton en pleine figure. Ce qui est fait est fait, tant pis. Il suffit qu'on sache que je n'ai jamais collaboré à ça en quoi que ce soit' (I was struck by that film like a club across the face. What is done is done, too bad. It suffices for people to know that I played no part in making it) (Mény 1980: 61). Giono demanded that his name be removed from the film's opening credits; only Brun's intervention and Pagnol's contractual obligations prevented him from complying (Citron 1990: 228).

As for *Regain*, Giono briefly visited Aubignane during construction, wrote a brief, lyrical homage to the collective effort involved, and recorded a short voice-over introducing the film (Giono 1937; Citron 1983: 153). The voice-over disappeared from the final montage, but Giono was still pleased with the result. In a November 1937 letter he noted that the 'la réussite du film m'a très heureusement réjoui. Je suis persuadé qu'on ne pourra guère être plus fidèle' (the film's success pleased me enormously. I am convinced that one could not have done a more faithful adaptation) and enthusiastically granted Pagnol permission to adapt his short story 'La femme du boulanger' (Anon. 1942). Giono and Les Editions Grasset also signed a contract allowing Pagnol to publish a low-cost illustrated edition of the *Regain* film's script in exchange for 4 per cent of the net sales figure, 2 per cent of which would go to Giono (Anon. 1941). However, the novelist's attitude abruptly changed upon seeing that Pagnol had reproduced *verbatim* substantial portions of the novel's dialogue. As he wrote to Brun:

> Si je n'ai pas été consulté pour le tournage du film, je ne suis pas loin de comprendre que c'est nécessaire pour le cinéma. Ceci posé, il serait

---

frail lungs that no longer know the taste of air; those who return from the factory with heads hung low, broken fingernails, and black oil in the cuts on their fingers: he who makes them momentarily forget miseries such as fatigue, worry, and death – he who makes laugh those who have so many reasons to cry, he gives them the strength to live, and he is loved like a benefactor.

assez curieux que le livre passe tel quel sous le nom de Marcel Pagnol, avec mon titre, avec mes phrases, avec mon esprit, sans autre forme de procès. Tu sais l'importance populaire du cinéma et de l'édition à bon marché. On ne parlerait bientôt plus que de '*Regain* de Marcel Pagnol', alors que j'ai la faiblesse de tenir à ce qu'on continue à parler de '*Regain* de Jean Giono'. C'est ce qu'il faut sauvegarder. C'est ce que je veux défendre. (Mény 1978: 64)[22]

He travelled to Marseilles in mid-December hoping to reach an arrangement with Pagnol but left prematurely, disgusted with what he perceived as the filmmaker's greed and moral bankruptcy: 'j'ai trouvé un homme à bout, vidé, faible, désemparé. Je n'ai rien osé demander de ce qui m'était dû. Il a donné en autographe de lui, signées par lui sur le grand programme mondial de la première de *Regain*, dix lignes qui sont de moi. Touchant' (I found a man overextended, empty, distraught. I didn't dare ask for what was owed me. He gave me a signed copy of the programme from *Regain*'s world premiere with ten lines of mine written in his hand. Touching) (Giono 1995: 229).

While not particularly egregious by cinema industry standards, Pagnol's conduct is surprising in light of his highly publicised stance on authorship and prior commitment to defending writers' intellectual and financial rights against usurpation by filmmakers. The initial adaptation contract that the two men signed on 8 November 1932 provided Giono generous compensation – a flat advance payment for each of five planned adaptations (50,000 francs for the first; 30,000 for each subsequent one), plus 6 per cent of the net box-office take – in exchange for his input on the screenplays and granting Pagnol authority to make 'toute modification pour les nécessités de la production et de l'exploitation' (all modifications necessary for production and commercialisation) (Anon. 1941; Anon. 1942).

Yet by December 1937 Pagnol had paid Giono only a portion of the prescribed percentage for *Jofroi*, *Angèle*, and *Regain*. In addition, Giono did not know how much he was owed, since Pagnol had disclosed no accounting records (Anon. 1941; Anon. 1942). Having

22 I can readily understand not being consulted about the film's production; that's a normal part of cinema. Even so, it would be strange for the book to appear under Marcel Pagnol's name, with my title, with my words, with my sensibility, but without any other form of legal proceedings. You know the public impact of film and of low-cost publishing. People will soon speak only of 'Marcel Pagnol's *Regain*', yet I am flawed enough to insist that people continue speaking of 'Jean Giono's *Regain*'. That's what must be preserved. That's what I want to protect.

himself been denied that same right in mid-1932 by Paramount during its 'hostile' adaptation of *Topaze*, Pagnol perhaps viewed subjecting Giono to the same treatment as an opportunity to enact a kind of Nietzschean justice, confirming the novelist's first impression of him as 'un charmant garçon en sable sec et qui fuit entre les doigts' (a charming guy who like dry sand slips through the fingers) (Citron 1990: 199).

Giono subsequently denounced Pagnol's *Regain* adaptation as 'essoufflé, boursouflé, et adipeux' (drained of vitality, turgid and flabby), a fundamental betrayal of his own 'œuvre maigre' (spartan work) (Giono 1971–89: VII, 660). In early January 1938 that dissatisfaction prompted him to take up the camera himself for the first time with the intention of making a short experimental film 'pour donner celui qui est dans son fauteuil de cinéma au milieu de la foule le sens et la grandeur de la solitude' (to give the spectators seated in the crowded cinema the uplifting feeling of solitude) (Giono 1995: 231). To be shot in the first person, from the perspective of a narrator walking alone through a snowy landscape, the images were to be accompanied by the noise of the narrator's steps and breathing, a spoken excerpt from Giono's novel *Poids du ciel*, and a choral version of Bach's 'Joy of Man's Desiring'. Though Giono only shot a few scenes and the project never came to fruition, it does clearly differentiate his aesthetic and social priorities from Pagnol's (Giono 1995: 232).

Giono's resentment towards Pagnol soon subsided, paving the way for the release of *La Femme du boulanger* and the publication of its script – which this time borrowed key characters and the basic premise of the original short story but relatively little dialogue. However, when Pagnol subsequently purchased the copyright to the title 'La Femme du boulanger' via an American lawyer in late 1940 with the intention of producing a new stage play, Giono again became irate (Anon. 1941). On 15 February 1941 he filed a lawsuit seeking the full 6 per cent of box-office receipts stipulated in the original contract, 2 per cent of the proceeds from the printed screenplays, a million francs in damages, and the immediate removal of all four films and both screenplays from circulation.

For the civil tribunal in Marseilles that heard the case eight months later, the central issue was whether Giono had fulfilled his contractual duty to participate in writing the screenplays. Whereas Giono asserted that he had drafted and mailed nearly complete scripts for *Angèle* and

Regain, as well as a detailed treatment for *La Femme du boulanger*, Pagnol claimed never to have received anything. Citing a lack of physical evidence in the form of registered mail receipts or duplicate manuscript copies, the court dismissed all four of Giono's complaints, ordered him to pay nine-tenths of the legal fees, and released Pagnol from making any additional royalty payments from the films' profits. However, the judges did order Pagnol to pay Giono 2 per cent of gross sales figures from the screenplays of both *Regain* – per the contract with Les Editions Grasset – and *La Femme du Boulanger*, for which no agreement had been signed. More important, Giono was also awarded joint copyright over the title 'La Femme du boulanger' by virtue of the eponymous short story he had published in the *Nouvelle Revue Française* in 1932, thereby effectively preventing Pagnol from staging it as a play (Anon. 1941; Anon. 1942).

Giono immediately appealed the unfavourable portions of the judgment. Eight months later a superior court in Aix reaffirmed his right to 6 per cent of the net profits from all four screen adaptations, appointed a panel of three auditors to determine the exact amount owed to him, and reduced his responsibility for administrative costs, but without awarding any punitive damages. Symptomatically, the adversaries each issued national press releases claiming victory. In the end Giono received a back payment of 1.5 million francs for the films and 3,000 francs for the screenplays (Anon. 1942; Giono 1995: 351).

While awaiting the result of his appeal, Giono renewed plans to make films on his own terms, drafting a screenplay sequel to *Regain* entitled *Triomphe de la vie* and a detailed shooting script based on his novella *Le Chant du monde* (Giono 1971–89: VII, 779–842; Mény 1978: 69–78; Mény 1980: 31–234). After negotiations with director Abel Gance and producer Léon Garganoff fell through (Giono 1971–89: VII, 1232–7), Giono resolved to found his own production company, noting in an interview that 'je réussirai ou j'échouerai, mais du moins je n'aurai à m'en prendre qu'à moi-même' (I will succeed or fail, but at least I will have only myself to blame) (Giono 1943). In a further effort to reclaim his work and supplant Pagnol, Giono wrote stage versions of *Jofroi* and *La Femme du boulanger* that were performed in Paris during the 1943–44 season to lukewarm reviews and little revenue (Citron 1990: 342–5; Giono 1995: 447–8). Though repeatedly postponed and resulting in only two pictures – *Crésus* (1960) and *Un roi sans divertissement* (1963) – Giono's short career behind the camera did finally capture his ascetic vision of the rough Provençal countryside and its residents (Mény 1978: 153–208).

By that time he had again reconciled with Pagnol, who as post-war president of the Société des Auteurs et des Compositeurs Dramatiques publicly supported his former antagonist against accusations of ideological sympathy for Vichy (Citron 1990: 402). In 1953, acting as 'cultural adviser' to Prince Rainier, Pagnol also arranged for Giono to receive the Grand Prix Littéraire de Monaco and accompanying million-franc honorarium, simultaneously proposing to sponsor his election to the Académie Française (Citron 1990: 469–72). Though Giono declined the latter offer in favour of the Académie Goncourt, like René Clair he felt a renewed sense of respect and gratitude towards 'un ami complet sans réticence' (a complete friend without reservation) (Giono 2008: 166).

An art of the commonplace

In the end, of course, neither Giono's books nor his films ever came close to bridging the cultural divide between urban and rural France or rivalling the impact of Pagnol's adaptations. From 1920 to 1939 more than a million peasants left the underdeveloped countryside in search of a better life (Sauvy 1984: II, 66). Whatever hardships they encountered, few of them duplicated Angèle and Arsule's joyous return to the earth. In this sense, Pagnol's representation of the peasantry was highly conventional, perpetuating a discourse that had characterised French literature and painting for centuries. As sociologist Pierre Bourdieu writes:

> La classe paysanne est l'exemple par excellence de la classe objet, contrainte de former sa propre subjectivité à partir de son objectivation. Il est certain que l'on ne pense à peu près jamais les paysans en eux-mêmes et pour eux-mêmes, et que les discours mêmes qui exaltent leurs vertus ou celles de la campagne ne sont jamais qu'une manière euphémisée de parler des vices des ouvriers et de la ville. (Bourdieu 1977: 4)[23]

23 The peasantry is the quintessential example of an objectified class, forced to construct its subjectivity from its own objectification. It is certain that one almost never conceives peasants by and for themselves, and that the very discourses exalting their virtues or those of the countryside are never anything but a roundabout way of speaking about the vices of the industrial working classes and the city.

By soliciting urban, working-class spectators to alternatively laugh at and admire their rural compatriots, Pagnol's ethnographic melodramas did objectify one class in order to better serve the psychological needs of another. Yet even in a Marxist perspective these films cannot properly be construed as socially regressive, for they offered literally millions of struggling French citizens a powerful sense of solidarity and comfort against the increasing material and psychological hardships of the Great Depression.

Cinematically, Pagnol's rural pictures were nothing short of revolutionary, inaugurating a new phase in the evolution of location shooting and cinematic authenticity that echoed French 'pictorialist naturalism' of the late 1910s and early 1920s while foreshadowing post-war Italian neo-realism. As early as 1947 André Bazin identified the influence of *Angèle* on Roberto Rossellini's *Paisà* (1946), and Vittorio De Sica's *Sciuscià* (1946). While Bazin acknowledged the films' shared use of 'une trame documentaire (a documentary framework) that incorporated humour, social critique, and a fictional plot 'qui atteint au tragique sans céder à l'amertume' (which achieves tragedy without succumbing to bitterness), he emphasised that 'la comparaison n'est pas à l'avantage du nouvel Académicien' (the comparison is not flattering for the newest member of the French Academy), asserting that Pagnol's *mise en scène* and montage lacked 'la force descriptive' (the descriptive power) of his Italian counterparts (Bazin 1947).

For their part, Rossellini and De Sica confirmed the filiation in more positive terms. Rossellini, who discovered *Angèle* and *La Femme du boulanger* just as he was beginning his directorial career in 1937–38, later characterised Pagnol's films as 'neo-realism before the fact' and recalled that 'they hit me like a fantastic gust of truth' (Gallagher 1998: 100). In an interview for French television shortly after Pagnol's death, he added that 'je me suis totalement amouraché de Pagnol avant la guerre, et il a influencé mes choix qui sont venus après' (I was completely infatuated with Pagnol, and he influenced the choices I made afterwards) (Rossellini 1976).

At the 1955 Cannes festival De Sica went a step further by revealing that he conceived *L'oro di Napoli* (1954) specifically as a homage to Pagnol: 'Les Napolitains sont pareils aux Marseillais. Avec chaque épisode du film, mon souvenir va à *Marius* et *La Femme du boulanger*. Par exemple, la *pizzaiola*, c'est la femme du boulanger, c'est la même histoire' (Neapolitans are similar to the residents of Marseilles.

With each episode of the film, I remember *Marius* and *La Femme du boulanger*. For example, the *pizzaiola* is the baker's wife) (De Sica 1955). Following Pagnol, the film's six episodes portray the working class and petty bourgeoisie with both affectionate humour and genuine pathos, emphasising regional dialect, the irascible Mediterranean temperament, and excessive performative speech that conceals uncomfortable psychological, social, and economic fractures within families and communities.

The best example is indeed 'Pizze a credito', in which a young, smoulderingly sensual pizza vendor's wife played by Sophia Loren leaves her wedding ring at a lover's house and lies to her middle-aged husband that she lost it kneading dough for the morning service. Their frantic visitation of the day's clients ends when her lover, alerted to the ruse, returns the ring claiming that he found it in a pie from the restaurant. Despite these thematic similarities, the film ends with a striking counterpoint to *La Femme du boulanger* that underscores the contextual shift from late 1930s France to mid-1950s Italy. Whereas Aimable and Aurélie share a private moment of marital reconciliation by relighting their hearth hand in hand, De Sica suggests the enduring triumph of undomesticated female sexuality in a tracking shot of the unfaithful *pizzaiola* strutting smugly down a crowded street as her cuckold husband follows passively behind, struggling to match her pace and utterly emasculated by his neighbours' alternatively lustful and incredulous gazes.

The degree to which Pagnol might rightfully be considered the grandfather of Italian neo-realism or the French new wave is of course open to debate, but his influence on those movements is undeniable, not only in his intrepid use of location shooting, improvisation, and non- or semi-professional actors, but in the application of those methods to illustrate his philosophy that 'il n'y a pas d'art en dehors des lieux communs' (there is no art beyond the commonplace) (Pagnol 1966). Even the iconic Jean-Luc Godard, whose style and sensibility are in many ways antithetical to Pagnol's, acknowledged his seminal influence in his speech accepting a career achievement honour at the 1987 César Awards. Responding in part to the multiple wins registered by Claude Berri's adaptations of *Jean de Florette* and *Manon des sources*, Godard remarked that '*Angèle*, c'est l'un des plus beaux films qu'on ait jamais tourné. Nous lui devons tous quelque chose, mais souvent sans le savoir et encore plus souvent sans l'avouer' (*Angèle* is one of the most beautiful films ever made. We all owe him something, but often without knowing it and even more often without admitting it) (Godard 1987).

References

Abel, Richard (1984). *French Cinema: The First Wave, 1915–1929*, Princeton, Princeton University Press.
Achard, Marcel (1937), 'La semaine à l'écran: *Angèle*', *Marianne*, 7 July.
Achard, Marcel (1937a), 'La semaine à l'écran: *Regain*', *Marianne*, 11 November.
Adriano (1993), 'The Film Music of Arthur Honegger' notes to *Arthur Honegger: Mayerling, Regain, Le Démon de l'Himalaya*, CD no. 8.223467, London, Marco Polo.
Airelle, Françoise (1937), '*Regain* de Marcel Pagnol', *Minerva*, 16 November.
Andrew, Dudley (1995), *Mists of Regret: Culture and Sensibility in Classic French Film*, Princeton, Princeton University Press.
Anon. (1931), 'On tourne *Marius* de Marcel Pagnol', *Le Petit Marseillais*, 7 July.
Anon. (1933), 'Marcel Pagnol magicien', *Cinémonde*, 19 October.
Anon. (1933a), 'Les nouveaux films: *Jofroi*', *Comœdia*, 22 December.
Anon. (1933b), '*Jofroi*', *La Cinématographie française*, 23 December.
Anon. (1934), 'Dans la campagne provençale, Marcel Pagnol tourne *Angèle*', *Paris Soir*, 16 June.
Anon. (1934a), 'La réouverture de *l'Odéon* à Marseilles', *La Revue de l'écran*, 1 October.
Anon. (1934b), '*Angèle*, le chef-d'œuvre du larmoyant', *La Dépêche de Toulouse*, 16 November.
Anon. (1935), 'La carrière du film *Angèle* depuis sa sortie', *La Cinématographie française*, 27 April.
Anon. (1935a), '*Angèle*, grand succès de l'exploitation', *Cinéma-Spectacles*, 25 May.
Anon. (1936), 'Films ruraux', *La France rurale*, 8 August.
Anon. (1937), 'Analyse et critique des films: *Regain*', *La Cinématographie française*, 22 October.
Anon. (1937a), 'La parole est aux spectateurs: *Regain*', *Pour Vous*, 10 November.
Anon. (1938), 'La parole est aux spectateurs: *La Femme du boulanger*', *Pour Vous*, 12 October.
Anon. (1939), 'L'Académie Féminine vous recommande...', *Minerva*, 26 February.
Anon. (1941), Arrêt de la Troisième Chambre du Tribunal Civil de Marseilles, Archives Départementales des Bouches-du-Rhône (Marseilles), series 63W, box 566, 14 October.
Anon. (1942), Arrêt de la Troisième Chambre de la Cour d'Appel d'Aix-en-Provence, Archives Départementales des Bouches-du-Rhône (Aix), series 1490 W, box 10, 8 June.
Anon. (1950), 'Fox Scores Sweep of Critics' Awards', *New York Times*, 28 December.

Antoine, André (1934), 'Les premières de l'écran: *Angèle*', *Le Journal*, 2 November.
Apostolidès, Jean-Marie (1987), 'Impudique Aurélie', in Philippe Perrot and Olivier Burgelin (eds), 'Parure, pudeur, étiquette', *Communications*, no. 46, 199–220.
Balzac, Honoré de (1976–81), *La Comédie humaine*, eds Pierre-Georges Castex et al., 12 vols, Paris, Gallimard.
Bard, Christine (1995), *Les Filles de Marianne: histoire des féminismes, 1914–1940*, Paris, Fayard.
Bazin, André (1947), '*Quatre pas dans les nuages:* nouveau triomphe de l'école italienne', *Le Parisien libéré*, 2 April.
Bazin, André (1958–1962), *Qu'est-ce que le cinéma?*, 4 vols, Paris, Editions du Cerf.
Blavette, Charles (1961), *Ma Provence en cuisine*, Paris, Editions France Empire.
Bost, Pierre (1936), '*Les Bas-fonds* de Jean Renoir', *Vendredi*, 18 December.
Bost, Pierre (1937), '*Regain* de Giono et *Regain* de Pagnol', *Vendredi*, 5 November.
Bourdieu, Pierre (1977), 'Une classe objet', *Actes de la Recherche en Sciences Sociales* no. 17– 18, November, 2–5.
Boverat, Fernand (1936), 'Les causes d'accélération de la dénatalité', *La Revue de l'Alliance Nationale pour l'Accroissement de la Population Française*, May.
Brunet, Louis (1934), 'Les beaux films: *Jofroi*', *La Revue de la famille*, 15 May.
Burch, Noël and Geneviève Sellier (1996), *La Drôle de guerre des sexes du cinéma français, 1930–1956*, Paris, Nathan.
Cachin, Françoise (1997), 'Le paysage du peintre', in Pierre Nora (ed.), *Les Lieux de mémoire*, Paris, Gallimard, 957–93.
Caldicott, C.E.J. (1977), *Marcel Pagnol*, Boston, Twayne Publishers.
Champeaux, Georges (1937), 'Le cinéma: *Regain*', *Gringoire*, 5 November.
Chantal, Suzanne (1934), 'En revenant de Provence', *Cinémonde*, 28 June.
Chantal, Suzanne (1934a), 'Un film nouveau: *Angèle*', *Le Journal de la femme*, 17 November.
Chantal, Suzanne (1938), 'Un film nouveau: *La Femme du boulanger*', 16 September.
Chazal, Robert (1937), '*Regain*, un chef-d'œuvre', *La Griffe cinématographique*, 16 November.
Chevignard, Marie-Geneviève and Nicole Faure (1978), 'Système de valeurs et de références dans la presse féminine', in René Rémond and Janine Bourdin (eds), *La France et les Français en 1938–39*, Paris, Presses de la Fondation Nationale des Sciences Politiques, 43–58.
Citron, Pierre (1983), 'Correspondance Jean Giono-Lucien Jacques, 1930–1961', *Cahiers Giono* no. 3, Paris, Gallimard.
Citron, Pierre (1990), *Giono, 1895–1970*, Paris, Seuil.
Contadin, Fernand [Fernandel] (1934), Letter to Pagnol, Archives of the Compagnie Méditerranéenne de Film, 19 November.
Crisp, Colin (2002), *Genre, Myth, and Convention in the French Cinema, 1929–1939*, Bloomington, Indiana University Press.
D'Aubarède, Gabriel (1934), 'Loin des studios, Marcel Pagnol tourne *Angèle*', *Comœdia*, 6 July 1934.

Déjan, Maurice (1938), 'La musique et le cinéma', *Journal d'Alsace et de Lorraine*, 14 March.

De Sica, Vittorio (1955), 'Reflets de Cannes: Vittorio De Sica à propos de son film *L'Or de Naples*', interview for French news filmed on 27 April (available at: www.ina.fr).

Duhamel, Georges (1930), *Scènes de la vie future*, Paris, Mercure de France.

Epardaud, Edmond (1936), 'Marcel Pagnol, roi de Marseille et empereur de Marcelin', *La Cinématographie française*, 26 December.

Fayard, Jean (1934), '*Angèle* aux Agriculteurs', *Je Suis Partout*, 10 November.

Fayard, Jean (1937), '*L'Habit vert* et *Regain*', *Candide*, 11 November.

Fieschi, Jean-André et al. (1965), 'Pagnol au travail par ses collaborateurs: rencontres avec Marius Brouquier, Suzanne de Troye, Jean Lecocq, et Charles Blavette', *Cahiers du cinéma* no. 173, December, 56–62.

Gallagher, Tag (1998), *The Adventures of Roberto Rossellini: his life and films*, New York, Da Capo Press.

Giono, Jean (1937), 'Jean Giono, auteur de *Regain*, retrace ici l'émouvante construction du village édifié pour le film de Marcel Pagnol', *Cinémonde*, 23 September.

Giono, Jean (1943), 'Jean Giono va devenir metteur en scène', *Dimanche illustré*, 24 April.

Giono, Jean (1971–89), *Œuvres romanesques complètes*, eds Robert Ricatte, Pierre Citron et al., 8 vols, Paris, Gallimard.

Giono, Jean (1995), *Journal, poèmes, essais*, eds Pierre Citron et al., Paris, Gallimard.

Giono, Jean (2008), *J'ai ce que j'ai donné*, ed. Sylvie Durbet-Giono, Paris, Gallimard.

Godard, Jean-Luc (1987), 'La 12e soirée des Césars décernés par l'Académie des arts et techniques cinématographiques', broadcast on TF1, 21 February.

Godefroy, Christian (1934), 'En Provence, Marcel Pagnol tourne *Angèle*', *La Cinématographie française*, 30 June.

Guégan, Gérard, Jean-André Fieschi and Jacques Rivette (1965), 'Une aventure de la parole: entretien avec Marcel Pagnol', *Cahiers du cinéma* no. 173, December, 24–37.

Halbreich, Harry (1992), *Arthur Honegger: un musicien dans la cité des hommes*, Paris, Fayard.

Halbreich, Harry (1994), *L'œuvre d'Arthur Honegger: chronologie, catalogue raisonné, analyses, discographie*, Paris, Honoré Champion.

Hay, James (1987), *Popular Film in Fascist Italy*, Bloomington, Indiana University Press.

Idestam-Almquist, Bengt (1952), *Classics of the Swedish Cinema: the Stiller and Sjöstrom Period*, Stockholm, Swedish Film Institute.

Imbs, Paul, ed. (1971–94), *Trésor de la langue française: dictionnaire de la langue du XIXe siècle et du XXe siècle*, 16 vols, Paris, Gallimard.

Jeancolas, Jean-Pierre (1983), *Quinze ans d'années trente: le cinéma des Français, 1929–1944*, Paris, Stock.

Kenez, Peter (1992), *Soviet Cinema and Society, 1917–1953*, Cambridge, Cambridge University Press.

Koos, Cheryl (1996), 'Gender, Anti-Individualism, and Nationalism: the Alliance Nationale and the Pronatalist Backlash against the *Femme Moderne*, 1933–1940', *French Historical Studies* 19.3: Spring, 699–723.

Lamy, J.-P. (1935), '*Angèle* s'avère le succès de la saison', *Ciné d'Afric*, February.

Liausu, Jean-Pierre (1933), '*Jofroi*, une paysannerie de Marcel Pagnol', *Comœdia*, 28 December.

London, Kurt (1936), *Film Music*, trans. Eric Bensinger, London, Faber & Faber.

Mény, Jacques (1978), *Jean Giono et le cinéma*, Paris, Editions Jean-Claude Simoën.

Mény, Jacques (1980), *Giono: œuvres cinématographiques, 1938–1959*, Paris, Gallimard.

Michelet, Jules (1974), *Le Peuple*, Paris, Flammarion.

Mistler, Jean (1961), *Epinal et l'imagerie populaire*, Paris, Hachette.

Offen, Karen (2000), *European Feminisms, 1700–1950: a Political History*, Stanford, Stanford University Press.

Ory, Pascal (1994), *La Belle illusion: culture et politique sous le signe du Front Populaire*, Paris, Plon.

Pagnol, Marcel (1937), '*Regain*: manuel de publicité', Bibliothèque Nationale de France, Département des Arts du Spectacle, 4–ICO-CIN-10335.

Pagnol, Marcel (1966), 'Marcel Pagnol, ou le cinéma tel qu'on le parle', television documentary broadcast on Antenne 2, 12 May.

Pagnol, Marcel (1995), *Œuvres complètes*, 3 vols, Paris, Fallois.

Peer, Shanny (1998), *France on Display: Peasants, Provincials, and Folklore in the 1937 Paris World's Fair*, Albany, State University of New York Press.

Petley, Julian (1979), *Capital and Culture: German Cinema, 1933–1945*, London, British Film Institute.

Peyrusse, Claudette (1986), *Le Cinéma méridional: le midi dans le cinéma français, 1929–1944*, Toulouse, Eché.

Proust, Pierre-Henry (1934), 'La Force de la race', *Comœdia*, 10 November.

Raoul, Jean (1934), 'On a donné le premier tour de manivelle d'*Angèle*', *L'Effort cinématographique*, 1 June.

Régent, Roger (1934), 'Avec Marcel Pagnol pendant les prises de vue d'*Angèle* dans la campagne marseillaise', *L'Intransigeant*, 9 June.

Renoir, Jean (1934), 'Un nouveau film de Jean Renoir: comment a été conçu *Toni*', *Les Cahiers du film* no. 5, November, 7–8.

Renoir, Jean (1938), 'Souvenirs', *Le Point* no. 18, December, 275–86.

Rivette, Jacques and François Truffaut (1957), 'Nouvel entretien avec Jean Renoir', *Cahiers du cinéma* no. 78, Christmas, 11–54.

Rohl, Francia (1937), 'Marcel Pagnol a construit un village pour y tourner *Regain*', *Pour Vous*, 18 February.

Rohl, Francia (1937a), 'M. Pagnol a abandonné son village, où il retournera faire la moisson des images', *Pour Vous*, 27 May 1937.

Rossellini, Roberto (1976), 'Le Masque et la plume: entretien autour des films de Marcel Pagnol', television interview broadcast on France 3, 18 January (available at www.ina.fr).

Sand, George (1979–80), *Œuvres complètes*, 27 vols, Geneva, Slatkine Reprints.

Sauvy, Alfred (1984), *Histoire économique de la France entre les deux guerres*, 2 vols, Paris, Editions Economica.

Scotto, Vincent (1947), *Souvenirs de Paris*, Toulouse, Editions STAEL.

Silver, Catherine (1982), *Frédéric Le Play: on Family, Work, and Social Change*, Chicago, University of Chicago Press.

Thébaud, Françoise (1986), *Quand nos grand-mères donnaient la vie: la maternité en France dans l'entre-deux-guerres*, Lyon, Presses Universitaires de Lyon.

Thierry, Gaston (1934), 'La conversion d'*Angèle*', 3 November.

Vuillermoz, Emile (1934), 'D'*Angèle* à *Caravane*', *Le Temps*, 3 November.

Williams, Alan (1992). *Republic of Images: A History of French Filmmaking*, Cambridge, Harvard University Press.

5

Pagnol and the French cinema industry

As a supplement to Pagnol's controversial theory of 'cinématurgie', the inaugural issue of *Les Cahiers du film* featured negative reviews of several recent British and American releases, including RKO's hit *King Kong* (1933).

> Si la réalisation de cette inepte histoire n'avait coûté que des sommes fabuleuses, l'aventure aurait un côté comique, du moins de ce côté-ci de l'Atlantique. Mais on pense à l'ingéniosité dépensée, à la science des perspectives, à toute la patience, à tout le travail sacrifiés par des hommes à cet horrible singe mécanique, et ceci est affligeant ... Quand j'ai vu King Kong broyer toute une rame de métro entre ses énormes doigts, j'ai regretté qu'une petite erreur de 'technique' ne lui ait pas fait anéantir de préférence le studio, les appareils de prises de vue, et tous les sunlights braqués sur lui. (D'Aubarède 1933: 31)[1]

Though written by long-time friend Gabriel d'Aubarède, the article bears a strong resemblance to Pagnol's own polemical style and clearly echoes the neophyte director's aesthetic and commercial priorities: disdain for technical embellishment, attachment to realism, and the ambition to craft a distinctly French production model capable of rivalling the largest Hollywood studios. Motivated by his contentious

---

1 If the cost of producing this inane story were limited only to fabulous sums of money, the endeavour would have a comical dimension, at least on this side of the Atlantic. But it is distressing when one thinks about the ingenuity expended, the science of scale models, all the patient human labour sacrificed to that horrible mechanic ape ... When I saw King Kong smash an entire subway train between his enormous fingers, I regretted that an error in 'technique' did not instead have him annihilate the studio, the cameras, and the lights trained on him.

break with Paramount over the adaptation of *Topaze*, Pagnol wasted no time in realising his vision. In less than five years he transformed himself from an upstart playwright with only the vaguest knowledge of the cinema industry into France's only fully independent filmmaker. In addition to serving as writer, producer and director, Pagnol built and ran his own studio and development laboratory in Marseilles, even acquiring two cinemas that served as outlets for his work. In an industry plagued by seemingly incurable fiscal and administrative problems and threatened by a rising tide of imports from the United States and Germany, Les Films Marcel Pagnol was one of only a few French companies to maintain an efficient organisational structure and a healthy bottom line.

The success of Pagnol's business model was unmatched in 1930s French cinema, offering industry insiders and the general public welcome proof that their nation could not only defend its unique cultural identity against Americanisation, but that it could compete economically with foreign pictures at home and abroad. Throughout the decade Pagnol's work was enormously popular across the French colonial empire and the world, enjoying special acclaim in the United States. His skill at mass marketing echoed that of large foreign studios, yet he clung stubbornly to a hands-on approach to making movies, proudly demonstrating that France could excel in a high-tech field without renouncing its prized reputation for quality craftsmanship. Equal parts cosmopolitan businessman and hometown artisan, Pagnol quickly earned folk hero status in the popular press.

An industry in crisis

From Louis Lumière's invention of the 'cinématographe' in 1895 through the end of the First World War, French films accounted for roughly 80 per cent of all those in circulation worldwide. In the 1920s, however, Hollywood gradually acquired a dominant market share that would subsequently prove essential in helping it weather the Great Depression. Lacking the capital reserves and vertical integration of American and German studios, French production was fragmented among hundreds of small, financially vulnerable companies (Crisp 1993: 39–41). At the peak of the crisis between 1933 and 1936, some 260 French producers declared bankruptcy (Leglise 1970: I, 106) and the cinema industry operated at a deficit of between 50 and 90 million francs annually (Renaitour 1937: 20). Among the victims were the country's two oldest and largest firms: Gaumont closed its doors in July 1934, while Pathé succumbed in February 1936, bought by Kodak (Crisp 1993: 26–32). A new crop of small companies immediately emerged to fill the vacuum, ensuring a steady stream of films and the growth of box-office revenues, but further exacerbating the systemic problems of undercapitalisation. Of the 202 film production firms registered in 1937, 80 per cent had a total liquid value of less than 50,000 francs. Because the typical feature film required an initial investment of about 2 million francs, most French producers faced ruin each time they undertook a new project (Créton 2004: 35–40).

The industry also suffered from a lack of rational, effective state regulation. Between 1932 and 1938 seven different ministerial initiatives to reform French cinema fell through, undermined by ongoing political divisions and rapid turnover of governments (Leglise 1970: 97–178; Crisp 1993: 33–8). A special governmental commission formed in 1934 following Gaumont's demise estimated that restructuring and refinancing French cinema would require a state investment of 200 million francs, a figure rejected by a succession of finance ministers (Renaitour 1937: 56–7). To make matters worse, cinema was the most heavily taxed of France's entertainment activities, with state deductions alone reaching 20 per cent, compared to 15 per cent for music halls and 10 per cent for cabarets. Factoring in the myriad of local taxes that existed, nearly half of all film box-office receipts were consumed by the dreaded *fisc*, which grew heavier as economic conditions worsened (Leglise 1970: I, 58).

While French cinema foundered, German filmmaking quickly transformed into a model of discipline and efficiency under the Nazis, who immediately moved to exploit their feeble neighbour. The massive UFA and Tobis studios, both nationalised by Propaganda Minister Joseph Goebbels in 1933, invested heavily in France via a Paris-based subsidiary known as the Alliance Cinématographique Européenne (ACE). By late 1934 it represented 15 per cent of the French film industry's total finance capital, serving as a nationwide distributor for both German- and French-made productions and running theatres in several key metropolitan markets. Building on the successful example of René Clair's *Le Million* (1931) and *Quatorze Juillet* (1932), both made at Tobis' studio complex in Epinay, the

Nazis also devoted substantial resources to making French-language pictures in Berlin, releasing nearly a hundred in all between 1934 and 1939. Lured by cutting-edge technology, high salaries, unmatched production efficiency, and comfortable working conditions, a growing stream of French talent flowed across the Rhine as the financial crisis in Paris deepened. In addition to signing respected directors such as Jacques Feyder, Jean Grémillon, Yves Mirande, Jacques de Baroncelli, and Marc Allégret, the Nazis attracted an even more impressive pool of stars featuring Jean Gabin, Pierre Blanchar, Danielle Darrieux, Arletty, Charles Vanel, Jules Berry, Michèle Morgan, Mireille Balin, Raimu, and Michel Simon (Courtade 1991; Chateau 1995: 11–13).

French spectators welcomed the chance to see their favourite stars in high-quality productions, which enjoyed consistent box-office success thanks to ACE's effective marketing and vigilant depublicisation of the Nazi money at work behind the scenes. For French intellectuals committed to stopping the spread of fascism and preventing the economic colonisation of their country, the situation was nothing short of treasonous. In a January 1934 speech Radical-Socialist deputy Henri Clerc identified cinema as 'l'instrument le plus dangereux de l'influence étrangère sur les esprits français' (the most dangerous instrument of foreign influence on the French mind) (Garcin 1934). Such fears grew as the decade wore on and the Third Reich's foreign policy became increasingly belligerent. In June 1938 cinema columnist Henri Jeanson openly denounced *L'Etrange Monsieur Victor*, Jean Grémillon's latest UFA-financed work, as a betrayal of French national interests: 'Comme tant d'autres soi-disant "films français" de nos jours, celui de Grémillon permet à l'Allemagne de se procurer en France les devises étrangères indispensables à l'exploitation intensive de ses usines de guerre' (Like so many other 'French' films today, Grémillon's lets Germany acquire in France the foreign currency essential to the intensive operation of its war factories (Jeanson 1939). His assessment was alarmist but accurate: between January 1937 and August 1938, French imports of German films totalled 33 million francs, while the Third Reich spent only 7 million francs to bring French productions across the Rhine.

Even the Popular Front failed to effectively address France's cinema problem. Between December 1936 and April 1937 a multi-party commission of legislators led by Jean-Michel Renaitour conducted an inquiry emphasising yet again the urgent need for reform. In his report to the committee, Minister of Education Jean Zay characterised the film industry as 'un marasme' (a quagmire) and 'une faillite quasi-générale' (approaching general bankruptcy) (Renaitour 1937: 114). Zay created a special commission to draft a national cinema bill, but its implementation proved excruciatingly slow (Leglise 1970: I, 179–98). Even the Popular Front's most loyal supporters showed frustration at its failure to reorganise French cinema. In the Christmas Eve edition of *Vendredi*, Jean Renoir, whose *La Grande Illusion* had just been banned in Germany, published an acerbic open letter urging the government to action.

> Si les dictateurs se permettent d'interdire des films, au moins en contrepartie ont-ils la clairvoyance de soutenir matériellement la production de leur pays. Il n'en est pas même chez nous, et reconnaissons que c'est dommage. Je ne sais pas ce que devra être le rôle de l'Etat demain. Mais j'affirme qu'aujourd'hui son devoir le plus strict est de faire confiance au génie français et de ressusciter une grande industrie, source de richesse nationale, que les capitalistes mauvais Français sont en train de laisser mourir.[2] (Renoir 1937)

Renoir's plea had little effect, and Zay's cinema legislation did not reach the National Assembly until March 1939, too late to do any good before the outbreak of war.

Though bureaucratic inefficiency was partially to blame, cultural mentalities played a more decisive role. If a small minority on the left and right strongly supported nationalising the film industry based on the German, Italian, or Soviet models, most French commentators rejected the principle of tightening governmental control, and censorship in particular, as fundamentally anti-democratic and inconsistent with their national character. Equally important was the pervasive fear – expressed on-screen in René Clair's hit *A nous la liberté* (1931) – that unchecked, American-style 'Taylorisation' of business and industry was exacerbating class conflict, dehumanising workers and consumers alike, and threatening the survival of French cultural identity (Crisp 1993: 22–5). In addition, those working in the film industry had little

---

2 If dictators allow themselves to ban films, at least in exchange they have the foresight to provide material support for their national production. Such is not the case in our country and that's a shame. I do not know what the role of the state will be in the future. But I believe that today its most pressing duty is to have faith in French ingenuity and to revive a great industry, a source of national wealth, that bad French capitalists are allowing to die.

faith in the ability of the government to help their cause. As *Ciné-Phono Magazine* columnist Charles Duclaux stated bluntly in a March 1934 article: 'L'ingérence de l'Etat dans notre industrie équivaut à la mort sans phrases. Tout ce que l'Etat gère périclite rapidement' (State interference in our industry simply amounts to death. Everything that the state manages collapses rapidly) (Duclaux 1934). Duclaux instead recommended that the industry help itself by reinforcing corporate structures and instituting stricter standards of professional conduct – neither of which materialised in any effective form.

A millionaire artisan

With a large reserve of capital at his disposal from his career as a playwright and the immensely successful screen adaptations of *Marius* and *Fanny* on-screen, Pagnol was uniquely positioned to implement an artisanal model of filmmaking that was immune to the problems plaguing the rest of the industry. Motivated in part by the financial troubles facing *Fanny* co-producer Roger Richebé and his own desire for complete creative autonomy, Pagnol's decision to acquire his own production infrastructure while shooting *Angèle* was ultimately made for logistical and financial reasons (Pagnol 2008: 17–21). The substantial delay and prohibitive cost of sending rushes to Paris for development by a third party justified the purchase and renovation of a modest development laboratory in Marseilles co-owned by childhood friend and chemical engineer Albert Assouad, whom Pagnol retained as general manager (Anon. 1934; Lechatellier 1934). The same logic prompted him to install a studio in the abandoned saw mill next door and to buy custom-built mobile sound equipment from Philips (Anon. 1934a). At just under 100 square metres, the studio was small but functional, comprising a single sound stage and administrative offices. Completed in early 1935, it served as the principal shooting venue for *Topaze* and *César*, as well as interior scenes for *Regain* and *Le Schpountz*.

At about the same time Pagnol founded distribution offices in Bordeaux, Lyon, and Lille to complement those already present since mid-1932 in Paris and Marseilles. The final step in achieving total self-sufficiency from the rest of the industry was to control the conditions under which his films were screened and keep the totality of box-office receipts. As he told a reporter in March 1935: 'Les directeurs de salles en prennent trop à leur aise. Pour me défendre, j'aurai mes propres cinémas. Dans deux ans je compte bien en avoir cent' (Theatre owners do as they like with my films. To protect myself, I will have my own cinemas. In two years I plan to have a hundred) (Anon. 1935). He took that step in September 1935 with the opening of 'Le Noailles', a 400-seat venue in the heart of Marseilles near the old Variétés music hall. It opened with an extended director's cut of *Angèle* and for the next two years screened Pagnol's work almost exclusively with great success (Anon. 1935a).

Pagnol managed his multimillion-franc portfolio like a traditional family business, performing multiple duties in the studios and labs alongside his fifteen employees, many of whom were childhood friends. In addition to participating in every phase of the initial construction, he regularly lent a hand building sets, repairing equipment, and developing filmstock (Bessy 1938). Yet that artisanal approach belied a revolutionary goal cited in a press release: to implement 'une décentralisation industrielle et artistique autour d'un centre cinématographique ultra-moderne ne cédant rien aux établissements parisiens si ce n'est que le prix de location plus bas' (an industrial and artistic decentralisation around an ultra-modern film hub that is equal to facilities in Paris except for lower rental fees) (Anon. 1934a). Though in practice the studio proved too cramped to divert much business from the capital or to compete with a larger facility in Nice known as La Victorine, other directors occasionally used Pagnol's set for brief indoor sequences while shooting outdoors nearby (Peyrusse 1986: 31–3). In contrast, the development laboratory ran steadily almost year-round and during peak months printed as many as 280,000 metres of film, the equivalent of 120 standard-length features (Epardaud 1938).

Pagnol was both immensely proud of his accomplishments as an industrialist and distressed by the time and effort they diverted from writing. As he confided to André Antoine in late 1936 during the pre-production of *Regain*:

De ma plume au public, tout est chez moi, sous ma direction constante, selon ma volonté, par une équipe qui travaille avec moi depuis quatre ans, avec une confiance totale, et un véritable amour de l'œuvre entreprise. Un auteur me disait un jour: 'Tu as une chance inouïe de te trouver dans une pareille situation'. A quoi j'ai répondu:

'Je ne m'y suis pas trouvé. Je m'y suis mis'. C'est d'ailleurs mon plus grand mérite, si j'en ai, car la construction et la mise au point d'une organisation pareille m'ont certainement coûté un ou deux *Marius* et autant de *Topaze*. Je ne parle pas de l'argent: je parle de ceux que je n'ai pas écrits pendant ce temps-là. Enfin, maintenant le ménage est fait, la machine tourne. Elle peut même tourner sans moi, et je redeviens écrivain. (Pagnol 1936)[3]

However, less than a year later Pagnol's ambitions again overwhelmed his creative instincts and he began building entirely new studios a few blocks away to serve as the hub of 'un Hollywood français' (a French Hollywood) that would transform Marseilles as Charlie Chaplin and Douglas Fairbanks had Los Angeles in the 1920s. In addition to a trio of 525 square metre stages each featuring the latest Debrie cameras, Philips sound equipment, and 100 metres of tracking rails, there was a 400 square metre courtyard for shooting outdoor scenes, a 5,000 ampere electric generator, a small fleet of service vehicles, mobile sound trucks, a canteen, and apartments for visiting actors and personnel (Anon. 1938; Epardaud 1938).

Inaugurated in April 1938 with *La Femme du boulanger*, over the following eighteen months another dozen pictures were shot, edited, and printed in their entirety at the new complex. Following the Munich crisis in September, Pagnol publicly offered his services to the French government as part of the industrial preparation for a new war, announced plans to build new laboratories on his estate near Le Mans, and opened another cinema in Marseilles – this time a large luxury venue dubbed 'Le César' (Pagnol 1938; Epardaud 1938a). Controlling every aspect of production and distribution enabled Pagnol to achieve an unequalled economy of scale and profit margin. At a time when the typical return on a French feature film was a million francs, he reported a per-film net average of 10 million (Bessy 1938).

---

3 From writing to exhibition, everything is under my constant control, done as I see fit, by a team that has worked alongside me for four years with complete trust and a genuine love for our endeavours. A writer said to me one day: 'You are incredibly lucky to find yourself in such a situation'. To which I responded: 'I didn't find myself in it. I put myself in it'. That is my greatest merit, if I have any, for the construction and refining of such an enterprise has certainly cost me one or two *Marius* and as many *Topaze*. I'm not talking about the money: I'm talking about the texts that I didn't write during that period. Finally, now my house is in order and the machine is running. It can even run without me, and I am becoming a writer again.

Unfortunately, the high operating expenses of his expanding empire soon put Pagnol under financial pressure and left him feeling 'pâle de terreur, la machine que j'avais passionnément construite me dévora' (pale with terror; the machine that I had enthusiastically built devoured me) (Pagnol 2008: 21). In the end his dream of becoming France's most powerful cinema mogul was dashed by the restrictions of the Occupation, which by mid-1942 had obliged him to liquidate his cinemas, labs, and studios.

Publicly, however, Pagnol's worries remained hidden from view and his unique approach to filmmaking drew nearly constant media attention, affording him a level of celebrity normally reserved for France's best-loved on-screen talent. By combining the business acumen of a large industrialist with the craftsmanship of a small artisan, he personified a French socio-economic ideal: profitability and efficiency without sacrificing quality or exacerbating class tensions and the other dehumanising effects so often associated with large-scale capitalism during the mid-1930s. Even Jean Renoir, who lobbied tirelessly in favour of nationalising the film industry, expressed admiration for Pagnol's philosophy of rugged self-sufficiency.

> Le cinéma français existe parce qu'il y a encore des indépendants, des gens qui ne sont pas soumis aux trusts. La plupart de mes collègues, du plus petit au plus illustre, travaillent pour les grandes maisons américaines ou pour la Tobis et la UFA, qui sont sous le contrôle de Hitler et Goebbels. Je ne les blâme pas. Il faut bien vivre. Je blâme les pouvoirs publics qui laissent nos adversaires s'emparer lentement, mais sûrement, de notre marché national. Rendons hommage à Marcel Pagnol qui s'est soustrait à toutes ces combinaisons, et qui est resté absolument libre. On aime ou on n'aime pas ses films, mais ce qu'il dit, il le pense et il ne va pas prendre de mot d'ordre nulle part. (Renoir 1938).[4]

Renoir implemented that method himself in late 1934 by borrowing Pagnol's equipment and technicians to make *Toni* on location near

---

4 French cinema exists because there are still independents, people who are not beholden to the trusts. Most of my peers, from the lowest to the most famous, work for the big American companies or for Tobis and UFA, which are under the direct control of Hitler and Goebbels. I don't blame them. I blame the public officials who are letting our adversaries slowly but surely take over our national market. Let us pay tribute to Marcel Pagnol for avoiding such schemes and remaining absolutely free. One either likes or doesn't like his films, but he says what he thinks and he doesn't take orders from anyone.

Marseilles. He later credited the shoot with allowing him to experience for the first time 'cette liberté d'esprit et de corps sans laquelle personne au monde n'est capable de faire du bon travail' (that freedom of mind and body without which no one in the world is capable of doing good work) (Renoir 1938a: 286).

Consciously mimicking the practices of his idol Molière, Pagnol worked consistently with a small band of collaborators who formed a loyal 'troupe' around him for much of the decade. By living together on location in the countryside during the shooting of *Angèle* and *Regain*, they acquired the reputation as living counterparts to the cohesive micro-communities celebrated on-screen in Pagnol's films. Journalists eagerly promoted this meta-textual narrative, reinforcing the appeal of his work as a symbolic antidote to national decadence and a source of French cultural renewal. 'Peu d'auteurs dramatiques célèbres ont autant de simplicité vraie et d'affable cordialité' (Few famous dramatic authors have as much genuine simplicity and affable warmth), wrote a reporter for *La Cinématographie française* in 1936 after visiting Aubignane.

> Il n'est pas de Marseillais plus populaire, plus admiré, et plus aimé. Mais ce qu'il faut surtout admirer, c'est l'esprit d'équipe qui règne entre le 'patron' et ses collaborateurs. C'est un grand exemple de probe labeur, de solidarité, de confiant enthousiasme que nous donne Marcel Pagnol en un temps où l'insécurité de l'avenir paralyse tout effort courageux et toute production soutenue. (Epardaud 1936)[5]

The succulent communal meals prepared during filming by actor Charles Blavette, an accomplished amateur chef, as well as the spirited games of *pétanque* and stories told by Pagnol between takes became the stuff of legend in the popular press, which offered readers a glimpse of these convivial scenes in a constant stream of publicity photos (see Figure 16). *Angèle* was all the more captivating for cinema audiences since it was the first French sound picture to be made entirely outdoors on location. The account that ran in France's largest daily paper, *Paris-Soir*, was typical in its lyricism:

---

[5] There is no more popular, more admired, and better loved Marseillais. But special admiration is reserved for the team spirit that unites the 'boss' and his collaborators. Marcel Pagnol provides a wonderful example of honest labour, solidarity, and confident enthusiasm at a time when an uncertain future seems to be paralysing all initiative and productivity.

> Des Camoins à Marcellin, il y a environ huit kilomètres d'une route en lacets, surplombant de magnifiques vallées et bordée de lavande qui dégagent une odeur pénétrante. A droite, à gauche, les hautes collines semblent écraser la maisonnette autour de laquelle, pareils à des fourmis, les hommes s'agitent. On travaille beaucoup là-bas et c'est avec plaisir que l'on voit arriver l'heure du déjeuner. C'est le meilleur moment de la journée. On discute, on blague, on joue aux boules, une charmante camaraderie règne entre tous les gens de la troupe. La rivalité entre l'image et le son, Willy et Lecocq, fait la joie de tous. Marcel Pagnol, entre deux plats, déguste un pastis et ajoute quelques mots en souriant. (Godefroy 1934)[6]

Thanks to such accounts, the making of *Angèle* and *Regain* became real-life allegories of the return to the earth dramatised in the films, with all the attendant associations of healthful open-air living, pleasure in hard work, and above all rediscovery of true community and cultural authenticity. 'Nous sommes tous devenus de vrais paysans' (We all became real peasants), Orane Demazis proudly told a reporter while shooting *Regain*. 'Personne d'entre nous n'a eu un seul instant l'impression de jouer. Descendus de voiture, nous entrions dans le village, le vrai village en pierres, et c'était une vraie vie qui commençait pour nous' (None of us felt for a single instant as though we were acting. When we got out of the car, we entered the village, the real stone village, and a new existence began for us) (Wahl 1937).

Based on her experiences playing Fanny in the Marseilles Trilogy, Demazis knew the utility of blurring the line between fact and fiction, which for her involved playing up her screen image as a peasant mother by including in the interview the son she had with Pagnol. Whatever the case, readers were treated to a taste of charmingly naïve commentary by the 3-and-a-half-year-old Jean-Pierre, a 'solide petit gars' (solid little guy) who reportedly expressed his desire to stay in

---

6 Camoins and Marcellin are separated by 8 kilometres of winding road overlooking magnificent valleys and bordered with lavender that gives off a pungent odour. To the right and left, high hills seems poised to crush the small house around which men busy themselves like ants. There is much to do down there and the arrival of the lunch hour is much appreciated. People talk, joke, play pétanque, and a charming camaraderie unites the members of the troupe. The rivalry between the image and sound technicians, Willy and Lecocq, amuses everyone thoroughly. Between two courses, Marcel Pagnol savours a glass of pastis and smiles while interjecting a few words.

the countryside away from Paris as long as possible. Given by many members of the cast and crew, such interviews provided the public evidence that in Pagnol's cinema, art perfectly imitated real life, and vice versa. Spectators who attended a Pagnol film were thus encouraged not to see actors simply playing the roles of peasants, but urbanites like themselves actually transforming into peasants before their very eyes, as Demazis contended.

For a nation plagued by a sense of its own decadence, such a suspension of disbelief in the fiction of *Angèle* and *Regain* had a powerful psychological pay-off, heightening the films' reassurance value as a manifestation of French cultural renewal. Little matter that the 'real stone village' of Aubignane was in fact a custom-built movie set or that it had never been nor would ever be home to a single genuine peasant. As for Demazis, she was a city slicker and society woman of the first order, but that identity made her supposed transformation all the more captivating and allowed her to indulge in some promotional hyperbole. When asked about the cast's plans after finishing the film, she replied: 'Nous allons faire la moisson et nous amuser à la foire du pays, puis nous attendrons le jugement des villes' (We are going to do some harvesting and have fun at the local fair, then we will wait for urbanites to judge the film). The idea of a prominent leading lady such as Demazis actually performing the hard physical labour of harvesting wheat was of course ludicrous, yet journalists and spectators willingly suspended disbelief in the off-screen return to the earth surrounding Pagnol's rural films.

A national hero

In addition to their appeal as allegories of French national cohesion, Pagnol's films offered compelling evidence that French cinema could hold its own against better-financed, technologically superior American and German competitors. Told with great delectation, this part of the meta-narrative adopted the conventions of a classic French folktale in which the protagonist, inevitably a 'little guy' overmatched in size and strength, conquers adversity and bests his more powerful rivals through cunning and ingenuity (Darnton 1984: 59–65). In an early 1937 article for the fan magazine *Ciné-France*, Roger Régent described Pagnol's working habits in exactly those terms:

Pagnol à l'œuvre, c'est un spectacle! J'imagine l'ahurissement d'un metteur en scène américain, habitué à l'incroyable perfection technique des studios d'Hollywood, allant rendre visite à Marcel Pagnol dans son impasse des Peupliers! On est en pleine bohème, dans la fantaisie jusqu'aux oreilles! Les décors sont construits au fur et à mesure, et si on ferme la porte pour tourner, c'est parce que les machines d'une chocolaterie voisine troublent le silence de l'impasse. Alors, on décide de réaliser les scènes difficiles le samedi après-midi, parce que la chocolaterie fait la semaine anglaise! (Régent 1937)[7]

Here the reference to working only on weekdays, the so-called 'semaine anglaise', functions as a strong marker of French difference from Anglo-American culture, with Pagnol's willingness to shoot on Saturday afternoons suggesting both a superior work ethic and enhanced creativity through improvisation. Though the image of Pagnol labouring on a Saturday may on the surface seem inconsistent with his reputation as convivial pétanque player and pastis drinker, this aspect of the narrative does not reveal a contradiction so much as it exemplifies the French belief that one must strike a balance between work and leisure in order to lead a meaningful, fulfilling life – this in contrast to American, British, and German cultures that supposedly prioritise work and productivity above all else. For visiting observers as well as his actors and crew, Pagnol took that ideal a step further, blending the necessary with the pleasurable so that the two became indistinguishable. As Fernandel told an interviewer shortly after the release of *Regain*: 'Avec Marcel Pagnol, faire un film, c'est d'abord manger une bouillabaisse entre amis, parler de la pluie et du beau temps, et enfin, s'il reste un moment, on tourne quelques scènes' (With Marcel Pagnol, making a film means first eating a fish soup with friends, chatting about the weather, and finally, if there is a moment to spare, shooting a few scenes) (Millaud 1937).

Yet Pagnol's appeal as a national folk hero ran deeper than his talent for Gallic *savoir vivre*. From mid-1934 on, a steady parade of

[7] Pagnol at work is a spectacle! I imagine the stupefaction of an American director, accustomed to the incredible technical perfection of Hollywood studios, visiting Pagnol in his small Marseilles facility. One is immersed in a bohemian fantasy. The sets are built as needed, and if someone closes the door while shooting, it's because the machinery of a neighbouring chocolate maker is disturbing the silence of the cul-de-sac. So the decision is made to shoot challenging scenes on Saturday afternoon because the chocolate maker works does not work on weekends.

reporters brought readers first-hand accounts of his exploits during location shooting, which during the making of *Angèle* purportedly ranged from dynamiting massive boulders blocking his trucks' path on narrow, serpentine access roads to quenching the thirst of his crew by magically locating underground springs. One spirited account read in part:

> Saviez-vous que Marcel Pagnol, cumulait outre ses dons naturels, celui du sourcier? Lors d'une pause dans le tournage, ce fut Pagnol lui-même qui découvrit, à très peu de profondeur, une nappe d'eau. Cette découverte se fit en présence de plusieurs personnes desséchées qui restèrent surprises de la facilité avec laquelle l'auteur de *Fanny* maniait la baguette de coudrier. Fernandel voulut l'imiter, mais il ne savait pas et la baguette se mit à remuer violemment au point de tordre le poignet du sympathique artiste. (Reboul 1934)[8]

Like the trickster characters omnipresent in French storytelling from Puss in Boots and Tom Thumb of early modern folktales, to Scapin and Scaramouche in Molière's plays, to twentieth-century comic-book hero Astérix the Gaul, Pagnol was cast as a real-life cinematic trickster who symbolically defended his nation's cultural style against threatening foreign juggernauts. The editor-in-chief of France's main corporate film journal praised *Angèle* specifically for having been made 'sans concession à la rigueur mathématique des découpages et des montages à l'américaine' (without succumbing to the mathematical rigour of American shooting and editing methods (Harlé 1934). Not to be outdone, a reviewer from Toulon crowed that 'il faut pouvoir dire avant tout et sans nationalisme qu'en face des idioties américaines, une bande comme *Angèle* fait honneur à la France' (above all, and without nationalism, one must be allowed to say that in comparison with American-made idiocies, a picture like *Angèle* does honour to France) (Merentir 1934).

When an interviewer characterised *Angèle* as 'inexportable' (unexportable) because of its slow, dialogue-heavy style and asked Pagnol

---

8 Did you know that water divining is among Marcel Pagnol's natural talents? During a break in the shooting, it was Pagnol himself who discovered water not far below the ground. That discovery was made in the presence of several parched persons who were surprised by the expertise with which the author of *Fanny* handled the hazelwood rod. Fernandel tried to imitate him, but he did not know how and the wand began to tremble violently enough to sprain the amiable actor's wrist.

whether he would ever make Hollywood-style films to boost French box-office revenue abroad, the filmmaker replied: 'Votre objection est uniquement d'ordre commercial. Ce genre de films, où tout est sacrifié à l'image, est essentiellement international. Je n'ai fait jusqu'ici que des films français destinés avant tout au public français' (Your objection is of a purely commercial nature. That type of film, which sacrifices everything to the image, is essentially international. Thus far I've only made French films intended for a French audience) (Novy 1935). Orane Demazis defended Pagnol's slow-moving, dialogue-heavy style in even more emphatic terms:

> Sa méthode a du bon, les résultats l'ont prouvé. Il me serait pénible de me plier aux formules américaines, à ces saccades, à ces césures, à ces heurts qui vous morcellent et vous dispersent tout au long de l'intrigue, faisant que l'acteur dépend presque entièrement des spécialistes du montage. (Jauniaux 1934)[9]

In this strikingly anthropomorphic account, American filmmaking methods caused a painful dismemberment of artistic consciousness, whereas Pagnol's approach safeguarded both the actor's sensibility and the continuity of the film as a whole. More generally, the comparison suggests the dehumanising, socially destructive effects of American business and implicitly validates French culture as more humane and cohesive.

The flaws that critics often distinguished in Pagnol's 'cinématurgie' thus became assets as a patriotic counterpoint to foreign competition. Even critics who deplored Pagnol's disdain for the visual aspects of filmmaking applauded his work for exemplifying the French national character. Lucien Rebatet could thus dismiss Pagnol's photography as 'd'une composition quelconque' (haphazardly composed) and his editing as 'médiocre, par endroits détestable' (mediocre, in places reprehensible), yet conclude approvingly that 'Pagnol sait être de chez lui dans un métier où la plupart du temps on est de nulle part' (Pagnol knows how to be French in a profession where most of the time one is from nowhere) (Rebatet 1934).

The quip that the majority of those working in French cinema came from 'nowhere' was a xenophobic allusion to the many technicians

9 His method has its advantages; the results prove so. I would find it unpleasant to bow to American conventions, to the abrupt cuts, breaks, and jolts that cut you into pieces and redistribute you across the story, leaving the actor almost entirely dependent on the editors.

and artistic personnel from central and eastern Europe, many of them Jews, who had come to France in the late 1920s and early 1930s. Though these immigrants enhanced the technical quality and stylistic range of French national production, contributing in particular to the emergence of poetic realism (Phillips 2003), they were frequently blamed for the myriad of problems that plagued French cinema in light of the highly publicised scandals surrounding Ukranian-born financier Alexandre Stavisky and transplanted Romanian producer Bernard Natan (Trumpbour 2002: 231–9). Echoing the justifications used by Hitler in 1933 to exclude Jews and other 'undesirable' foreigners from German cinema, French commentators of all political colours demanded the 'sanitisation' of their industry as a necessary step towards recovering economic solvency and national grandeur.

In mid-1934 film labour unions established quotas stipulating that non-citizens could not exceed 10 per cent of the major artistic personnel or 25 per cent of the total crew on any given production. In his successful novella *France la Doulce* published that same year, Paul Morand offered a darkly satirical behind-the-scenes look at the making of a 'typically French' feature film by scheming Moldavian Jews, noting that 'en écrivant ce livre, je demande seulement pour nos compatriotes une place, une toute petite place, dans le cinéma national. En défendant les Français, je revendique simplement le droit des minorités' (by writing this book, I am simply requesting a small place for our compatriots in our film industry. By defending the French, I am simply asserting the rights of a minority) (Morand 2005: 358).

Appeals for more severe measures flourished and became increasingly violent in tone as unemployment figures rose and the economic crisis deepened. By mid-1938 the same industry observers who lauded Pagnol were openly calling for a 'une Saint-Barthélemy du cinéma, qui ne sera plus le massacre d'innocents, mais le geste qui nettoiera notre industrie à tous les étages' (a new Saint Bartholomew's Day [the state-sponsored massacre of Protestants by Catholics in 1572] which this time will not be a massacre of innocents, but an act that will clean up all levels of our industry) (Reboul 1938). A few months later a film labour union conducted a census of foreigners employed in Paris studios and called for the immediate revocation of all work visas granted during the previous three years, limiting foreigners to 10 per cent of the total workforce, and forbidding them from Gallicising their names to escape detection (Anon. 1938a).

Satirical xenophobia in *Le Schpountz*

Such anxieties further reinforced Pagnol's reputation as the champion of Franco-French filmmaking – an image he emphatically underscored in *Le Schpountz*. Starring Fernandel as Irénée Fabre, a naïve small-town clerk who blunders his way to a successful movie career in comedy, the picture satirises the French cinema industry by detailing the swindles of a Jewish film producer from central Europe named Meyerboom, who with his partner Yaourt runs the ironically named 'Compagnie Française du Film Français'. In a meeting with his attorney, Meyerboom unabashedly explains how to create a movie on paper and divert investors' money to fund a different project through a Byzantine web of fake contracts. When Meyerboom's lawyer, thoroughly scandalised, objects in the name of honesty, the producer replies: 'Vous comprenez, je suis juif' (You understand, I'm Jewish).

Pagnol is equally scathing in his caricature of imaginary expatriate director Bogidar Glazounow, described as 'un Allemand ou un Turc, qui a pris un nom russe et parle avec un accent italien, ce qui lui a permis de devenir un grand metteur en scène français' (a German or a Turk, who took a Russian surname and speaks with an Italian accent, which allowed him to become a great French director). Hired by Meyerboom to remake Abel Gance's 1927 epic *Napoléon*, Glazounow speaks a variety of French whose comical atrocity is matched only by his incompetence in directing, and histrionics when things go awry.

While in some respects the film echoes Morand's *France la Doulce* and the real-life accusations of fraud levelled against Bernard Natan in 1936, Pagnol also undermines xenophobic, anti-Semitic stereotypes by humanising Meyerboom as pitiable and even sympathetic. When a mischievous production crew tricks Irénée into sabotaging the climactic scene of the big-budget epic about Napoléon, Meyerboom is upset not by their lack of professionalism or the significant financial cost incurred, but that he was not invited to participate. He tells them so in a monologue lamenting the alienation that wealth creates and the sadness of growing old alone. Shortly thereafter, he compassionately offers the humiliated Irénée a job in the studio's accessory department so that the aspiring actor will not have to return home in shame.

That equivocation drew criticism on both sides of the political spectrum upon the film's release in April 1938. The socialist weekly *La Lumière* expressed disappointment with Pagnol, noting that 'on pourrait applaudir de bon cœur une attaque en règle contre certains milieux cinématographiques si la xénophobie n'en faisait un peu trop souvent les frais' (one could readily applaud a legitimate attack on certain elements of the film industry if not for the xenophobia that too often accompanies it) (Decaris 1938). In the Popular Front's official weekly, Pierre Bost puzzled over what to make of 'le producteur véreux, qui a servi de prétexte à un couplet antisémite absolument navrant, et qui fait tout à coup, sans aucune espèce de raison, un discours sur la tristesse de vieillir' (the sleazy producer, who serves as a pretext for a thoroughly deplorable anti-Semitic line, and who suddenly, without any reason at all, gives a speech on the sadness of growing old) (Bost 1938).

Right-wing commentators were equally frustrated by Pagnol's equivocation. Jean Fayard enthusiastically endorsed the caricature of 'un affreux faisan juif qui ne vit que de combines' (an awful Jewish shark who lives only on swindles), but deplored the attempt 'de nous attendrir sur le bandit qui se sent isolé par son âge. Il fallait choisir' (to make us feel sympathy for the crook who feels isolated by his age. Pagnol needed to choose) (Fayard 1938). Lucien Rebatet was more dissatisfied still, arguing that:

> tout le bénéfice de la satire est perdu. Pagnol nous indique que si Meyerboom a un certain nombre d'irrégularités sur sa conscience, son cas n'est pas pendable. Ces Juifs sont, après tout, de bonnes pâtes d'hommes, au chèque facile, le cœur sur la main, et Pagnol semble bien conclure qu'on ne saurait se passer d'eux. (Rebatet 1938).[10]

Significantly, there is no evidence to suggest that Pagnol was himself an anti-Semite. On the contrary, he had numerous Jewish friends and colleagues: Alexander Korda, who taught him the basics of filmmaking while shooting *Marius*; cinematographer Willy Faktorovich, a naturalised citizen originally from Kiev who provided the film's title, 'schpountz' being a Yiddish slang term for an irritating groupie such as those who flocked to Pagnol's outdoor shooting locations with the hope of appearing on-screen; most notably, writer Albert Cohen, a childhood classmate from Marseilles. In a December

10 All the benefit of the satire is lost. Pagnol points out that if Meyerboom has a certain number of irregularities on his conscience, he doesn't deserve to be hanged. These Jews are, after all, essentially good, financially generous men who wear their hearts on their sleeve, and Pagnol clearly seems to conclude that we could not do without them.

1938 review article for *Les Nouvelles littéraires*, Pagnol denounced the Kristallnacht pogrom carried out a month earlier by the Nazis in Berlin and welcomed Cohen's novel *Mangeclous* as an important step towards dissipating anti-Semitic prejudice.

> Ce qu'il faudrait, tout d'abord, ce serait de nous expliquer les Juifs, nous les faire comprendre, nous les faire aimer ... Toujours bernés mais jamais déçus, ses personnages sont toujours prêts à croire et à espérer. Ils sont vivants. Ils n'ont rien de ces Juifs schématiques qu'on voit dans certains romans pour illustrer une thèse ou pour symboliser tel aspect de l'âme juive *ad usum gentilium*. Ils sont Juifs comme on est Breton ou Basque ou Marseillais.[11] (Pagnol 1938a)

Seen in relation to *Le Schpountz*, Pagnol's praise of Cohen can be understood as an implicit critique of his own awkward attempt to accomplish the same goal. The last sentence in particular speaks to Pagnol's intentions: Jews may have their own distinct cultural identity, but they are no less French than any other regional minority, including the characters in the Marseilles Trilogy or the filmmaker himself. That reading is consistent with his initial response to the scandal surrounding the film: less than a week after its release he took the unusual and expensive measure of recalling all copies in circulation and removing the entire scene between Meyerboom and the lawyer.

In one sense an act of conscience that defied xenophobic, right-wing reviewers such as Fayard and Rebatet, the decision was almost certainly also intended to protect Pagnol's image and his financial interests by erasing any appearance of anti-Semitism that might alienate potential clients. Indeed, it was likely the same commercial logic that had initially prompted Pagnol to engage in Jewish carica-ture, which by 1938 was a well-established and profitable convention in French cinema. The actor he cast to play Meyerboom, Léon Bélières, was already famous for playing miserly yet sympathetic businessman Moïse Lévy in a series of successful comedies directed by André Hugon: *Lévy et compagnie* (1930), *Les galeries Lévy et compagnie* (1932),

---

11 What would be required, first of all, is to explain Jews to us, to make us understand them, to make us love them ... Always downtrodden yet never dispirited, his characters are always ready to believe and to hope. They are alive. They bear no resemblance to the one-dimensional Jews that one sees in certain novels to illustrate an argument or symbolise for Gentiles some aspect of the Jewish soul. They are Jewish as one is Breton or Basque or Marseillais.

Moïse et Salomon, parfumeurs (1935), and *Les mariages de Mademoiselle Lévy* (1936) (Sorlin 1981). Ever the ambitious opportunist, Pagnol was not above suspending his personal convictions to exploit prevailing cultural stereotypes as a means of enhancing the public appeal and commercial value of his work.

Once the incriminating scene was removed, *Le Schpountz* quickly regained crucial favour. André Antoine noted his satisfaction at seeing 'une satire et une critique impitoyables des mœurs et des gens de l'écran' (a merciless satire and critique of the film industry mores and people), concluding that 'l'ensemble forme un spectacle d'une substance et d'une saveur vraiment nouvelles' (the final product is a spectacle of truly original substance and flavour) (Antoine 1938). In the end most reviewers concurred with René Bizet, who concluded approvingly that 'Pagnol a une verve purement française. Il est le seul dont la bouffonnerie soit dans son genre comparable à l'humour anglo-saxon, et soit spécifiquement de chez nous' (Pagnol has a purely French wit. He is the only one whose bawdy comedy is a distinct genre comparable to Anglo-American humour and is specifically our own) (Bizet 1938). Spectators agreed, making *Le Schpountz* the fourteenth highest-grossing film of 1938 according to a poll of theatre owners (Crisp 2002: 300).

Resisting Hollywood

At the same time he satirised foreigners working in the film industry, Pagnol publicly denounced the government's failure to support French cinema and make it competitive internationally. 'Non seulement on ne nous donne pas les moyens de nous défendre' (Not only are we not given the means to defend ourselves), he told Henri Jeanson, 'on nous désarme, on nous bâillonne, on nous ligote et on nous livre à Hollywood' (we are disarmed, gagged, tied up, and delivered to Hollywood). Pagnol added bitterly that with the exception of his own work, the theatre he owned in Marseilles projected mostly American films 'qui se louent pour rien chez nous parce qu'ils sont déjà amortis. Pour quelques centaines de francs, j'ai un grand film récent, les actualités, un documentaire et un dessin animé. Avec la recette d'un soir, je paye mes frais de la semaine. Tout le reste est bénéfice (which rent for nothing here because their production costs have already been recouped at home. For a few hundred francs, I get a recent feature film, a newsreel, a documentary, and an animated short. One evening's receipts pay my expenses for the week. The rest is profit) (Jeanson 1939).

Even after selling his studios, laboratories, and cinemas Pagnol continued to lobby for protection against American competition. In June 1946 he published an open letter that gave voice to industry-wide outrage over the Léon Blum–James Byrnes trade agreement abolishing all French restrictions and taxes on Hollywood imports in exchange for massive loan forgiveness, additional credit, and the bulk purchase of desperately needed products such as wheat and petrol at reduced rates (Crisp 1993: 73–7). Printed in *France-Soir*, the country's largest-circulation newspaper, Pagnol's acerbic text characterised the agreement as a misguided 'sacrifice' intended to save France economically that would quickly turn to economic and cultural 'suicide' by ensuring unchecked Americanisation. While referring to the United States as 'la plus noble et la plus puissante nation du monde' (the most noble and the most powerful nation in the world) and thanking it for liberating France, he equated Hollywood's high-volume, low-cost 'dumping' practises with Nazi film propaganda disseminated during the Occupation.

Within five years, Pagnol claimed, 'nos enfants penseront américain, ils s'habilleront à l'américaine, ils parleront anglais, ils voudront des stylos américains, des barattes, des Frigidaires' (our children will think American, they will dress American, they will speak American, they will want American pens, barrettes, and Frigidaires) (Pagnol 1946). Pagnol concluded by accusing Blum 'de nous avoir vendu à l'Amérique au prix de 250 milliards' (having sold us to America for 250 billion francs) and demanding that the government provide French filmmakers a production subsidy of 5 billion francs as well as American-made colour filmstock – at the time a rare and expensive commodity – to make their work technologically competitive.

Although neither Pagnol's sensationalistic predictions nor the concessions he sought ever materialised, over the next year the American share of the French market did increase dramatically from 41 to 54 per cent. Responding to a new wave of outrage, in September 1948 the Centre National de la Cinématographie began subsidising domestic production via an additional tax on ticket sales (Crisp 1993: 76–7). By that time the maverick director had already taken combating

American hegemony into his own hands by shooting *La Belle Meunière* with an experimental colour process invented by French engineers Lucien and Armand Roux. In contrast to other existing colour technologies, Rouxcolor was optical rather than chemical in nature and involved recording four separate images per frame on standard black-and-white filmstock, then combining them into a single colour image during projection via a set of filters.

Seduced by the new invention's high quality and lower cost compared to American Technicolor, Pagnol saw it as a magic bullet that would liberate France from its dependence on imported filmstock, restore the French cinema industry to financial stability, and finally make it a serious rival to Hollywood on the international market (Pagnol 2008: 121–31). Yet theatre owners were reluctant to invest in the expensive, specialised equipment required for projection. A *New York Times* correspondent who attended the premiere of *La Belle Meunière* in Paris noted that the film 'was applauded for its technical magnificence and derided for its outrageous miscasting [of Tino Rossi as Franz Schubert]' (James 1948). Predictably, the film was a commercial flop and definitively put an end to Rouxcolor.

A marketing pioneer

While proudly proclaiming his commitment to artisanal, quintessentially Gallic production methods, from the outset of his career Pagnol embraced mass-market capitalism by using American promotional strategies learned from Paramount during the making of *Marius*. As he bluntly wrote in the first issue of *Les Cahiers du film*: 'Un art, pour réaliser ses œuvres d'abord et pour les répandre ensuite, a besoin d'être nourri par un commerce. Pour faire plaisir aux idéalistes, disons que ce commerce est le fumier qui nourrit la fleur' (All art, from its initial creation to its subsequent dissemination, needs to be fed by a business. To placate idealists, let's say that this business is the manure that feeds the flower) (Pagnol 1933: 3). Combined with his redefinition of sound cinema as a machine for recording and disseminating theatre, Pagnol's rejection of art as the pursuit of an aesthetic ideal beyond vulgar material considerations incurred enduring scorn and unacknowledged envy from many French critics. Like the dull-witted villains in classic folktales, they failed to understand that public accusations of venality and technical incompetence had exactly the opposite of their intended effect, providing Pagnol an invaluable opportunity to establish and perpetually renew his image as a champion of the common people against elitism. He never tired of asserting that the success or failure of his work lay exclusively in the hands of the public and that 'la critique est absolument impuissante à le détourner d'un film qui lui plaît, comme elle ne peut lui imposer un film qui l'ennuie' (critics are utterly powerless to dissuade it from a film that it likes, just as they cannot force upon it a film that it finds boring) (Pagnol 1995: I, 1039).

In his *Critique des critiques* (1949) he revealed the extent to which that dynamic depended on his own carefully orchestrated marketing campaign.

> Les journaux de cinéma ont raconté la vie privée de mes acteurs, on a inventé des échos pittoresques sur les incidents survenus pendant la réalisation; le metteur en scène a donné des interviews, dont le texte, rédigé par mon spécialiste, fut illustré de photos choisies par moi. On a ainsi déclenché dans le public du cinéma une vive curiosité qui sera ensuite savamment entretenue. (Pagnol 1995: I, 1037–8)[12]

Pagnol's philosophy was simple: use saturation advertising to create 'une trompette géante qui sonne le rappel du public et auprès duquel les plus bruyants de nos critiques ne font que musique de chambre' (a giant trumpet that calls the public to it and beside which even the noisiest critics make only chamber music) (Pagnol 1995: I, 1038).

In practice this meant spending several hundred thousand francs to flood mass-circulation film magazines and general newspapers with publicity in the weeks immediately preceding and following the release of each new picture. For example, between June and December 1934 photo spreads promoting *Angèle* appeared on the cover of every significant French cinema fan magazine and corporate journal at least once; twice for *Pour Vous* and *Ciné-Miroir*; three times for *Cinémonde*. A related move consisted of negotiating long-term screening agreements with exclusive theatres in Paris while his films were still in production to guarantee a profit. On rare occasions

---

12 Film magazines have recounted the private lives of my actors; we have invented picturesque echoes of things that happened during production; the director gave interviews written by my specialist and illustrated with photos that I chose. We have thus sparked among the movie-going public a strong curiosity that will be skilfully maintained.

when the previous success of his work proved an insufficient signing incentive, he sometimes offered theatre owners cash advances above the minimums guaranteed by standard rental contracts. The value of *Angèle* was such that it enjoyed the unusual distinction of premiering simultaneously in Paris at three normally exclusive-contract theatres on 26 October 1934, running for an exceptionally long fifteen weeks at the *Ciné-Opéra* and seven weeks each at the *Agriculteurs* and *Bonaparte*.

Adopting a systematised approach that was not widely used by French producers or distributors at the time, Pagnol's publicity department sent a mass mailing of marketing prospectuses to provincial theatre owners within three weeks of each new film's release in the capital. These glossy *manuels de publicité*, whose dual purpose was to incite competition for rental contracts and to assist already-signed clients in preparing their own local advertising campaigns, consisted of four to six pages divided into three sections. The first compiled fifteen to twenty laudatory excerpts from reviews in prominent Paris newspapers and magazines, systematically eliminating any shadow of criticism and in some cases misrepresenting the overall tenor of the reviewers' comments. The second showed the various mural poster designs (typically five to seven) available in formats ranging from small 60 x 80 centimetre single sheets for lobby display to 320 x 240 centimetre, four-sheet monsters intended as outdoor façade decoration. The third and final section offered a selection of five or six illustrated black-and-white newspaper advertisements. Beyond achieving an exceptional degree of efficiency in communicating with exhibitors, Pagnol's system balanced variety with continuity, ensuring that promotional materials were readily available for every size theatre and budget while maintaining visual coherence and an easily recognisable brand image from one picture to the next.

Pagnol worked consistently with three of the era's most talented graphic artists. The first was Henri Cerutti, a trained lithographer who began drawing film posters in 1929 at the age of 18 and quickly earned a reputation as an industry leader (Auzel 1988: 240). He worked on all but one of Pagnol's pre-war films, highlighting their dramatic power through a realist style that placed near-photographic likenesses of the actors in evocative poses against multi-layered, carefully filtered and stylised backgrounds. The wistful black-and-blue poster he prepared for *Fanny* instantly captures the unavoidable tragedy of Marius' wanderlust: in the foreground Pierre Fresnay and Orane Demazis look longingly upwards across the Old Port towards towering three-mast sailboats – she with anguish, he with resolve – while Notre Dame de la Garde, presumptive site of the couple's aborted wedding, Fanny's tortured pilgrimage after learning of her pregnancy, and her subsequent loveless marriage to Panisse, looms partially obscured in the background (see Figure 17). In his poster for *Angèle*, Cerutti made more explicit use of the same motif to emphasise the female protagonist's predicament and salvation: Orane Demazis, now at the centre of the image and surrounded by the film's other characters, absorbs their gazes while herself looking sorrowfully towards nothing into the distance, unaware that her eventual rescuer Albin is watching over her from above, leaning against a tree in an idyllic landscape (see Figure 18).

In mid-1933 Pagnol recruited another rising star to head his newly founded publicity department: Antoine Antona, a young political cartoonist for *Le Petit Marseillais* newspaper known to readers under the pen name Toé (Capitaine 1988: 79). He soon proved himself one of the most innovative and efficient French publicists of the decade, drawing recognition from *La Cinématographie française* on two occasions as 'exceptionnel' (outstanding) for his creation of lobby cards that blended still photos with text to promote *Angèle* and *La Femme du boulanger* (Derain 1937; Guimberlaud 1938). The modular poster system that he conceived to launch *Regain* – four 120 x 160 centimetre images of the film's four principal stars accompanied by a separate band of text to be placed below – drew special praise for offering theatre owners the flexibility to create different configurations and emphasise the actors preferred by their clientele. The system was used with particular success in the Paris subway 'où on ne pouvait faire un pas sans voir ce panneau, le premier de ce genre' (where one could not take a step without seeing this display, the first of its type) (Anon. 1937) (see Figure 19).

Like Pagnol, Toé took a hands-on approach to his duties that involved drawing numerous promotional images for newspapers and magazines, writing advertising copy, and designing posters. Whereas Cerutti highlighted the pathos of Pagnol's work by evoking the complex emotional bonds between characters, Toé devoted himself to accentuating the comedic through individual caricature that identified the defining trait actors brought to their respective roles: Charpin's smiling, gentle Panisse; Raimu's bug-eyed, ever-exasperated César;

and Fernandel's naïvely affable grin as both Saturnin in *Angèle* and Irenée Fabre in *Le Schpountz* (see Figure 20).

The stylistic link between Cerutti and Toé's poster designs was provided by Albert Dubout, another Marseillais renowned for his skills as a caricaturist specialising in ribald, extraordinarily detailed crowd scenes. His collaboration with Pagnol began in 1936 with *César*, for which he crafted a massive four-sheet poster depicting Panisse's tragi-comic funeral procession set against the complex spatial and human geography of the Old Port (see Figure 21). Prior to the war Dubout produced only one other image for Pagnol – a memorably farcical representation of angry studio employees chasing the hapless Fernandel in *Le Schpountz* – but in 1945 he became the filmmaker's primary artist, designing original posters not only for *Naïs*, *Manon des sources*, and *Les Lettres de mon moulin*, but the 1950–51 rerelease of the Trilogy, *Angèle*, *Le Schpountz*, *La Femme du boulanger*, and *La Fille du puisatier* as well (Dubout 1994).

The effectiveness of Pagnol's marketing was further enhanced by the extensive use of test screenings, a Hollywood innovation which in the 1930s had just begun to catch on in Europe. Pagnol observed the effectiveness of the technique for the first time during the editing of *Marius*, when Paramount producer Robert Kane had used the technique to thwart studio executives' demands for extensive cuts (Anon. 1931). For a converted playwright intent on applying stage production practices to cinema, the technique naturally perpetuated his longstanding habit of recording audience reaction during the first performances, then reworking his text accordingly. With a cinema of his own at his disposal in Marseilles from September 1935 on, Pagnol enjoyed the rare ability to refine his screenplays during production by showing a reel or two to spectators after the advertised feature, or to inform his editing of the finished product by screening an entire rough cut after shooting wrapped (Jeanson 1939).

Most of the time these showings were impromptu, but those that were announced constituted valuable advertising in the days immediately preceding the film's official release as well as an opportunity for Pagnol to publicly snub professional critics and reaffirm the populist character of his work. As he wrote in a newspaper ad announcing the sneak preview of *La Femme du boulanger* in Marseilles: 'Le public collabore à toutes les œuvres dramatiques. C'est sur les réactions de la salle pleine que l'on choisit les coupures. Voilà pourquoi nous allons présenter officiellement notre dernier film à la seule critique digne de le juger. J'ai voulu connaître l'avis du public' (The public participates in the creation of all dramatic works. It's based on the reactions of a full theatre that one makes cuts. That is why we are going to officially present our latest film to the only critics worthy of judging it. I wanted to know the public's opinion) (Pagnol 1938b).

Yet in fact Pagnol sought to reach the broadest possible audience, testing *La Femme du boulanger* on a highbrow audience at the Lutétia cinema in Biarritz during the height of the summer resort season so that he could compare their reaction with that of working-class customers in Marseilles (Parrot-Lagarenne 1938; Anon. 1938b). He also recognised the importance of upholding certain standard industry practices and did regularly organise private advance showings for critics, as well as exclusive gala screenings in the capital. The Parisian release of *César* on 10 November 1936 was used to inaugurate a new luxury cinema on the Champs-Elysées named in honour of the film (Wolff 1936); the following fall *Regain*'s first public screening served as a fundraiser for the Fondation Lyautey, a youth education and leadership development programme focused on France's colonies (Régent 1937a).

To publicise *Regain* Pagnol employed another tactic that is today standard fare in the cinema industry but was virtually unknown in 1930s France: releasing a 24-minute 'making of' documentary about the construction of Aubignane. Shown in his Marseilles cinema and nationally through his various distribution agencies, the short film generated such interest that a bus company in Marseilles began running weekly excursions to the Marcellin valley. Within a few months souvenir hunters had begun to visibly dismantle the stone walls of Angèle's farmhouse and the village buildings on the overlooking bluff, necessitating the installation of signs claiming the presence of mines. That measure had little effect, and several years later the base of Aubignane's church clock tower had become so unstable that Pagnol had mason Marius Brouquier demolish it entirely (Labarthe 1966: I).

The release of *Regain* also marked his first foray into what is currently known as 'cluster merchandising'; that is, using the popularity of a film to sell related products. While photos of movie stars were often sold in French theatre lobbies during the 1930s, Les Films Pagnol was the first to offer spectators multiple sets of postcards recycling production photos previously disseminated in the press and complete screenplays in book form, illustrated with glossy still-frame images from the film. With a suggested retail price of five francs, these 'films que l'on peut lire' (films that one can read), as their cover put it, cost about the same as an average movie ticket and were a good value for spectators (Pagnol 1937, 1938c, 1938d). For exhibitors who purchased them wholesale at three-and-a-half francs and in some markets resold them at six or eight, they provided welcome supplementary income.

To achieve maximum effect, Toé's marketing prospectus suggested that exhibitors display the merchandise in their lobbies two weeks before the film's release just as they began running its 'trailer' announcement. Those who placed orders received not only a special version of the trailer promoting the books and postcards, but an assurance that unsold copies could be returned for a full refund (Toé 1937, 1938, 1938a). According to records subpoenaed by the court during the Giono–Pagnol lawsuit, the volumes devoted to *Regain* and *La Femme du boulanger* sold approximately 50,000 copies each – a figure that far surpassed the initial print runs of Giono's source texts (Anon. 1942).

In a related move that underscored Pagnol's attachment to 'cinématurgie' and defiance of critics who attacked him for prioritising word over image, he had Columbia Records release portions of the dialogue from *Marius*, *Fanny*, and *César* within a year of their cinematic premieres. Appearing in 78 rpm format on the company's 'Magic Notes' label in five-, four-, and six-disc sets, respectively, these excerpts capture the Trilogy's best moments of performative speech – most of them featuring Raimu – in both the comic and dramatic register: César explaining how to mix a 'proper' cocktail composed of four thirds over Marius' objections; the patriarch's stern warning to his son that 'honour is like matches' and 'can only be used once' when dealing with women; Marius' tearful, barely reciprocated 'I love you, Dad' just prior to his unannounced midnight departure; César's disingenuous diatribe to his friends claiming that he has no interest in receiving a letter from 'that unnatural navigator'; his excitedly dictating a reply through Fanny, then sending Marius away when he finally returns; Panisse's public deathbed confession; finally, the card games before and after the sailmaker's death that frame cheating as a heartfelt expression of friendship.

The *Marius* and *Fanny* recordings were among the most popular spoken-word recordings of the decade, reportedly selling several hundred thousand copies in addition to enjoying frequent radio broadcasts. As screenwriter and journalist Marcel Achard observed in late 1936, the single most popular disc contained the first card game, 'ce court chef-d'œuvre que le disque et la radio ont popularisé à un tel point que les jeunes Français d'aujourd'hui le connaissent mieux que leurs pères les imprécations de Camille et *Après la bataille* de Victor Hugo' (that short comic masterpiece that records and radio have popularised to such a degree that today young French men and women know it better than their parents did the rantings of Camille [in Pierre Corneille's classic play *Horace*] and Victor Hugo's poem *After the Battle*) (Achard 1936). Three years later another high-profile critic asserted that the *Fanny* records had made Escartefigue's indignant, unexpected retort to César's bullying – 'La Marine Française te dit "merde"!' (The French navy says 'shit' to you!) – 'l'une des deux répliques les plus connues de tout le théâtre français' (one of the two best-known lines in all of French theatre), the other being 'Rodrigue, as-tu du cœur?' (Rodrigue, have you any heart?) from Corneille's *Le Cid* (Jeanson 1939).

A proud international export

In addition to ensuring that his work reached virtually every town in metropolitan France with a functioning sound cinema, Pagnol's decidedly un-artisanal approach to marketing produced impressive results abroad as well. The voluminous books of press clippings preserved at the Compagnie Méditerranéenne de Films show that within a year of their release in Paris the Marseilles and rural trilogies enjoyed successful runs in French North Africa at Algiers, Tunis, Dakar, Casablanca, Fes, and Rabat, eventually reaching overseas outposts as far flung as Pointe-à-Pitre (Guadeloupe), St Denis (Réunion), Tananarive (Madagascar), Hanoi (Indochina), Nouméa (New Caledonia), and Djibouti (French Somaliland). Echoing the logic of economic competition and cultural expansion that fuelled French colonialism itself, expatriate cinema entrepreneurs often attempted to secure exclusive contracts by including gifts (coffee in particular) with their requests or stating their case as a matter of patriotic resistance against foreign encroachment. As Romuald Robert, proprietor of several theatres in Madagascar and Réunion put it:

Je suis dans l'océan indien le seul Français qui fait du cinéma. Comme nous sommes inondés de mauvais films américains, nous aimerions passer certains bons films français du genre *Fanny, Angèle*, ou *La Femme du boulanger*. Dès réception de cette lettre, fixez-moi votre prix et je vous ouvre paiement par la Banque coloniale de Marseilles. (Robert 1941)[13]

At a time when French officials were intent on disseminating the image of a strong, unified nation and earning foreign revenue to combat the ongoing economic crisis, Pagnol's films made perfect exports, not only for their thematic emphasis on social cohesion and moral redemption, but their creator's unique skill in marketing and familiarity to an international audience from his career as a playwright. Overtaxed and underfinanced, most French producers did not have the capital to invest in dubbing or subtitling their films for non-francophone markets. From 1930 on, French films sent to the United States faced the additional obstacle and expense of censorship under the infamous Production Code, which frequently required several months of negotiations and multiple rounds of editing prior to approval.

As a result, the potential world market for French pictures was typically limited to 75 million viewers and 5,000 theatres (3,800 of them in metropolitan France), whereas anglophone films benefited from a natural audience of 225 million served by 30,000 screens. Those endemic handicaps were exacerbated by disadvantageous film trade agreements negotiated with Germany in 1934 and the United States in 1936 which flooded France with high-quality foreign competition. Between 1935 and 1939 French-made films accounted for only 12 per cent of the imports shown in American theatres, while Hollywood's share in France rose from 47 per cent to 56 per cent. During the same period French producers' portion of their own domestic market slipped from 35 per cent to 29 per cent, the lowest level ever (Crisp 1993: 76; Leglise 1970: I, 261–70).

Several dossiers of contracts held at the CMF attest to the exceptionally broad international appeal of Pagnol's work. Between October 1937 and March 1941 *Angèle, Regain,* and *La Femme du boulanger* played

13 I am the only Frenchman in the Indian Ocean who works in cinema. Since we are flooded with bad American films, we would like to show certain good French films like *Fanny, Angèle,* and *The Baker's Wife*. As soon as you receive this letter, tell me your price and I will pay you through the Colonial Bank of Marseilles.

Table 1 Export rental fees (in French francs), 1937–41

Country	*Angèle* Amount	*Regain* Amount	*La Femme du boulanger* Amount
United States		114,000	83,000
Canada	25,000	40,000	48,000
UK			128,000
Italy			90,000
Spain			90,000
Portugal			20,000
Sweden			27,000
Norway			13,000
Holland			24,000
Finland			24,000
Hungary	12,000	25,000	25,000
Romania			9,000
Bulgaria	19,000	19,000	19,000
Greece			11,000
Brazil	1,000	40,000	27,000
Argentina		20,000	48,000
Mexico	32,000		67,000
Central America			7,000
Chile/Peru	15,000	10,000	10,000
Bolivia/Ecuador	15,000	10,000	
Uruguay/Paraguay		10,000	
Egypt			18,000
Syria/Lebanon		10,000	
Belgian Congo	1,000		
Total	120,000	388,000	698,000
Grand total			1,206,000

Source: Archives of the Compagnie Méditerranéenne de Films

in at least twenty-five countries across Europe, North America, South America, and the Middle East, generating over 1.2 million francs in rental fees. Table 1 summarises the surviving data.

The data in Table 1 are far from complete. Notably absent are figures for Belgium and Switzerland, where all three films enjoyed long, highly lucrative runs documented in the local press. *Angèle*, originally released in late 1934, received its broadest international distribution between 1935 and 1937, with particular success in Montréal. The film also played in several large American cities in 1939, as did *Regain* for several weeks in London, but no financial records have survived. A smattering of additional contracts shows that the Marseilles Trilogy and *Le Schpountz* were also exported during the 1930s, but less widely than the titles cited above because of unfavourable market conditions. By the time Pagnol had his distribution network in place, *Marius* and *Fanny* were already several years old and faced competition from quality foreign adaptations including Paramount's German *Zum goldenen Anker* (Alexander Korda, 1931) and Swedish *Längtan till havet* (John Brunius, 1931), as well as an Italian *Fanny* (Mario Almirante, 1933), *Der schwarze Walfisch* (Fritz Wendhausen, 1934), a German compression of *Marius* and *Fanny* starring Emil Jannings, and Metro Goldwyn Mayer's *Port of Seven Seas* (1938), a quintessential Hollywood programme picture directed by James Whale and scripted by Preston Sturges.

Audiences unfamiliar with the originals or exposed only to remakes would have likely found *César* difficult to appreciate, thus justifying its selective release. The same was true of *Le Schpountz*, whose satirical punch depended in large part on familiarity with the culture of the French film industry. On the other hand, *Angèle*, *Regain*, and *La Femme du boulanger* were self-contained works whose power lay in working through the consequences of marital infidelity, changing gender roles, and the disappearance of traditional rural communities – all well-established, pan-national phenomena to which viewers from all over the world could easily relate.

The reception of Pagnol's work in New York offers an especially memorable illustration of his unique ability to promote French cinema and culture abroad while touching on universal themes. The first of his films to open there was *Marius*, in April 1933, followed by *Merlusse* in March 1938, and *Angèle* (renamed *Heartbeat* because Paramount held copyright over the title *Angel*), in September 1939. As with most French films, they played for only two weeks each and went largely unnoticed. A reviewer for the *New York Times* praised *Marius* for its 'blend of the picturesque and realistic, a far cry from the fluffy musical comedies we have come to expect from the Paramount studios in Joinville', but found the picture 'far too long' and noted that 'it could be considerably abbreviated to good advantage' (H.T.S. 1933). *Merlusse* received a less enthusiastic verdict – 'interesting dramatically but technically awkward' (Nugent 1938) – while *Heartbeat* was panned outright as 'a trite pastoral about the farmer's daughter' (Nugent 1939) and 'tediously told, lacking dramatic flexibility' (Crowther 1939).

Yet *Regain*, renamed *Harvest* and submitted to the state Motion Picture Review Board in July 1939, encountered an entirely different fate. Despite having being pre-emptively edited by distributor André Heymann for both length (to satisfy exhibitors) and content (to avoid censorship), the picture received the harshest possible sanction – outright rejection rather than a recommendation for eliminations and resubmission – on the grounds that it was 'immoral' and 'would tend to corrupt morals' (Anon. 1939). After personally re-screening the picture on Heymann's request, board head Irwin Esmond reaffirmed that picture was 'utterly immoral' because it 'shows a woman who is the mistress of two men' and 'glorifies an adulterous relationship that results in pregnancy, without the least recognition of marital rites or obligations, thus teaching that regeneration may best be obtained through the free exercise of animal passion' (Esmond 1939a).

Heymann immediately hired one of New York's most prominent trial lawyers, Arthur Garfield Hays, to file an appeal with the state Board of Regents, held several private screenings for journalists to win support for his cause, and notified the French Embassy, which lodged a protest. By mid-August nearly every major newspaper and magazine in the city had denounced the ban. The *New York Daily News* cited it as 'proof that our censorship grows ever more ridiculous' and called for the censorship board's abolishment (Winsten 1939), while an editor for *The Nation* lamented 'a new height of idiotic hypocrisy applied to a picture that is reverential almost to the point of immaculate conception' (Hoellering 1939).The *New York Times* added ironically that:

> The only fault of this film is that it concerns living human beings, two lonely people who find each other amid a world of accident and sordid contacts and who cause dead fields to flourish anew by the miracle of their happiness. It is a masterpiece, a picture so touching and beautiful that the ruling of the censors becomes merely a bad joke, like a belch during a harp solo. Of all the motion pictures we have seen, *Harvest* is the most profoundly moral and tending to incite morality, the most noble and eloquent defense of the monogamous ideal. (Crisler 1939)

The press campaign sparked an unprecedented movement against film censorship in New York that united organisations as diverse as the American Civil Liberties Union, the Modern Museum of Art, the Federal Council of Churches, the National Education Association, and the New York League of Women Shoppers. At its 15 September 1939 meeting the Board of Regents bowed to the pressure and in a split vote approved *Harvest* without eliminations, despite vehement opposition from two dissenting members, one of whom threatened independent litigation to uphold the ban (Anon. 1939a). On the other side of the Atlantic the French trade press followed the scandal closely. *La Cinématographie française* deplored the initial ban as 'typique de la censure américaine, qui est impitoyable pour les films français, avec tout ce que le mot peut comporter d'injustice' (typical of American censorship, which is merciless towards French films, with all the injustice inherent in that word) (Jahrblum 1939), but subsequently rejoiced at *Harvest*'s approval: 'c'est avec fierté que nous enregistrons ce triomphe du cinéma français. Pagnol maintient en terre américaine notre production à une place digne de sa valeur' (it is with pride that we record this triumph of French cinema. On American soil Pagnol maintains our production at a rank commensurate with its value) (Anon. 1939b).

Following its 2 October 1939 premiere *Harvest* played for a record forty-eight consecutive weeks in Manhattan and enjoyed short periodic revivals at second-run theatres through mid-1943. In December 1939 it was named best foreign-language film of the year by the New York Film Critics Association (Anon. 1939c) and over the next few months made its way across the country with screenings in Boston, Philadelphia, Baltimore, Cleveland, Chicago, San Francisco, and Los Angeles. Its notoriety paved the way for the New York release of *La Femme du boulanger*, which premiered without incident on 26 February 1940 after minor eliminations of sexually charged dialogue and imagery (Anon. 1940). On the strength of Raimu's masterful performance, the film surpassed *Regain* on all counts, winning the 1940 New York Film Critics' award for best foreign picture in a landslide vote and grossing $65,000 during its first eleven weeks at the World Theater (Anon. 1940a; Weinberg 1940), where its run was eventually extended to a full year to satisfy popular demand. It subsequently played uninterrupted for another full year at second-run cinemas, with occasional re-screenings into July 1944. The version of *La Fille du puisatier* that arrived in September 1946 – notable for its pre-censorship excision of the reconciliation sequence anchored around Pétain's armistice announcement (Anon. 1946) – met with similar success: a seven-month exclusive stint at the Avenue Playhouse, followed by a string of other engagements through September 1947. It took second in the balloting for best foreign picture for 1946, losing narrowly to Rossellini's classic *Open City* (Anon. 1946a).

The massive acclaim Raimu and Pagnol had acquired among American critics finally prompted the release of the Marseilles Trilogy in 1948 as a six-and-a-half-hour triple bill that drew rave reviews. 'Though they are all superb', wrote a critic in the *New Yorker*, '*César* is the best of the lot and offers a lesson in picture-making that a good many of our local boys could afford to study' (McCarten 1948). For a director who had defined himself largely in opposition to American cinema, such comments offered not only the sweetest possible affirmation of his reputation as a French national hero, but the ultimate revenge on Paramount and vindication of his unique approach to filmmaking, proving definitively that mass-market commercialism could fuse seamlessly with artisanal craftsmanship. As Pagnol commented wryly in a letter to the *New York Times* announcing that he had decided to come work in Hollywood: 'When *Fanny* first was released in France in 1932, critics suggested that I go to America and learn. That is why I am so surprised at the success of my films there now. Now that I have critical approval, I know I shall learn a lot' (Pagnol 1948).

Despite several similar announcements in the years that followed and multiple invitations from friends in the US – most notably John Huston, who wanted to adapt Pagnol's play *Judas* for the screen (Huston 1955), and Joshua Logan, who staged a hit Broadway production of *Fanny* that ran for two full years (Carey 1955) – Pagnol never worked in Hollywood or even crossed the Atlantic. Dissuaded by his attachment to France and a paralysing fear of air travel, the first filmmaker elected to the French Academy had little to gain from taking yet another ambitious career leap. In the end more Escartefigue than Marius, Pagnol understandably declined the excitement and risk of overseas adventure in favour of navigating comfortable waters close to home.

References

Achard, Marcel (1936), 'La semaine à l'écran: *César*', *Marianne*, 18 November.

Anon. (1931), 'Trying Supers out on French before Editing', *Variety*, 20 October.

Anon. (1934), 'Une usine Marcel Pagnol à Marseilles', *L'Effort cinématographique*, 1 April.

Anon. (1934a), 'Marcel Pagnol possède ses propres camions sonores', *L'Effort cinématographique*, 1 December.

Anon. (1935), 'Marcel Pagnol exploitant', *Cinéma Spectacles*, 2 March.

Anon. (1935a), 'L'ouverture du *Noailles*', *Marseilles matin*, 6 September.

Anon. (1937), 'Le lancement de *Regain*', *La Cinématographie française*, 19 November.

Anon. (1938), 'Dans le soleil Marcel Pagnol a construit de vastes studios modernes', *La Cinématographie française*, 23 September.

Anon. (1938a), '4.040 étrangers dans le cinéma français: ce que demande le Syndicat Professionnel Français', *La Cinématographie française*, 25 November.

Anon. (1938b), 'Deux "previews" de *La Femme du boulanger*', *La Revue de l'écran*, 27 August.

Anon. (1939), *Harvest*, New York State Archives (Albany), Record Series A1418 (Motion Picture License Application Files), 37196-721.

Anon. (1939a), Minutes of the Meetings of the Board of Regents of the University of the State of New York, New York State Archives (Albany), Record Series 17267, Volume 23.

Anon. (1939b), 'La représentation triomphale de *Regain* à New York', *La Cinématographie française*, 28 October 1939.

Anon. (1939c), 'Winners of 1939 Awards by Motion Picture Critics', *New York Times*, 28 December.

Anon. (1940), *The Baker's Wife*, New York State Archives (Albany), Record Series A1418 (Motion Picture License Application Files), 37343-729 and 38264-773.

Anon. (1940a), '*Baker's Wife* Honored', *New York Times*, 23 December.

Anon. (1942), Arrêt de la Troisième Chambre de la Cour d'Appel d'Aix-en-Provence, Archives Départementales des Bouches-du-Rhône (Aix), series 1490W, box 10, 8 June.

Anon. (1946), *The Well-Digger's Daughter*, New York State Archives (Albany), Record Series A1418 (Motion Picture License Application Files), 48709-1241.

Anon. (1946a), 'British Score High with Film Critics', *New York Times*, 31 December.

Antoine, André (1938), 'Le film du jour: *Schpountz* à l'Olympia', *Le Journal*, 24 April.

Antona, Antoine [Toé] (1937), '*Regain*: manuel de publicité', Bibliothèque Nationale de France, Département des Arts du Spectacle, 4-ICO-CIN-10335.

Antona, Antoine [Toé] (1938), '*Le Schpountz*: manuel de publicité', author's personal collection.

Antona, Antoine [Toé] (1938a), '*La Femme du boulanger*: manuel de publicité', author's personal collection.

Auzel, Dominique (1988), *Affiches du 7e art: le cinéma français à l'affiche*, Paris, Henri Veyrier.
Bessy, Maurice (1938), '"Il n'y a rien de plus bête que la technique", déclare Marcel Pagnol', *Cinémonde*, 6 October.
Bizet, René (1938), '*Le Schpountz* de Marcel Pagnol', *Le Jour*, 17 April.
Bost, Pierre (1938), 'Le cinéma: *Le Schpountz*', *Vendredi*, 29 April.
Capitaine, Jean-Louis (1988), *Les Affiches du cinéma français*, Paris, Seghers.
Carey, Alida (1955), 'Pagnol: Portrait of a Gallic Triple Threat', *New York Times*, 5 June.
Chateau, René (1995), *Le Cinéma français sous l'Occupation (1940–44)*, Paris, Editions René Chateau.
Courtade, Francis (1991), 'Les co-productions franco-allemandes et versions multiples des années 30', in Heike Hurst and Heiner Gassen (eds), *Tendres ennemis: cent ans de cinéma entre la France et l'Allemagne*, Paris, Harmattan, 172–83.
Créton, Laurent (2004), 'Années trente: une économie du cinéma en mal de réforme', in Créton (ed.), *Histoire économique du cinéma français: production et financement, 1940–1959*, Paris, CNRS Editions, 2004, 33–57.
Crisler, B.R. (1939), 'Our Prudish Censors', *New York Times*, 23 July.
Crisp, Colin (1993), *The Classic French Cinema, 1930–1960*, Bloomington, Indiana University Press.
Crisp, Colin (2002), *Genre, Myth, and Convention in the French Cinema, 1929–1939*, Bloomington, Indiana University Press.
Crowther, Bosley (1939), 'At the Little Carnegie', *New York Times*, 5 September.
Darnton, Robert (1984), *The Great Cat Massacre and Other Episodes in French Cultural History*, New York, Basic Books.
D'Aubarède, Gabriel (1933), 'Critique de quelques films', *Les Cahiers du film* no. 1, December, 31.
Decaris, Germaine (1938), '*Le Schpountz* de Marcel Pagnol', *La Lumière*, 29 April.
Derain, Lucie (1937), 'Comment on lance un film: étude sur la publicité de cinéma', *La Cinématographie française*, 26 March.
Dubout, Albert (1994), *Pagnol: le livre des livres*, Paris, Editions Michèle Trinckvel.
Duclaux, Charles (1934), 'Sauvons le film parlant français', *Ciné-Phono Magazine*, March.
Epardaud, Edmond (1936), 'Marcel Pagnol, roi de Marseilles et empereur de Marcellin', *La Cinématographie française*, 26 December.
Epardaud, Edmond (1937), 'Marcel Pagnol agrandit ses studios', *La Cinématographie française*, 31 December.
Epardaud, Edmond (1938), 'Grâce à Marcel Pagnol, un centre important de production se crée à Marseilles', *La Cinématographie française*, 25 March.
Epardaud, Edmond (1938a), 'Marcel Pagnol ouvre *Le César* à Marseilles', 24 June.
Esmond, Irwin (1939a), Affidavit of 31 July submitted to New York State Board of Regents, New York State Archives (Albany), Record Series A1418 (Motion Picture License Application Files), 37196-721.
Fayard, Jean (1938), '*Le Schpountz*', *Candide*, 21 April.
Garcin, Paul (1934), 'Henri Clerc parle à Lyon de la querelle du cinéma et du

théâtre', *Comœdia*, 3 Janaury.

Godefroy, Christian (1934), 'Dans la campagne provençale, Marcel Pagnol tourne *Angèle*', *Paris-Soir*, 16 June.

Guimberlaud, Gabriel (1938), 'Comment utiliser les photos: un bel exemple que donnent Les Films Pagnol', *La Cinématographie française*, 9 September.

Harlé, Pierre (1934), '*Angèle*', *La Cinématographie française*, 3 November.

Hoellering, Franz (1939), 'Films', *The Nation*, 5 August.

H.T.S. (1939), 'Romance in Marseilles', *New York Times*, 14 April.

Huston, John (1955), Letter to Pagnol, Margaret Herrick Library, Special Collections Department, John Huston Papers, F 691, 1 July.

Jahrblum, Charles (1939), '*Regain* interdit en Amérique mais toute la presse proteste', *La Cinématographie française*, 26 August.

James, Michael (1948), 'New Film Color Process Unveiled in France', *New York Times*, 24 November.

Jauniaux, René (1934), 'De onze heures à midi avec Orane Demazis', *Libre Belgique*, 26 October.

Jeanson, Henri (1939), 'Souvenirs d'une conversation avec Marcel Pagnol', *Paris-Spectacles*, 3 May.

Labarthe, André (1966), *Marcel Pagnol, ou le cinéma tel qu'on le parle*, French television documentary broadcast on Antenne 2, 5 and 12 May. Archived at the Inathèque de France.

Lechatellier, Pierre (1934), 'Un essai de décentralisation: une usine moderne de tirage à Marseille', *Les Cahiers du film* no. 4, September, 16.

Leglise, Paul (1970), *Histoire de la politique du cinéma français*, 2 vols, Paris, Librairie Générale de Droit et de Jurisprudence.

McCarten, John (1948), 'Last and Best: *César*', *New Yorker*, 6 November.

Merentir, Henry (1934), '*Angèle* au *Fémina*', *La République du Var*, 20 October.

Millaud, Fernand (1937), 'Mon ami Marcel Pagnol', *Ciné-France*, 19 November.

Morand, Paul (2005), *Romans*, eds Michel Collomb et al., Paris, Gallimard.

Novy, Yvon (1935), '"Je ne fais que du théâtre", nous dit Marcel Pagnol', *Le Jour*, 23 February.

Nugent, Frank (1938), '*Merlusse* by Marcel Pagnol Opens at the Continental', *New York Times*, 17 March.

Nugent, Frank (1939), 'Circling the Square', *New York Times*, 10 September.

Pagnol, Marcel (1933), 'Cinématurgie de Paris', *Les Cahiers du film* no. 1, December, 3–8.

Pagnol, Marcel (1936), Undated letter to André Antoine, Bibliothèque Nationale de France, Département des Arts du Spectacle, MS-78 [late November / early December].

Pagnol, Marcel (1937), *Regain: film de Marcel Pagnol*, Paris, Les Editions Marcel Pagnol.

Pagnol, Marcel (1938), 'Marcel Pagnol signale l'existence de son usine de tirage à Marseilles', *La Cinématographie française*, 14 October.

Pagnol, Marcel (1938a), 'En marge du problème juif', *Nouvelles littéraires, artistiques, et scientifiques*, no. 844, 17 December.

Pagnol, Marcel (1938b), 'Aujourd'hui, à 21 h au César, unique soirée pour la présentation au public de *La Femme du boulanger*', *Le Petit Marseillais*, 25 August.

Pagnol, Marcel (1938c), *Le Schpountz: film de Marcel Pagnol*, Paris, Les Editions Marcel Pagnol.
Pagnol, Marcel (1938d), *La Femme du boulanger: film de Marcel Pagnol*, Paris, Les Editions Marcel Pagnol.
Pagnol, Marcel (1946), 'Lettre ouverte de Marcel Pagnol, de l'Académie Française, à Monsieur le Ministre de l'Information', *France Soir*, 29 June. Reprinted in Pagnol (2008), 107-16.
Pagnol, Marcel (1995), *Œuvres complètes*, 3 vols, Paris, Fallois.
Pagnol, Marcel (2008), *Carnets de cinéma*, Paris, Editions de la Treille.
Parrot-Lagarenne, Michel (1938), 'Une première à Biarritz: *La Femme du boulanger*', *La Petite Gironde*, 19 August.
Peyrusse, Claudette (1986), *Le Cinéma méridional: le Midi dans le cinéma français, 1929–1944*, Toulouse, Eché.
Phillips, Alastair (2003), *City of Darkness, City of Light: émigré filmmakers in Paris, 1929–1939*, Amsterdam, Amsterdam University Press.
Rebatet, Lucien [François Vinneuil] (1934), 'L'écran de la semaine: *Angèle*', *L'Action française*, 9 November.
Rebatet, Lucien [François Vinneuil] (1938), 'L'écran de la semaine: *Le Schpountz*', *L'Action française*, 15 April.
Reboul, Jacques (1934), 'En voyant tourner *Angèle*', *L'Effort cinématographique*, 15 June.
Reboul, Jacques (1938), 'Sur quelques projets de chambardement', *Cinéma-Spectacles*, 6 May.
Régent, Roger (1937), 'Pagnol tourne au Prado', *Ciné-France*, 1 January.
Régent, Roger (1937a), 'Le premier et éclatant gala de cinéma de la saison: *Regain*', *L'Intransigeant*, 30 October.
Renaitour, Jean-Michel (1937), *Où va le cinéma français?*, Paris, Editions de la Baudinière.
Renoir, Jean (1937), 'Le cinéma et l'Etat', *Vendredi*, 24 December.
Renoir, Jean (1938), 'Une journée avec Marcel Pagnol', *Regards*, 4 August.
Renoir, Jean (1938a), 'Souvenirs', *Le Point* no. 18, December, 275–86.
Robert, Romuald (1941), Letter to Les Films Marcel Pagnol, Archives of the Compagnie Méditerranéenne de Films, 24 July.
Sorlin, Pierre (1981), 'Jewish Images in the French Cinema of the 1930s', *Historical Journal of Film, Radio, and Television* 1.1, March, 15–32.
Trumpbour, John (2002), *Selling Hollywood to the World: US and European Struggles for Mastery of the Global Film Industry, 1920–1950*, Cambridge, Cambridge University Press.
Wahl, Lucien (1937), '"Nous sommes tous devenus de vrais paysans", nous dit Orane Demazis entre deux scènes de *Regain*', *L'Intransigeant*, 5 July.
Weiler, A.H. (1948), 'By Way of Report: Pagnol Coming Here', *New York Times*, 7 March.
Weinberg, Herman (1940), 'The Funny Business of Picking Hits', *New York Times*, 12 May.
Winsten, Archer (1939), '*Harvest*: Censors Pull Another Boner', *New York Daily News*, 4 August.
Wolff, Pierre (1936), '*César* inaugure Le César', *Paris Soir*, 12 November.

Epilogue
Pagnol's legacy

In the interval between his retirement from filmmaking in 1955 and his death in 1974, Pagnol solidified his status as a French national icon by reinventing himself yet again in two new modes of storytelling. *La gloire de mon père* and *Le château de ma mère*, nostalgic memoirs of childhood summers spent in the countryside near Aubagne, became immediate bestsellers upon their release in 1957, followed by a third instalment two years later entitled *Le temps des secrets*. In 1963 he published an equally acclaimed pair of novels under the title *L'eau des collines*, adding substantial depth to his cinematic treatment of *Manon des sources*. Pagnol spent the final decade of his life preparing the first edition of his complete works, which appeared between 1964 and 1973, as well as writing the fourth and final chapter of his *Souvenirs d'enfance*, which appeared posthumously as *Le temps des amours* in 1977 just after *La gloire* and *Le château* became part of the national curriculum for French middle schools.

Rather than overshadowing Pagnol's work as a director, these late-career literary triumphs helped ensure the longevity of his pictures by introducing them to new generations of spectators, albeit in a roundabout way. In 1986 Claude Berri's *Jean de Florette* and *Manon des sources*, both adapted from *L'eau des collines*, became the most successful French 'heritage films' ever made. They ran for 70 and 58 weeks, respectively, selling 7.2 and 6.6 million tickets as the year's top box-office performers (Powrie 1997: 188). Yves Robert's faithful adaptations of *La gloire* and *Le château* followed suit in 1990, scoring 6.3 and 4.3 million entries on their way to claiming first and third place nationally for the year (Simsi 2000: 92).

Thanks to frequent television rebroadcasts and numerous re-adaptations for stage and screen, Pagnol's original work as a director has also enjoyed a thriving afterlife and continued to evolve in relation to changing cultural preoccupations. One noteworthy example was Jérôme Savary's 1985 production of *La Femme du boulanger* at the Théâtre Mogador using a script Pagnol had originally drafted in 1946 but left unpublished and unperformed following Raimu's untimely death that same year (Savary 1985). Starring Michel Galabru, who accomplished the difficult task of reprising a role already imprinted on collective memory, the play was a smash success and gave rise to a series of national tours lasting until 1998.

In a subtle yet significant change of emphasis compared to Pagnol's original, Savary portrayed Aurélie's adultery not as a selfish act of betrayal, but as a natural response to a mismatched marriage of convenience that frustrates the much younger woman's legitimate desire for sexual satisfaction. In so doing, the play draws out the critique of failed masculinity latent in Pagnol's line, delivered by the baker during his drunken soliloquy, that 'c'est un beau jeune qui mérite Aurélie. On dit qu'elle me trompe avec le berger. Pas du tout. C'est moi qui, depuis cinq ans, ai trompé le berger avec elle!' ('A handsome young man deserves Aurélie. People say that she is cheating on me with the shepherd. Not at all. I am the one who for five years has been cheating on the shepherd with her!) (Pagnol 1995: II, 828).

In 1999 Nicolas Ribowski's made-for-television movie endorsed that updated view of gender roles by presenting Aurélie and the shepherd's tryst as the result of genuine romance and mutual attraction rather than a predatory seduction. Ribowski also eliminated several other elements that were culturally or ideologically dated, such as the priest and the schoolteacher's vitriolic debate over whether Joan of Arc was God's divine messenger or simply a patriotic peasant girl given to 'auditory hallucinations'. Yet the film's visual style and production values offered an intensely nostalgic homage to Pagnol. Shot entirely on location in and around the picturesque Provençal village of Artignosc-sur-Verdon, it features numerous landscape shots absent from the original. Sweeping views of lavender fields, olive groves, and rolling, brush-covered hills open up the story, nicely complementing a strong performance from Roger Hanin as the baker. The film was a success, drawing a very good 34 per cent market share for its premiere (Inathèque 1999).

EPILOGUE: PAGNOL'S LEGACY 239

Several months later renowned comedic director Gérard Oury released a reworking of *Le Schpountz* that maintained the original's tribute to the redemptive power of laughter while incorporating a tongue-in-cheek commentary on ethnicity, stardom, and cultural stereotyping at the turn of the twenty-first century. Responding implicitly to Pagnol's portrait of French cinema as overrun by foreigners, Oury cast popular Beur comedian Smaïn in Fernandel's role as the naïve, small-town dreamer from the south who goes to Paris and blunders his way into a lucrative acting contract. Though perfectly integrated into French culture with the hyper-traditional first name 'Irénée' and no signs of 'otherness' apart from his skin colour, Smaïn's character is hassled by Parisian cops who ask for his identity papers and denied the chance to audition for dramatic roles, instead being steered into comedy – the only performance genre in which entertainers of North African origin have traditionally enjoyed success in France. Characterized by a reviewer as 'aimable mais pas vraiment nécessaire' (likeable but not really necessary) (Coppermann 1999: 45), Oury's clever meta-satire was overlooked by critics and the public, selling fewer than 200,000 tickets and prompting his retirement from filmmaking (Oury 2001).

Since the early 1990s there has been a particularly strong renewal of interest in the Marseilles Trilogy beginning with Jean-Luc Tardieu's three-act play *La Trilogie marseillaise*, which compresses the action into a single narrative but faithfully recreates the best-loved scenes from each of the movies. After a successful five-month run in 1992 at the Variétés theatre where *Marius* and *Fanny* were originally performed, the show enjoyed several national tours lasting two-and-a-half years in all (Dhaussy 1994). Flush from the success of his adaptation of *La Femme du boulanger*, in 2000 Ribowski remade the Trilogy as a three-part television mini-series co-financed by the French, Belgian, and Québécois governments. Conceived as a patrimonial project whose goal was to expose a young international audience to Pagnol's classic story, the films drew solid market shares of between 34 and 36 per cent on initial broadcast, thanks in large part to the casting of Hanin as César (Inathèque 2000).

The most recent and most creative flourish of remakes has included Vladimir Cosma's two-act opera *Marius et Fanny* (2007), Irène Bonnaud's three-act *mise en scène* of *Fanny* for the Comédie Française (2008), and Francis Huster's two-act stage play *César – Fanny – Marius*

(2009) at the Théâtre Antoine. Described by Cosma as 'une rentrée aux sources de l'opéra populaire et de l'ancien opéra-comique, avec une histoire toute simple et des interprètes de premier plan' (a return to the origins of popular opera and the old style of comic opera, with a very simple story and first-rate performers) (Wachthausen 2007: 34), *Marius et Fanny* required three years of planning, the most difficult aspect of which was securing commitments from international superstars Robert Alagna (Marius) and Angela Gheorghiu (Fanny).

The premiere was greeted with rave reviews in the French press. A critic for *Le Monde* called it 'un miel lyrique' (a lyrical nectar) and 'une œuvre travaillée, avec de grands airs dramatiques un peu kitsch, écrits pour des grandes voix, et remarquablement orchestrée' (a finely crafted work, with sweeping, slightly kitschy dramatic arias, written for big voices, and remarkably orchestrated) (Roux 2007: 26). In addition to six performances in Mareille during September 2007, excerpts of the opera were recorded with the London Symphony Orchestra and released on CD, with a recording of the full performance broadcast on the Arte television channel in November 2008.

The goal of Bonnaud's *Fanny*, as Comédie Française general manager Muriel Mayette put it, was 'de rendre à la prose dramatique de Pagnol une dimension universelle' (to give Pagnol's dramatic prose a universal dimension) by highlighting the themes of inter-gender and intergenerational conflict, individual versus collective forms of identity, and the weight of tradition (Mayette 2008: 6). Though Bonnaud's dialogue and plot are virtually identical to Pagnol's play, her adaptation de-historicised and de-regionalised the action by abandoning the southern accent, dressing the actors in simple, contemporary attire, and using minimalist staging techniques that included only two sets constructed from ephemeral, recycled materials gathered on the streets of Paris: wooden crates, canvas, and cardboard. Critical response was divided and highly polemic, but the play generated good ticket sales during its six-week run. Its official endorsement by the Comédie Française – one of Pagnol's few unrealised ambitions during his lifetime – was further enhanced by being the first play ever to be broadcast live in digital high definition on French television.

As for Huster, he conceived his *César – Fanny – Marius* largely as a reaction against Bonnaud's work, instead offering an intensely nostalgic tribute that attempted to recreate the atmosphere and performance style of Pagnol's original stage versions of *Marius* and

Fanny. As Huster explained, his intention was '[de] réunir en une pièce unique ce qui dans ces trois œuvres m'apparaissait spécifiquement théâtral, compact, rare, et bouleversant' (to bring together in a single play aspects of the three works that struck me as specifically theatrical, succinct, distinctive, and emotionally moving) (Huster 2009: 107–8). The performance featured Huster, who cast himself as Panisse, alongside Jacques Weber as César, thus reuniting former veterans of the Comédie Française and two of the most celebrated French theatre actors of the last thirty years. While both drew unanimous praise for their performances, so did relative newcomers Stanley Weber (Jacques' son) as Marius and Hafsia Herzi, a 22-year-old of Tunisian–Algerian ancestry from Marseilles, as Fanny. Despite the omission of key scenes from the films – César's receiving Marius' first letter and dictating a response to Fanny, Marius' return and futile attempt to reclaim Fanny and their baby, Panisse's deathbed confession in front of his friends – the play drew packed houses in Paris and eventually completed a thirty-show tour of France, Switzerland, and Belgium by mid-2010.

During that same period, spectators interested in an intimate look at the real-life drama behind the Trilogy attended *Jules et Marcel*, a one-act 'mise en espace' of the tumultuous friendship between Pagnol and Raimu. Directed by Jean-Pierre Bernard, the show featured Michel Galabru (Raimu) and Philippe Caubère (Pagnol) doing dramatic readings of letters the legendary actor and filmmaker exchanged between 1929 and 1946, supplemented with embellishments by scriptwriter Pierre Tré-Hardy. The show's four-month inaugural run at the Théâtre Hébertot between March and June 2009 prompted a successful national tour the following year. A related and equally popular dramatisation of Pagnol's work in the last two years has been the organisation of *randonnées théâtrales*, or theatrical walking tours through the hills surrounding the Marcellin Valley near Aubagne. In addition to experiencing firsthand the scenery captured in Pagnol's rural films, visitors have the opportunity to interact with costumed characters from *Jean de Florette*, *Manon des sources*, and the *Souvenirs d'enfance*.

In April 2011 Pagnol's work returned to the big screen for the first time in over a decade thanks to Daniel Auteuil's remake of *La Fille du puisatier*. A long-time Pagnolophile who launched his acting career by playing Ugolin in Claude Berri's adaptations, Auteuil mimicked his idol by writing the screenplay and directing, but went a step further by also starring as the well-digger. Auteuil's rendering, which displaces the unwed-mother melodrama from the Second World War back to the First, is even more nostalgic than the 1940 original, yet that strategy proved an asset rather than a liability. The film sold over 1.3 million tickets in France, surpassing a range of competing Hollywood fare (*Scream 4*, *The Adjustment Bureau*, *Rango*, *Tron*, *The Fighter*, *Tree of Life*) and ranking thirteenth overall for the first half of the year (Cinefeed 2011). In so doing, it proved that the heritage film is still a viable genre in France and prompted Auteuil to remake the Marseilles Trilogy beginning in 2012.

The ongoing appeal of Pagnol's work can be attributed in no small part to the ongoing efforts of La Compagnie Méditerranéenne de Films (CMF), which Pagnol himself founded shortly after the Second World War to promote and disseminate his work. Managed today by grandson Nicolas, the CMF still operates as a small but influential family business thanks to long-standing relationships with the town of Aubagne, the city of Marseilles, television networks France 2/France 3, and a range of other cultural institutions. In the past several years the CMF has focused on creating a recognisable Pagnol 'brand' through a variety of new marketing initiatives: the digitally restored DVD editions of his films (a process slowed by ongoing copyright disputes with Jean Giono's descendants), the publication of recently discovered diaries and letters, and a dual-language website (www.marcel-pagnol.com) that offers direct sales of those products, blog discussions, and a host of information about Pagnol.

In a larger cultural perspective, the strong renewal of interest in Pagnol over the past two decades can be appreciated as a reaction against the perceived dilution of French national identity in the middle of intensifying globalisation and the creation of a supranational European Union (EU). The years 1992–94 marked the conclusion of the Uruguay round of the General Agreement on Tariffs and Trade (GATT) negotiations, which included the creation of the World Trade Organization and dealt a serious blow to French economic protectionism, exposing French business to international competition more fully than any time since the Second World War and sparking widespread protests.

In 1999–2000 there was furious debate over the formal introduction of the euro currency, which effectively linked the economies of the EU countries together by setting exchange rates for phasing out national currencies by early 2002. Building on the EU's incorporation of former Soviet bloc countries in 2004, 2007–2009 saw the controversial addition of Bulgaria and Romania, prompting French fears of further corporate delocalisations to the East and unchecked immigration in the opposite direction, as well as the ratification of the Treaty of Lisbon in an attempt to address French and Dutch rejection of the European Constitution in 2005. A final, lingering debate that continues today is the candidacy of Turkey for EU membership and the fundamental incompatibility that many French see between Islamic culture and the core values of both their nation and Europe as a whole.

Against this background, the purge of social conflict and performance of consensus that characterises nearly all of Pagnol's films has served as a kind of screen onto which French spectators can project their desire to reaffirm the traditional bonds of family, community, and nation as a form of resistance to increasingly rapid change. This is an especially potent form of nostalgia to the second degree – a retrospective longing for an idealised reality that never actually existed except on-screen and in the collective imagination of spectators suffering through the turmoil of the Great Depression. That Pagnol's films continue to fulfil the analgesic function that they already held in the 1930s is not only a testament to the enduring power of his unique brand of poetic realism, but a measure of the social and cultural malaise that has become a seemingly unshakable part of twenty-first-century French society.

If Pagnol deserves to be remembered as a provocative theorist of the relation between speech and image, the most complete auteur of his generation, and a precursor of the new wave and neo-realism, his legacy extends far beyond the field of cinema studies. While the work of more critically acclaimed peers such as Renoir, Carné, and Clair has gradually lost its visibility over time, Pagnol's has grown ever stronger, standing today as an indelible part of French popular culture, and national identity. This is perhaps the most fitting vindication for an artist who consistently flouted stylistic and industry conventions in order to preserve his independence and realise his own distinct creative vision.

References

Cinefeed (2011), Box-office statistics compiled weekly from the Centre National de la Cinématographie, www.cinefeed.com.

Coppermann, Annie (1999), '*Le Schpountz* de Gérard Oury: Pagnol revisité', *Les Echos*, 27 August.

Dhaussy, Jacques (1994), 'Pagnol sur les planches: *Marius, Fanny, César* en version théâtrale condensée', *Le Figaro*, 18 August.

Huster, Francis (2009), 'Marcel Pagnol, le Poquelin de Marseilles', *L'Avant-scène théâtre* no. 1259–60, March.

Inathèque de France (1999), HyperBase, television statistics for 7 June.

Inathèque de France (2000), HyperBase, television statistics for 17, 18 and 20 April.

Mayette, Muriel (2008), '*Fanny* à la Comédie Française, la perte d'une jeunesse volée', official programme distributed at the 24 September performance.

Oury, Gérard (2001), *Ma grande vadrouille de A à Z*, Paris, Plon.

Pagnol, Marcel (1995), *Œuvres complètes*, 3 vols, Paris, Fallois.

Powrie, Phil (1997), *French Cinema in the 1980s: Nostalgia and the Crisis of Masculinity*, Oxford University Press.

Roux, Marie-Aude (2007), 'Opéra: Marius et Fanny prennent le large', *Le Monde*, 6 September.

Savary, Jérôme (1985), '*La Femme du* boulanger: de la provocation à la séduction', *L'Avant-scène théâtre* no. 775, October.

Simsi, Simon (2000), *Ciné-Passions: 7e art et industrie de 1945 à 2000*, Paris, Editions Dixit.

Wachthausen, Jean-Luc (2007), 'Vladimir Cosma fait entrer Pagnol à l'opéra', *Le Figaro*, 3 September.

Filmography

In order to correct errors and fill gaps in previous filmographies, the information below was compiled and cross-referenced using multiple period sources, particularly *Comœdia, La Cinématographie française, Le Film, Le Film français, La Revue de l'écran, Paris-Soir, Le Petit Marseillais*, and the on-screen credits of the pictures themselves. Attendance statistics cited for post-war films come from the Centre National de la Cinématographie, as compiled in Simon Simsi, ed., *Ciné-Passions: 7e art et industrie de 1945 à 2000*, Paris, Editions Dixit, 2000.

Films directed or co-directed (with year of initial release)

Marius (1931), 132 min., b/w

Directors: Alexander Korda and Marcel Pagnol
Screenplay: Marcel Pagnol, from his stage play
Production company: Paramount
Producer: Robert T. Kane
Photography: Ted Pahle
Editor: Roger Spiri-Mercanton
Set design: Vincent Korda and Alfred Junge
Music: Francis Gromon
Shooting: June–August 1931 at Paramount Studios (Joinville) and in Marseilles (Old Port)
Distribution: Paramount
Premiere: 9 October 1931 at the Paramount Palace cinema (Paris)
Main cast: Raimu (César Olivier), Pierre Fresnay (Marius Olivier),

Orane Demazis (Fanny Cabanis), Fernand Charpin (Honoré Panisse), Alida Rouffe (Honorine Cabanis), Paul Dullac (Félix Escartefigue), Robert Vattier (Monsieur Brun), Alexandre Mihalesco (Piquoiseau)

Notes: An unannounced test screening was held on 5 October 1931 at the Paramount Palace in Paris.

Fanny (1932), 148 min., b/w

Directors: Marc Allégret and Marcel Pagnol
Screenplay: Marcel Pagnol, from his stage play
Production company: Les Etablissements Braunberger–Richebé
Producers: Roger Richebé and Marcel Pagnol
Photography: Nicolas Toporkoff, André Dantan, Georges Benoît, Julien Coutelen
Sound: William Bell
Editor: Jean Mamy
Set design: Gabriel Scognamillo
Music: Vincent Scotto and Georges Sellers
Shooting: June–August 1932 at Braunberger–Richebé Studios (Boulogne-Billancourt) and in Marseilles (Old Port)
Distribution: Les Films Marcel Pagnol
Premieres: 20 October 1932 at the Capitole cinema (Marseilles), 28 October 1932 at the Marigny cinema (Paris)
Main cast: Raimu (César), Pierre Fresnay (Marius), Orane Demazis (Fanny), Fernand Charpin (Panisse), Alida Rouffe (Honorine), Milly Mathis (Claudine), Auguste Mouriès (Escartefigue), Robert Vattier (Monsieur Brun), Maupi (Innocent Mangiapan)

Notes: The film was shown in two parts separated by an intermission, reportedly the first such case in France since the silent era.

Le Gendre de Monsieur Poirier (1933), 92 min., b/w

Director: Marcel Pagnol
Screenplay: Marcel Pagnol, from the stage play by Emile Augier and Jules Sandeau
Production company: Les Auteurs associés
Producer: René Pagnol
Photography: Willy Faktorovitch and Roger Ledru
Sound: Joseph de Bretagne
Editor: Suzanne de Troye
Set design: Jean Bijon and Jean Debucourt

Music: Vincent Scotto
Shooting: August–September 1933 at Braunberger–Richebé studios (Boulogne-Billancourt) and at Pagnol's estate near Parcé-sur-Sarthe
Distribution: Les Films Marcel Pagnol
Premiere: 16 December 1933 at the Rex cinema (Paris)
Main cast: Léon Bernard (Monsieur Poirier), Annie Ducaux (Antoinette Poirier de Presles), Jean Debucourt (Gaston de Presles), Fernand Charpin (Verdelet), Maurice Escande (Hector de Montmeyran)
Notes: A screening for theatre owners and distributors was held on 31 October 1933 at the Capitole cinema in Marseilles. Because of its initial failure both critically and at the box office, this is the only one of Pagnol's movies never rereleased theatrically in France. Pagnol made no effort to preserve the film, whose only surviving archival print is a subtitled copy released in the United States.

Jofroi (1933), 52 min., b/w

Director: Marcel Pagnol
Screenplay: Marcel Pagnol, from the short story *Jofroi de la Maussan* by Jean Giono
Production company: Les Auteurs associés
Producer: René Pagnol
Photography: Willy Faktorovitch and Roger Ledru
Sound: Pierre Calvet
Editors: Suzanne de Troye and André Robert
Set design: Jean Bijon
Music: Vincent Scotto
Shooting: November 1933 in La Treille (Bouches-du-Rhône) and Pathé-Natan Studios (Joinville)
Distribution: Les Films Marcel Pagnol
Premiere: 16 December 1933 at the Rex cinema (Paris)
Main cast: Vincent Scotto (Jofroi), Henri Poupon (Fonse Durbec), Annie Toinon (Barbe), Odette Roger (Marie Durbec), André Robert (the schoolteacher), José Tyrand (the priest), Charles Blavette (Antonin)
Notes: Initially released as a 'programme complement' to *Le Gendre de Monsieur Poirier*, the film won the 1950 New York Film Critics' award for best foreign picture. In the United States it was distributed in a package of short features with Jean Renoir's *Partie de campagne* (1936) and Roberto Rossellini's *Il Miracolo* (1948).

L'Article 330 (1934), 34 min., b/w

Director: Marcel Pagnol
Screenplay: Marcel Pagnol, from the stage play by Georges Courteline
Production company: Les Auteurs associés
Producer: René Pagnol
Photography: Willy Faktorovitch and Roger Ledru
Sound: Pierre Calvet
Editor: André Robert
Set design: Jean Bijon
Shooting: January–February 1934 at Paris-Studios-Cinéma (Boulogne-Billancourt)
Distribution: Les Films Marcel Pagnol
Premiere: 17 February 1934 at the Impérial cinema (Paris)
Main cast: Robert Le Vigan (La Brige), Jean d'Yd (the judge), Henry Darbrey (the public prosecutor), André Robert (the bailiff)
Notes: A 'programme complement' to *Léopold le bien-aimé* directed by Arno-Charles Brun, this forgotten short feature earned Pagnol the only cinema award of his career in France: the Prix Courteline given annually to recognise a film exemplifying the satirical spirit of the playwright's work.

Angèle (1934), 163 min., b/w

Director: Marcel Pagnol
Screenplay: Marcel Pagnol, from the novel *Un de Baumugnes* by Jean Giono
Production company: Les Films Marcel Pagnol
Producers: René Pagnol and Charles Brun
Photography: Willy Faktorovitch and Roger Ledru
Sound: Jean Lecoq
Editors: Suzanne de Troye and André Robert
Set design: Marius Brouquier
Music: Vincent Scotto and Georges Sellers
Shooting: April–June 1934 in the Marcelin Valley (near La Treille) and Marseilles
Premieres: 27 September 1934 at the Odéon cinema (Marseilles), 25 October 1934 at the Agriculteurs, Ciné-Opéra, and Bonaparte cinemas (Paris)
Main cast: Orane Demazis (Angèle Barbaroux), Fernandel (Saturnin), Henri Poupon (Clarius Barbaroux), Jean Servais (Albin), Edouard

Delmont (Amédée), Annie Toinon (Philomène Barbaroux), Andrex (Louis)

Notes: The film was cut to 138 minutes prior to its Paris release. The long version was shown again during the summer and autumn of 1935 at Pagnol's Noailles cinema in Marseilles and eventually played in Paris from June through September 1937 during the World's Fair.

Merlusse (1935), 72 min., b/w

Director: Marcel Pagnol
Screenplay: Marcel Pagnol
Production company: Les Films Marcel Pagnol
Producer: René Pagnol
Photography: Albert Assouad and Roger Ledru
Sound: Jean Lecoq
Editor: Suzanne de Troye
Music: Vincent Scotto
Shooting: January–February 1935 (first version), August–September 1935 (second version) at the Lycée Thiers (Marseilles) and Pagnol's studios (Impasse des Peupliers, Marseilles)
Distribution: Les Films Marcel Pagnol
Premiere: 7 December 1935 at the Marivaux cinema (Paris)
Main cast: Henri Poupon (Merlusse), André Pollack (the headmaster), Thommeray (the deputy headmaster), Rellys (the orderly), André Robert (the dormitory monitor), Jean Castan (Galubert), Jean Dubrou (Pic), Fernand Bruno (Catusse).

Notes: *Merlusse* was reshot six months after its initial recording to resolve sound reproduction problems. Originally slated for release with *Cigalon* to inaugurate Pagnol's newly acquired cinema Le Noailles in Marseilles, the films were replaced in that capacity by a reprise of *Angèle*.

Cigalon (1935), 65 min., b/w

Director: Marcel Pagnol
Screenplay: Marcel Pagnol
Production company: Les Films Marcel Pagnol
Producer: René Pagnol
Photography: Albert Assouad and Roger Ledru
Sound: Jean Lecoq

Editor: Suzanne de Troye
Music: Vincent Scotto
Shooting: January–February 1935 (first version), July–August 1935 (second version) in La Treille and at Pagnol's studios (Impasse des Peupliers, Marseilles)
Distribution: Les Films Marcel Pagnol
Premiere: 7 December 1935 at the Marivaux cinema (Paris)
Main cast: Antoine Arnaudy (Cigalon), Henri Poupon (the client), Marguerite Chabert (Madame Toffi), Jean Castan (Virgile), Alida Rouffe (Sidonie), Charles Blavette (a policeman)
Notes: Like its companion piece *Merlusse*, the first version of *Cigalon* was scrapped after printing because of poor sound quality. The film was rerecorded its entirety, with Arnaudy replacing Poupon in the title role, and eventually released with *Merlusse* after a six-month delay.

Topaze (1936), 110 min., b/w

Director: Marcel Pagnol
Screenplay: Marcel Pagnol, from his stage play
Production company: Les Films Marcel Pagnol
Producer: Charles Pons
Photography: Willy Faktorovitch and Roger Ledru
Sound: Julien Coutelen
Editor: Suzanne de Troye
Music: Vincent Scotto
Studios: Marcel Pagnol, Impasse des Peupliers (Marseilles)
Shooting: January–February 1936 at Pagnol's studios (Impasse des Peupliers, Marseilles)
Distribution: Les Films Marcel Pagnol
Premiere: 23 May 1936 at the Ciné-Opéra cinema (Paris)
Main cast: Antoine Arnaudy (Topaze), Léon Bélières (Régis Castel-Bénac), Délia-Col (Suzy Courtois), Léon Brouzet (Monsieur Muche), Pierre Asso (Tamise), Sylvia Bataille (Ernestine Muche), Jean Castan (a student), Henri Poupon (the old man)
Notes: Pagnol withdrew the film from circulation after only seven weeks to settle an ongoing copyright dispute with Paramount, which rereleased its 1933 adaptation of the play simultaneously.

César (1936), 168 min., b/w

Director: Marcel Pagnol
Screenplay: Marcel Pagnol
Production company: Les Films Marcel Pagnol
Producer: Charles Pons
Photography: Willy Faktorovitch and Roger Ledru
Sound: Julien Coutelen
Set design: Marius Brouquier
Editor: Suzanne de Troye
Music: Vincent Scotto
Shooting: July–September 1936 in Marseilles (Old Port), Les Lecques, a calanque near Cassis, Toulon, Pagnol's studios (Impasse des Peupliers, Marseilles)
Distribution: Les Films Marcel Pagnol
Premiere: 10 November 1936 at the César cinema (Paris)
Main cast: Raimu (César), Marius (Pierre Fresnay), Fanny (Orane Demazis), Panisse (Fernand Charpin), André Fouché (Césariot), Alida Rouffe (Honorine), Milly Mathis (Claudine), Paul Dullac (Escartefigue), Robert Vattier (Monsieur Brun), Maupi (Innocent Mangiapan), Doumel (Fernand), Edouard Delmont (Doctor Venelle), Thommeray (Elzéar the priest), Jean Castan (the altar boy)
Notes: The film was distributed in both 168-minute and 150-minute versions. In Paris it played simultaneously at four first-run cinemas: the Agriculteurs, Ciné-Opéra, Bonaparte, and César. Today a single copy of the long montage survives at the Cinémathèque de Toulouse.

Regain (1937), 155 min., b/w

Director: Marcel Pagnol
Assistant director: Roger Goupillières
Screenplay: Marcel Pagnol, from the novel by Jean Giono
Production company: Les Films Marcel Pagnol
Producer: Charles Pons
Photography: Willy Faktorovitch and Roger Ledru
Sound: Jean Lecoq
Set design: Marius Brouquier and René Paoletti
Editor: Suzanne de Troye
Music: Arthur Honegger

Shooting: February–May, July–August 1937 on the Barres de Saint-Esprit overlooking the Marcelin Valley, Aubagne, Roquevaire, Gémenos, and Pagnol's studios (Impasse des Peupliers, Marseilles)
Distribution: Les Films Marcel Pagnol
Premiere: 29 October 1937 at the Marignan cinema (Paris)
Main cast: Gabriel Gabrio (Panturle), Orane Demazis (Arsule), Fernandel (Gédémus), Marguerite Moreno (La Mamèche), Henri Poupon (L'Amoureux), Odette Roger (Alphonsine), Edouard Delmont (Gaubert), Charles Blavette (Jasmin), Robert Le Vigan (the police sergeant), Paul Dullac (Monsieur Astruc)
Notes: Initially banned by the New York State Board of Censors in July 1939 for 'approving the cohabitation of an unmarried couple' (Panturle and Arsule), the film was subsequently authorised by the New York State Board of Regents and given a special award for quality by the New York Film Critics Association.

Le Schpountz (1938), 129 min., b/w

Director: Marcel Pagnol
Screenplay: Marcel Pagnol
Production company: Les Films Marcel Pagnol
Producer: Charles Pons
Photography: Willy Faktorovitch and Roger Ledru
Sound: Jean Lecoq and Marcel Lavoignat
Set design: Marius Brouquier and René Paoletti
Editor: Suzanne de Troye
Music: Casimir Oberfeld and Jean Manse
Shooting: April–July 1937 in Eourres and at Pagnol's studios (Impasse des Peupliers and Avenue Jean Mermoz, Marseilles)
Distribution: Les Films Marcel Pagnol
Premiere: 15 April 1938 at the Olympia cinema (Paris)
Main cast: Fernandel (Irénée), Orane Demazis (Françoise), Fernand Charpin (Baptiste), Jean Castan (Casimir), Odette Roger (Clarisse), Léon Bélières (Meyerboom), Maupi (the bartender), Robert Vattier (Astruc), Henri Poupon (Galubert)
Notes: Amidst accusations of anti-Semitism, Pagnol recalled all copies of the film less than a week after its national release in order to cut a sequence explicitly identifying the dishonest film producer Meyerboom as Jewish.

La Femme du boulanger (1938), 127 min., b/w

Director: Marcel Pagnol
Assistant director: Roger Goupillières
Screenplay: Marcel Pagnol, from the short story *Le Boulanger, le berger, Aurélie* by Jean Giono
Production company: Les Films Marcel Pagnol
Producer: Charles Pons
Photography: Georges Benoît and Roger Ledru
Sound: Marcel Lavoignat
Set design: Marius Brouquier and René Paoletti
Editor: Suzanne de Troye
Music: Vincent Scotto and Georges Sellers
Shooting: May–July 1938 in Le Castellet (Var), the Giens peninsula (near Hyères), and Pagnol's studios (Avenue Jean Mermoz, Marseilles)
Distribution: Les Films Marcel Pagnol
Premiere: 7 September 1938 at the Marivaux cinema (Paris)
Main cast: Raimu (Aimable Castanier), Ginette Leclerc (Aurélie Castanier), Charles Moulin (Dominique), Fernand Charpin (Marquis Castan de Venelles), Robert Vattier (the priest), Robert Bassac (the schoolteacher), Charles Blavette (Antonin), Edouard Delmont (Maillefer), Maupi (Barnabé), Paul Dullac (Casimir), Jean Castan (Esprit), Alida Rouffe (Céleste)
Notes: This was the first film shot in Pagnol's expanded and re-equipped studios. Two test screenings were held: the first on 18 August at the Lutétia cinema in Biarritz and the second on 25 August at Pagnol's recently acquired cinema Le César in Marseilles. Following its American release in February 1940, the film ran for eleven months at the World Theatre in New York and was named best foreign picture of the year by both the National Motion Picture Review Board and the New York Film Critics Association.

La Fille du puisatier (1940), 170 min., b/w

Director: Marcel Pagnol
Screenplay: Marcel Pagnol
Production company: Les Films Marcel Pagnol
Producer: Marcel Pagnol
Photography: Willy Faktorovitch and Roger Forster
Sound: Marcel Lavoignat

Set design: Marius Brouquier
Editor: Jeannette Ginestet
Music: Vincent Scotto
Shooting: May–June, September–November 1940 in Aix-en-Provence, Gémenos, Pont de l'Etoile, and Pagnol's studios (Avenue Jean Mermoz, Marseilles)
Distribution: Les Films Marcel Pagnol
Premiere: 19 December 1940 at the Pathé Palace cinema (Lyon)
Main cast: Raimu (Pascal Amoretti), Josette Day (Patricia Amoretti), Fernandel (Félipe Rambert), Georges Grey (Jacques Mazel), Fernand Charpin (André Mazel), Line Noro (Madame Mazel), Milly Mathis (Nathalie), Félicien Tramel (the waiter), Maupi (the clerk), Charles Blavette (the dry cleaner)
Notes: Shooting was suspended for two months following France's defeat. The film opened in Marseilles and Toulouse on 24 December 1940 at the Pathé Palace. The original 170-minute version of the film was shown only in the unoccupied zone from late 1940 through spring 1941. The 150-minute version that premiered in Paris on 24 April 1941 at the Madeleine was subsequently distributed throughout both the occupied and unoccupied zones.

La Prière aux étoiles (1941), b/w

Director: Marcel Pagnol
Screenplay: Marcel Pagnol
Production company: Les Films Marcel Pagnol
Producer: Alexis Plumet
Photography: André Thomas
Set design: Robert Giordani
Shooting: August 1941–June 1942 in Pagnol's studios (Avenue Jean Mermoz, Marseilles), Cassis, the Château de la Buzine (near Aubagne), and Luna Park (Paris)
Main cast: Pierre Blanchar (Pierre), Josette Day (Florence), Julien Carette (Frédéric), Pauline Carton (Fernande), Jean Chevrier (Dominique), André Alerme (Albert), Fernand Charpin (Evariste), Milly Mathis (the maid), Jean Castan (Pétugue), Line Noro (Mademoiselle Reverdy), Marguerite Moreno (the fortune-teller)
Notes: Production was interrupted several times because of equipment failures, filmstock shortages, and other material or logistical problems associated with the war. The film was not completed

or shown publicly. A short sequence shot in Paris at Luna Park survived the war and is among the bonus features on the DVD version of *La Fille du puisatier* distributed by the Compagnie Méditerranéenne de Films.

Naïs (1945), 127 min., b/w

Directors: Raymond Leboursier and Marcel Pagnol
Screenplay: Marcel Pagnol, from the short story *Naïs Micoulin* by Emile Zola
Production company: La Société Nouvelle des Films Marcel Pagnol
Producer: Jean Martinetti
Photography: Charles Suin and Walter Wottitz
Set design: Robert Giordani
Sound: Privat, Jacques Legras
Editor: Jeanne Rongier
Music: Vincent Scotto and Henri Tomasi
Shooting: May–July 1945 in Cassis, the nearby calanques, and at the Château de la Buzine (near Aubagne)
Distribution: Gaumont
Premiere: 22 November 1945 at the Gaumont Palace cinema (Paris)
Main cast: Fernandel (Toine), Henri Poupon (Micoulin), Jacqueline Bouvier (Naïs Micoulin), Raymond Pellegrin (Frédéric Rostaing), Henri Arius (Monsieur Rostaing), Germaine Kerjean (Madame Rostaing), Charles Blavette (the engineer)
Notes: According to official Centre National de la Cinématographie figures, the film sold 3,467,792 tickets between its release and 1999, making it the eighth most popular picture of 1945.

La Belle Meunière (1948), 98 min., Rouxcolor

Directors: Marcel Pagnol and Raymond Lamy
Screenplay: Marcel Pagnol, inspired by the music of Franz Schubert
Production company: La Société Nouvelle des Films Marcel Pagnol
Producer: Jean Martinetti
Photography: Willy Faktorovitch and Roger Ledru
Technical adviser: Armand Roux
Set and costume design: Robert Giordani and Jean Mandaroux
Sound: Marcel Royné
Editor: Jeanne Rongier
Music: Franz Schubert, arranged by Tony Aubin and Raymond Legrand

Shooting: July–August 1948 in Castellaras (Alpes-Maritimes) and at Pagnol's estate near La Colle-sur-Loup (Alpes-Maritimes) and La Victorine studios (Nice)
Distribution: Gaumont
Premiere: 23 November 1948 at the Madeleine cinema (Paris)
Main cast: Tino Rossi (Franz Schubert), Jacqueline Pagnol (Brigitte), Raoul Marco (the miller), Raphaël Patorny (the count)
Notes: The film was initially recorded in black and white between June and September 1947, then reshot using a new optical colour process invented by Armand Roux. The result was good technically but expensive to project because of the specialised equipment required. Though the film generated a respectable attendance figure of 1.7 million, it was by far the least successful of Pagnol's post-war productions.

Topaze (1950), 135 min., b/w

Directors: Marcel Pagnol and François Gir
Screenplay: Marcel Pagnol, from his stage play
Production company: La Société Nouvelle des Films Marcel Pagnol
Producer: Jean Martinetti
Photography: Philippe Agostini and Jean-Marie Maillols
Set design: Hugues Laurent and Robert Giordani
Sound: Marcel Royné
Editor: Monique Lacombe and Jacqueline Bultez
Music: Raymond Legrand
Shooting: October 1950 at Franstudios (Saint Maurice)
Distribution: Gaumont
Premiere: 2 February 1951 at the Gaumont Palace, Berlitz, and Colisée cinemas (Paris)
Main cast: Fernandel (Topaze), Jacques Morel (Régis Castel-Bénac), Marcel Valée (Monsieur Muche), Jacqueline Pagnol (Ernestine Muche), Pierre Larquey (Tamise), Hélène Perdrière (Suzy Courtois)
Notes: This was Pagnol's third and final adaptation of his play, whose original dialogue it reproduces nearly verbatim. An advance screening to benefit the Red Cross was held on 25 January 1951 at the Beaux Arts cinema in Monaco. Despite having pre-approved the script, censors required Pagnol to modify three sections of dialogue referring to the sale of political influence and to include a written disclaimer at the outset of the film stating that any resemblance between the film and 'real facts' or 'living people' was purely

coincidental. These measures were intended to avoid inflaming public outrage over a series of scandals in 1949–50 involving high-ranking colonial officials in Algeria and Indochina, yet spectators still reportedly made the association. The film sold 3,184,380 tickets between its release and 1999, ranking tenth among all pictures released in 1951.

Manon des sources (1953), 190 min., b/w

Director: Marcel Pagnol
Screenplay: Marcel Pagnol
Production company: La Société Nouvelle des Films Marcel Pagnol
Producer: Charles Pons
Photography: Willy Faktorovitch and Roger Ledru
Set design: Eugène Delfau
Sound: Marcel Royné
Editor: Raymonde and Jacques Bianchi
Music: Raymond Legrand
Shooting: June–August 1952 in La Treille, the Marcelin Valley, and at Gaumont studios (Marseilles)
Distribution: Gaumont
Premiere: 16 January 1953 at the Gaumont Palace, Colisée, and Berlitz cinemas (Paris)
Main cast: Jacqueline Pagnol (Manon), Raymond Pellegrin (the schoolteacher), Henri Poupon (Papet), Rellys (Ugolin), Robert Vattier (Monsieur Belloiseau), Henri Vilbert (the priest), Alfred Goulin (Jean de Florette)
Notes: The original montage of the film, which was test screened on 3 November 1952 in Paris, ran 240 minutes. It was subsequently cut to 190 minutes and divided into two parts, *Manon des sources* and *Ugolin*, to facilitate distribution and screening. The film was the ninth most popular released in 1953, selling 4,278,645 tickets through 1999 and significantly outperforming all of Pagnol's other post-war pictures.

Les Lettres de mon moulin (1954), 160 min., b/w

Directors: Marcel Pagnol
Screenplay: Marcel Pagnol, from the short stories *La Diligence de Beaucaire*, *Les Trois messes basses*, *L'Elixir du Père Gaucher*, and *Le Secret de Maître Cornille* by Alphonse Daudet
Production company: La Compagnie Méditerranéenne de Films

Producer: Jean Martinetti
Photography: Willy Faktorovitch
Set design: Robert Giordani and Jean Mandaroux
Sound: Marcel Royné
Editor: Monique Lacombe and Jeanne Rongier
Music: Henri Tomasi
Shooting: June–August 1954 at Gaumont studios (Marseilles), Auriol, Ganagobie, Saint-Michel- de-Frigolet
Distribution: Gaumont
Premiere: 5 November 1954 at the Gaumont Palace, Le Paris, and Berlitz cinemas (Paris)
Main cast: *La Diligence de Beaucaire*: Roger Crouzet (Alphonse Daudet), Henri Crémieux (the notary), André Bervil (the baker), Edouard Delmont (Maître Cornille), Jean Daniel (the café owner); *Les Trois messes basses*: Henri Vilibert (Dom Balaguère), Marcel Daxely (Toinet Garrigou), René Sarvil (the cook), Yvonne Gamy (the old woman), Antonin Fabre (Arnoton); *L'Elixir du Père Gaucher*: Rellys (Father Gaucher), Robert Vattier (the Abbot), Christian Lude (Father Sylvestre), Jean Toscane (Father Joachim), Fernand Sardou (Monsieur Charnigue); *Le Secret de Maître Cornille*: Edouard Delmont (Maître Cornille), Roger Crouzet (Alphonse Daudet), Pierrette Bruno (Vivette), Serge Davin (Roumanille), Andrée Turcy (Marinette)
Notes: An advance screening of the film to benefit charity was held on 3 November 1954 at the Beaux Arts cinema in Monaco. The original montage of the film ran 180 minutes, but its prologue (*La Diligence de Beaucaire*) was cut to facilitate distribution and screening. Pagnol also shot footage for another 'letter' (*Le Curé de Cucugnan*) that was eventually completed in 1967 and broadcast on French television in December 1968. *Les Lettres* was the second-worst performer among Pagnol's post-war pictures, selling 2,399,645 tickets from 1954 through 1999.

Additional screenplays

Pagnol authored or co-authored a handful of screenplays for films he did not direct. Directors' names and original release dates are given parenthetically.

Direct au cœur (Roger Lion, 1933), from the stage play by Pagnol and Paul Nivoix

L'Agonie des aigles (Roger Richebé, 1933), from the novel *Les Demi-Soldes* by Georges d'Esparbès

Tartarin de Tarascon (Raymond Bernard, 1934), from the novel by Alphonse Daudet

Monsieur Brotonneau (Alexandre Esway, 1939), from the stage play by Robert de Flers and Gaston Arman de Caillavet

Arlette et l'amour (Robert Vernay, 1943), from the stage play *Atout cœur!* by Félix Gandera

Le Rosier de Madame Husson (Jean Boyer, 1950), from the short story by Guy de Maupassant

Carnaval (Henri Verneuil, 1953), from the stage play *Dardamelle* by Emile Mazeaux

Additional films produced and distributed

As a favour to friends in the cinema industry or to generate supplementary revenue during periods of financial need, particularly the Second World War, Pagnol occasionally produced and distributed films that he did not direct. Directors' names and initial release dates are given parenthetically.

Knock, ou le triomphe de la médecine (Roger Goupillières and Louis Jouvet, 1933): distributor

Léopold le Bien-Aimé (Charles-Arno Brun, 1934): distributor and co-producer

Toni (Jean Renoir, 1935): distributor and co-producer

Monsieur Brotonneau (Alexandre Esway, 1939): distributor and producer

Le Président Haudecœur (Jean Dréville, 1939): distributor

Marseilles mes amours (Jacques Daniel-Norman, 1939): distributor

La Tragédie de Mers-el-Kébir (French Navy Cinema Service newsreel, 1940): distributor

La France en Marche (French Army Cinema Service documentary series, 1940–42): distributor

La Croisée des chemins (André Berthomieu, 1942): producer

Seul dans Paris (Hervé Bromberger, 1951): producer

Carnaval (Henri Verneuil, 1953): producer

VHS/DVD editions

Between 1991 and 1996 the Compagnie Méditerranéenne de Films released VHS versions of all the films Pagnol directed or co-directed, as well as *L'Agonie des aigles*, *Léopold le Bien-Aimé*, *Le Rosier de Madame Husson*, *Carnaval*, and Paramount's 1933 adaptation of *Topaze*. These are now out of print. Restored DVD editions began to appear in 2003, with ten titles available as of late 2010. Unfortunately, in many cases the archival copies being used date from the 1950s or 1960s and are substantially shorter than the original theatrical releases, having been edited over the years to satisfy commercial exigencies (particularly the 120-minute norm for television broadcast) and various censor boards. On VHS and DVD, *Marius* thus loses ten minutes; *Fanny* thirty; *César* thirty-six; *Regain* thirty-eight. While the short versions of *Angèle* and *La Fille du puisatier* can be seen nearly intact, the long versions have unfortunately disappeared from all European cinema archives. Only *César* has survived unmodified in its original form at the Cinémathèque de Toulouse in a single glorious nitrate print of 168 minutes.

Select bibliography

The peculiar combination of critical disdain and mass popularity surrounding Pagnol has generated a large volume of books, most of which are descriptive and/or hagiographic rather than analytical. Similarly, no comprehensive critical edition of Pagnol's own writings has ever been published – a surprising oversight given his status as one of the twentieth century's most versatile and successful dramatic authors. The titles cited below are only the most useful. For a broader view of the literature available on Pagnol, see the introductory chapter and the list of references that follows it.

Texts by Pagnol

Œuvres complètes (1995), Paris, Fallois. This three-volume paperback set published to honour the centenary of Pagnol's birth is the most recent, most affordable, and most compact edition of his 'complete works'. Though lacking three film scripts (*L'Article 330, La Prière aux étoiles,* and *Manon des sources*) as well as the minor historical essay 'Le Masque de fer', and the early co-authored play *Tonton, ou Joseph veut rester pur,* it does include the rest of his screenplays, plays, novels, childhood memoirs, and essays related to dramatic art. One important caveat: like all previous editions of Pagnol's complete works, many of the texts do not correspond to their original published form (or in the case of screenplays, to the dialogue actually spoken on-screen), instead reflecting modifications made by the author as late as the mid-1960s. For example, the 'definitive' versions of *Marius* and *Fanny* omit social–

realist material highlighting race and class tensions in Marseilles, while *César* and 'Cinématurgie de Paris' incorporate substantial additions and organisational changes.

Marcel Pagnol: l'album d'une vie (2011), Paris, Flammarion. Edited by grandson Nicolas Pagnol, this selection of previously unpublished letters written and received by Pagnol sheds new light on his relationship with family members, actors, and other directors.

Texts about Pagnol

Bens, Jacques (1994), *Pagnol*, Paris, Seuil. A lavishly illustrated bio-thematic essay in the popular 'Ecrivains de toujours' series, its breadth and easy accessibility make it a perfect first introduction to Pagnol.

Beylie, Claude (1995), *Marcel Pagnol, ou le cinéma en liberté*, 3rd edn. Initially published in 1974 and updated a first time in 1986, this thematically organised essay was the first serious scholarly overview of Pagnol's career and the first major attempt to legitimise his work among French critics. Especially valuable for its detailed list of Pagnol's plays and films, as well as their posthumous adaptations through 1995.

Caldicott, C.E.J. (1977), *Marcel Pagnol*, Boston, Twayne Publishers. Organised chronologically, this was the first book devoted to Pagnol in English. Comprehensive in scope and descriptive in nature, it touches on virtually every key aspect of his work as a playwright and filmmaker, but lacks depth and suffers from some glaring gaps in research, as well as occasional factual inaccuracies.

Castans, Raymond (1987), *Marcel Pagnol: biographie*, Paris, J.C. Lattès. Written by Pagnol's most prolific hagiographer, this novelistic biography seamlessly blends documented fact with legend, speculation, and invented dialogue between the filmmaker and his entourage. Useful, but must be handled with great care.

Heath, Stephen (2004), *César*, London, British Film Institute. Cogent, perceptive, and beautifully written, this entry in the BFI's 'Film Classics' series in fact deals with the Trilogy as a whole, highlighting Pagnol's theory and practice of *cinématurgie* while reflecting on his singular place in French film history.

Jelot-Blanc, Jean-Jacques (1998), *Pagnol inconnu*, Paris, Editions de

La Treille. The most reliable and complete biography of Pagnol to date, it represents a middle ground between Castans and Luppi (see below) by injecting new research and insights to an admiring, novelistic narrative.

Labarthe, André (1966), *Marcel Pagnol, ou le cinéma tel qu'on le parle*, Paris, ORTF, 109 minutes. The first and best documentary about Pagnol, originally broadcast on French television in two segments as part of the acclaimed 'Cinéastes de notre temps' series. It skilfully blends interviews featuring Pagnol, technicians, friends, actors, critics, and other directors with substantial clips from nearly all his films. Currently available for viewing at the Inathèque de France in the Bibliothèque Nationale (Tolbiac site, Paris), this film and the rest of the series are being restored for broadcast on the Arte television channel and eventual release on DVD.

Leprohon, Pierre, 'Marcel Pagnol' (May 1976), *Anthologie du cinéma* no. 88 (supplement to *L'Avant-scène cinéma*). A short essay notable for recognising the seminal influence of Pagnol's rural films on Italian neo-realism, particularly Rossellini and De Sica.

Luppi, Jean-Baptiste (1995) *De Pagnol Marcel à Marcel Pagnol: voyage aux sources de sa gloire*, Marseilles, Editions Paul Tacussel. Thoroughly researched in local archives, this detailed portrait of the teacher, journalist, and playwright stops in 1931 just prior to his entry into filmmaking.

'Marcel Pagnol et Sacha Guitry, cinéastes malgré eux?' (December 1965), *Cahiers du cinéma* no. 173. A special issue juxtaposing France's two most famous 'theatrical' filmmakers, it includes long interviews with Pagnol and several of his technicians about their production habits, as well as a pioneering short essay by André Labarthe identifying recurring themes in Pagnol's cinema.

Index

Allégret, Marc 35, 46, 86–9, 101, 104–5, 110, 114, 201, 246
Angèle 5, 25, 29–30, 115, 118–20, 128, 140–1, 143, 145, 147, 151–8, 161–4, 167–74, 178–82, 184, 186, 188–92, 248–9
Antoine, André 8, 18–20, 23–4, 28, 33, 44–5, 52–5, 81, 105–6, 113, 117, 119, 125, 148, 155, 204, 217
Article 330, L' 248, 261

Ballard, Jean 13–20
Baur, Harry 20, 45, 57
Bazin, André 3–4, 7–8, 129–32, 168, 191
Becque, Henry 19, 23, 27–8
Bélières, Léon 216, 252
Belle meunière, La 4, 219, 255–6
Benjamin, Walter 35
Bergson, Henri 5–6, 30–1, 185
Berri, Claude 129, 192, 237, 241
Blavette, Charles 119, 122, 149–52, 156, 207, 247, 250, 252–5
Braunberger, Pierre 60, 63, 86, 110
Brouquier, Marius 152, 158, 224, 248, 251–4

Cahiers du film, Les 2, 16, 106, 111, 114, 156, 198, 219
Carné, Marcel 4, 75, 114, 159–61, 166, 243
Cerutti, Henri 144–5, 221–3
César 2, 5, 39, 43, 69, 93–100, 115, 119–26, 131, 136, 139, 146–7, 157–8, 203, 223–6, 229, 232, 251
  recent adaptions of 239–42
Chaplin, Charlie 4–7, 52, 103, 108–9, 122, 158, 185, 205
Charpin, Fernand 33, 104, 124–5, 137, 222, 246–7, 251–54
Chevalier, Maurice 57, 61–3
Cigalon 5, 118, 157, 249–50
cinématurgie 28, 85–132
Clair, René 8, 56–9, 75, 101, 109, 112–14, 121–3, 128–9, 159, 190, 200, 202, 243
Cocteau, Jean 7, 17, 50
comedy 5–7, 23–7, 36, 40, 44–5, 90–4, 102, 113, 122, 127, 147, 154, 161, 183

Deleuze, Gilles 90
Delmont, Edouard 143, 154, 156, 167, 249, 251–3, 258
Demazis, Orane 20, 33, 36, 42,

87, 125, 137, 140, 153, 155, 185, 208–9, 212, 221–2, 246, 248, 251–2
Derrida, Jacques 30
De Sica, Vittorio 149, 191–2
Dullac, Paul 33, 138, 246, 251–3

Faktorovitch, Willy 120, 143, 208, 215, 246–8, 250–3, 255, 257–8
Fanny
    film 2, 39–43, 81, 85–107, 110, 114, 116, 131, 139, 144, 148, 150, 154, 157, 180, 182, 203, 211, 221–2, 225–7, 229, 232, 246
    play 34–5, 38–43, 45–6
    recent adaptations of 232, 239–42
Femme du boulanger, La 5, 25, 30, 115, 121, 126, 128, 147, 175–82, 253
Fernandel 103, 118–19, 140, 143, 146, 154–5, 181, 183–4, 210–11, 214, 223, 239, 248, 252, 254–6
Fille du puisatier, La 5, 30, 115, 155, 182–3, 223, 231, 253–4
    remake of 241–5
Fortunio 12–17, 31, 50, 103
Fresnay, Pierre 33, 45–6, 70, 119–22, 125, 137, 221, 245–6, 251
Freud, Sigmund 26, 31, 176

Gance, Abel 14–15, 56, 70, 109, 113, 164, 189, 214
Gasnier, Louis 5, 46, 101–3
gender 7, 25, 40–3, 74–5, 95–6, 113, 173–82, 229, 238, 240
Gendre de Monsieur Poirier, Le 104–6, 148, 246–7
Gide, André 17, 35, 86
Giono, Jean 5, 115, 147–8, 152, 155, 158, 161–2, 182–90, 225, 242,

247–9, 251, 253
Godard, Jean-Luc 123, 192–3
Guitry, Sacha 63, 86, 110–11, 126–7

Hollywood 2, 8, 58–61, 64–5, 70, 101, 103, 155, 198–9, 205, 210–12, 217–19, 223, 227–32, 242
Honegger, Arthur 164–6, 251

Jeanson, Henri 19, 59, 201, 217, 223, 226
Jofroi 5, 115, 119, 143, 147–52, 163–4, 167–70, 181–9, 247
Jouvet, Louis 101–2, 159
Junge, Alfred 70, 76–8, 245

Kane, Robert 61–5, 75, 81, 85, 223, 245
Kant, Immanuel 93
Korda, Alexander 49, 64–77, 85, 87, 101, 104, 114, 136, 215, 229, 245

laughter 5–6, 30–1, 93–4, 185, 239
Leclerc, Ginette 141, 175, 180, 253
Lessing, Gotthold 106–7
Lettres de mon moulin, Les 4, 131, 223, 257–8

Manon des sources 5, 25, 30, 115, 120, 129–31, 151, 181–2, 192, 223, 237, 241, 257, 261
Marchands de gloire, Les 19–25
Marius
    film 2, 39–44, 49–81, 85–91, 95, 99–101, 103–5, 107, 114, 123, 131, 137–8, 148, 150, 157, 180, 191–2, 203, 205, 215, 219, 223, 225, 229, 245–6, 260–1
    play 25, 32–46, 205, 239–41, 261
    recent adaptations of 239–42

Mathis, Milly 33, 246, 251, 254
Maupi, Marcel 33, 150, 246, 251–4
Merlusse 5, 115–20, 131, 147, 151, 157, 162, 229–30, 249
Mihalesco, Alexandre 138, 246
Millet, Jean-François 148, 163–4
Mirande, Yves 58, 64, 201
Molière 3, 6–7, 18, 23, 25, 27, 52, 185, 207, 211
Montaigne, Michel de 18, 25

Naïs 5, 25, 115, 151, 155, 181–2, 223, 255
neo-realism 5, 119, 149, 191–2, 243
new wave 5, 118–19, 132, 192, 243
Nietzsche, Friedrich 25, 28–31
Nivoix, Paul 9, 16–20

Pagnol, Joseph 11, 23
Pagnol, Simonne Collin 12–13, 20, 42
Paramount 5, 14, 46, 60–6, 70, 75–7, 81, 245
pathos 6, 34, 44–5, 91, 96, 119, 122, 127, 149–51, 134, 161, 167, 183–5, 192, 222
Poupon, Henri 115, 119, 143, 150–1, 154, 167, 183, 248–50, 252, 255, 257
Prière aux étoiles, La 254–5, 261

Rabelais, François 6, 18, 23, 26
Raimu 33, 45–6, 52–3, 57, 65, 80, 86, 96, 99–100, 110, 119, 122, 125, 139, 142, 150, 175, 180, 183, 201, 222, 225, 231–2, 238, 241, 245–6, 251, 253–4
realism, poetic 8, 75, 147–93
Regain 5, 29, 115, 119–20, 126, 145, 147, 158–67, 170, 174, 176, 178, 180–9, 207–10, 222, 224–5, 227–31, 251–2

regionalism 7, 11, 31–4, 44–5, 96, 149, 192, 216, 240
Renoir, Jean 4, 8, 75, 86, 114, 120–3, 150, 152, 156, 159, 161, 166, 172, 202, 206–7, 243
Richebé, Roger 46, 60, 63, 85–6, 99, 103, 110, 114, 203, 246
Rossellini, Roberto 149, 152, 191, 232
Rouffe, Alida 33, 45, 96, 139, 246, 250–1, 253
Rouxcolor 4, 219, 255–6

Schpountz, Le 6, 115, 119–20, 126, 146, 185, 203, 214–17, 223, 228, 252
  remake of 239
Scotto, Vincent 143, 150–1, 164, 183, 246–51, 253–5
Sophocles 17, 50, 98
speech, performative 3, 5, 40, 44, 90–9, 113–14, 112–13, 129, 147, 159, 192, 225

Toé 103, 146, 222–5
Topaze
  films 5, 75, 85, 100–3, 118, 120, 162, 188, 199, 203, 205, 256–7
  play 20–5, 29–30, 32, 41–2, 46, 50, 57–8, 75, 113, 162, 205
Truffaut, François 118, 123

Vattier, Robert 33, 138, 246, 251–3, 257–8
Vigo, Jean 4, 114, 117–18
Volterra, Léon 44–5, 58

xenophobia 212–17

Zola, Emile 15, 54, 115, 148, 161, 181, 255